Home Businesses You Can Buy

Home Businesses You Can Buy

◆ ◆ ◆

The Definitive Guide
to Exploring Franchises,
Multi-Level Marketing,
and Business Opportunities
Plus: How to Avoid Scams

◆ ◆ ◆

PAUL AND SARAH EDWARDS
AND WALTER ZOOI

JEREMY P. TARCHER / PUTNAM
a member of Penguin Putnam Inc.
New York

Most Tarcher/Putnam books are available at special quantity discounts for bulk purchases for sales promotions, premiums, fund-raising, and educational needs. Special books or book excerpts also can be created to fit specific needs. For details, write or telephone Putnam Special Markets, 200 Madison Avenue, New York, NY 10016; (212) 951-8891.

Jeremy P. Tarcher/Putnam
a member of Penguin Putnam Inc.
200 Madison Avenue
New York, NY 10016
http://www.putnam.com

Library of Congress Cataloging-in-Publication Data

Edwards, Paul, date.
    Home businesses you can buy : the definitive guide to finding high-
potential franchises, multilevel marketing and business
opportunities—and avoiding scams / Paul and Sarah Edwards and
Walter Zooi.
      p. cm.
    "A Jeremy P. Tarcher/Putnam book."
    Includes bibliographical references and index.
    ISBN 0-87477-858-1 (alk. paper)
    1. Franchises (Retail trade)   2. Business enterprises—Purchasing.
I. Edwards, Sarah (Sarah A.) II. Zooi, Walter.   III. Title.
HF5429.23.E39   1997   96-52507 CIP
658.1'11—dc21

Book design by Lee Fukui

Printed in the United States of America
10 9 8 7 6 5 4 3 2 1

This book is printed on acid-free paper. ⊖

Acknowledgments

ROBERT WELSCH, the former marketing director for our publisher, the Tarcher imprint of the Putnam Publishing Group, suggested we write this book when in our conversations with him we discussed how many people wanted to be their own boss but didn't want to start a business from scratch. Robert saw this book as an outgrowth of our successful book *Best Home Businesses for the 90s*.

A number of people have contributed significantly to the research, writing, and fine-tuning of this book. First, we thank our coauthor, Walter Zooi, whose patience and good nature have made the arduous task of producing an information-intensive book bearable. Sidney Schwartz played a significant role in conducting many of the interviews of people featured in the book and provided valuable advice and insight. People who contributed their expertise include Jan Caldwell, a Maryland attorney in private practice who specializes in the direct selling industry; David Buchen of the University of Wisconsin Whitewater Business Outreach Program; Doris Woods, founder of the Multi-Level Marketing International Association and a consultant to the multilevel industry; Merry Schiff, who is both a franchisor and a vendor of business opportunities; James Chambers of the National Business Opportunity Bureau; and Liz Doherty of the Direct Selling Association. We also thank the people we interviewed who forthrightly shared both their positive and negative experiences.

We are grateful to the supportive team of people at Tarcher/Putnam, including our new publisher, Joel Fotinos, with whom we delight in working; the ever helpful editors, Irene Prokop, editor-in-chief, and her assistants, David Groff and Jennifer Greene; and the people whose importance cannot be underestimated in producing a readable book, Coral Tysliava and Claire Vaccaro, and the people with whom they work. We recognize the special contributions of our publicists, Joanna Pinsker and Ken Siman, and of Maria Liu, marketing coordinator.

Deserving of special note, too, is our assistant, Joyce Acosta, who enables us to complete the manuscripts that come from our home office and who makes hundreds of phone calls to verify telephone numbers and other information.

We hope the cumulative contributions people have made will lead you to finding rewarding ways of making a living and preventing costly mistakes.

Paul & Sarah Edwards

Contents

Introduction

New Alternatives to Career and Financial Success

WE DON'T NEED to tell you that the ways people can earn a living these days are changing. Jobs in corporate and industrial America that were once considered secure have been among the hardest hit by downsizing and cutbacks. College graduates who were once guaranteed a secure job future often settle for jobs well below their expectations. Real wages are down and consumer prices continue to rise. Most families require two incomes just to get by. Many people need to work multiple jobs to make ends meet. "Temp" jobs are among the fastest growing. The signs of change are everywhere and have probably directly affected your friends, family, and most likely, you. These changes are among the primary reasons growing numbers of people all across the country are taking the initiative to start their own businesses, most often from home.

The rapidly changing economic news is actually not as bad as it might seem at first glance, however. We still live in a country of growing wealth and opportunity. Our economy is in transition, not depression. Due to the very nature of this transition, never has the potential for starting a new business been greater, or the opportunities themselves more numerous. One of the greatest areas of opportunity and growth is having a home-based business. A 1996 *Money* magazine survey found that one in five home-based businesses are grossing between $100,000 and $500,000 a year and from fewer than three million in the early 1970s, there now are as many as fifteen million people in the United States earning their primary income from a home-based business.

But, you may ask, "Doesn't starting a home business mean I'll have to create my own business from scratch, and spend a lot of time learning the ropes before I ever earn any real money?" That's a fair question and, yes, that is the most common and often the best way of becoming successfully self-employed. Yet we know many of you reading this book don't have the interest, resources, or time to develop your own business from scratch. That's why so many people these days are interested in what could be called buying a "prepackaged" business you can run from your home.

What exactly is a "prepackaged" home business and can *you* really make money from one? We will help you answer that question in the following pages and demonstrate both the benefits and misconceptions of buying a prepackaged business. So if you decide to follow this path to your own business, you can do so with confidence. You'll see how sometimes prepackaged businesses can require less initial investment than starting a business by yourself. They may require less time to get under way and start generating income because all the initial legwork has been done by the company you are buying the business from. And, perhaps most important, with a prepackaged business, statistics indicate that you could begin earning real profits more quickly.

On the other hand, you'll also discover that many of the business opportunities people buy sit on a shelf collecting dust. The average gross income for the typical person active in multilevel marketing is less than $100 a month. And even buying a home-based franchise has been a disappointing experience for some. But with so many advantages to buying a home business, why doesn't it work out well for more people? Primarily, the reason people don't succeed in a home business they buy is because too often people get involved with businesses that aren't well suited to them or, rightly or wrongly, buy from a company that doesn't provide what they expected.

It's this very dilemma that caused us to write this book. We wanted to develop a comprehensive guide for understanding and evaluating the vast array of home businesses you can buy so you can make an informed and wise decision if you want to buy a home business and, if so, which one will be best suited to you. This book defines three categories of home-business packages you can buy: franchises, described in Chapter 1; multilevel marketing, described in Chapter 3; and business opportunities, described in Chapter 5.

In each of these chapters, you'll learn how this kind of prepackaged business works, what it will require of you, and what you can realistically expect from it. You'll learn about others who have bought and are running such businesses. You'll read firsthand accounts of problems people have encountered as well as what it's like to work and succeed in a prepackaged home-based business.

At any point when you decide you want to pursue purchasing one of the three types of prepackaged home businesses, you'll find specific guidelines for testing and evaluating the fitness, honesty, and marketability of the particular business package you're considering. For each type of packaged home business—franchises, MLMs, and business opportunities, you'll find three crucial tools that will help you to know if this type of business would be a good choice for you personally. These tools, the "Fitness Check," the "Honesty Check," and the "Market Check," make this book unique among all others, and you should apply these tests to any prepackaged home business you're considering before you decide to buy.

We've designed the book so you can go directly to the chapters addressing the kind of prepackaged business that is of most interest to you at the moment; or if you want to explore them all, we suggest that you read Chapters 1, 3, and 5 first and then do the assessments in Chapter 2, 4, or 6 for whichever prepackaged business option(s) interest you most. You will find that the structure of these chapters is similar because we want you to be able to weigh the pros and cons of each type of prepackaged business based on the same issues and criteria. While some of the questions are repetitive, the assessments and conclusions from each have subtle and sometimes substantial differences.

The "Fitness Check" will help you test out a particular business to see if it is what it's represented to be and how well it matches what you think, or hope, it is. You'll be able to find out if a business is suited to your personality, skills, interests, and experience and discover if what you're considering is a good match for you and your expectations. In particular, you'll find a detailed list of questions to ask and work sheets you can fill out to identify what we call the "Core Function," or actual work, you'll be doing when you buy a particular business you're considering. Knowing the Core Function of a prepackaged home business is vital because while, of course, you're thinking of the business as a way to make money, if you don't enjoy it or have any aptitude for the actual work involved, the odds are you won't be very successful at it.

The "Honesty Check" provides concrete steps you can take to ensure that a company you're considering buying from is an honest and reputable one with a healthy track record of success and fairness. We're sure you've heard the horror stories (and we'll recount a few as well) about dishonest franchises and fraudulent multilevel marketing and business opportunity companies. The Honesty Check will allow you to cut through all the hype and test out just how honest, fair, and responsible a company you're considering actually is. It will enable you to ask the right questions and show you how to do the right kind of homework to ensure that the business in question is forthright and representing itself with integrity.

No matter how strong the company is or how well a home business is suited to your interests, skills, and experience, however, if there aren't enough people you can reach who want what you'll be offering, you won't be able to succeed in that business. And unfortunately, some very good home businesses can sell marvelously well in one area and not at all in another. That's why we created the "Market Check."

The Market Check will help you determine if there are enough potential customers accessible to you to make a particular business you're considering viable. It will also show you how and where to find potential customers and how to determine how many potential customers the business you are considering actually has. And the work you do to carry out the Market Check before you buy won't be wasted after you buy. The Market Check will also serve as the groundwork you'll need to get your marketing efforts under way and build an ongoing client base after you do decide to buy a prepackaged business.

After considering what makes franchising, multilevel marketing, and business opportunities unique and separate in the first six chapters, in Chapter 7 you'll find general guidelines for picking any prepackaged business and a checklist you can take with you to protect yourself from being taken advantage of at a business and franchise expo.

These shows have proliferated over the past several years. In general, they're a good place to get acquainted with many prepackaged business opportunities and to gather important research from a number of resources, including your attorney general's office, the Federal Trade Commission (FTC), and other regulatory agencies who generally have a presence at these shows. But such shows can be overwhelming, too. That's why we heartily recommend that you bring this book with you and use it as a guide when you attend a show. The Fitness, Honesty, and Market Checks will help you sort out the wheat from the chaff at these shows.

At the close of Chapter 7, we provide you with one final test you can put a packaged business through. It's called *What's Wrong with This Picture*, and it will allow you to see if any potential business you're considering will fit into your picture of the future.

In Chapters 8, 9, 10, you'll find a comprehensive directory of literally hundreds of franchises, multilevel marketing companies, and business opportunities. Each company's listing includes a designation as to the "Core Function" it requires of you, so you'll know if the "Core" of the business relates to activities you enjoy, can do well, or are positioned for, because making money probably isn't the only reason you're thinking of buying a home business. Regardless of your need and desire to make money from home, a mismatch can result in wasting your time, money, and belief in yourself.

Finally, in the Appendices 1 through 7, you'll find a detailed list of regulatory agencies, trade organizations, publications, and other resources you can use to check out a particular business you may be considering, Such resources can also be quite helpful in terms of information, company background checks, and additional resources. You'll also find general resources for learning the wide range of things you'll need to know to become successful in any business you buy.

Interviews with people who have bought home-based business are scattered throughout the book. You'll meet people who have been successful and some who haven't been. You'll find out why they either were or weren't able to make their business work for them, so you can decide whether their problems might become problems for you, too, and how you can avoid them. Our goal is to provide you with a realistic picture of the many possibilities open to you today, so you can make the best possible choices for your life. And to do that we recommend keeping the following questions in the front of your mind at all times as you apply the principles of this book to shopping for any home business:

Just What Am I Buying? Is It Worth the Price?

Could I Do It Just as Well or Better on My Own?
As you consider buying any prepackaged home business, always ask yourself what you're buying that you don't already have or couldn't obtain on your own. Are you buying:

    ____ 1. A chance to sell something for some other company
    ____ 2. A territory
    ____ 3. A line of products
    ____ 4. A body of knowledge based on a proven track record of success
    ____ 5. A name-brand with a well-known valuable reputation
    ____ 6. Training, assistance, and support
    ____ 7. Marketing plans you can implement
    ____ 8. A national marketing or advertising campaign
    ____ 9. Leads and referrals for paying customers
    ____ 10. Software, equipment, and/or supplies
    ____ 11. Personnel to process or carry out services or products you sell
    ____ 12. Other

We wish you success on your adventure of starting a business you can run from your home. With the right amount of desire, hard work, and information, there is undoubtedly some way that you can join the millions of people who are creating successful, fulfilling lives for themselves by working from home.

1

Would a Home-Based Franchise Appeal to You?

YOU'VE PROBABLY HEARD it said, "Never break up a winning game." Well, franchising could be said to take this adage one step further: "Once you've got a winning game, duplicate it and get others to play, too."

Of course, not long ago, buying a franchise required investing large amounts of money to join that winning game and there were few opportunities to join the game as a home-based business. But today, home-based franchising is a dynamic and growing phenomenon. This chapter will give you an understanding of what franchising is and what opportunities it offers for starting a home-based business. You'll become acquainted with the kinds of people who are doing it and the products and services best offered through home-based franchising.

Most crucial to your success as a potential business owner is finding a business that is well matched to your interests, talents, experience, and skills, so we've devoted considerable space to defining which personality traits and skills are important to franchising success and what kinds of people tend to do better than others.

In this chapter you'll also find an overview of the legal issues involved in buying a franchise, and the groundwork for negotiating a favorable franchise agreement. Since most of us learn best by example, the chapter also includes case studies of people who've purchased home-based franchises.

A BRIEF HISTORY OF FRANCHISING
AND ITS DEVELOPMENT

Although it's been around for a couple of thousand years, franchising as we know it began with Ray Kroc in the 1950s. Kroc was a milk shake machine salesman unhappy with his job. In his travels, he heard about a burger restaurant in San Bernardino, California, that was doing an incredible amount of business. As a matter of fact, he received an order from them for three machines. None of his other customers had ever ordered more than one! He felt compelled to check this business out personally. Upon arriving at the location, he quickly saw, and tasted, the reasons for the success of the McDonald brothers' restaurant. One big reason was that the burgers and fries were among the best he'd ever tasted. Another was that the business could serve literally thousands of customers in a day due its unique drive-through system. Ray Kroc knew a great opportunity when he saw one. He quickly made a unique deal with the McDonald brothers. He purchased from them the rights to franchise the restaurant.

The franchises Ray Kroc sold with the conviction of a traveling preacher consisted of the McDonald's name, recipes, product names, the drive-through or drive-up services system, the golden arches—in short, a complete package that included the exact specifications as to how a McDonald's restaurant should look and operate and how the food should taste. His idea was that, in no matter what part of the country, or later the world, one's experience at a McDonald's restaurant should be exactly the same. Kroc's concept caught on pretty quickly, and the rest, as they say, is history.

The genius of Ray Kroc wasn't the great burger recipes—they weren't even his. Ray's genius was his ability to recognize an effective way of doing business, put it into an easily copied system, and market that system to interested entrepreneurs under a trademark. This is the essence of modern franchising.

Other entrepreneurs and businesspeople in the 1950s and early 1960s recognized a good thing when they saw it. Franchising presented a way for a business to distribute its products or services very quickly over great distances without having to invest significant amounts of money. In fact, franchising was proving to be a moneymaker. The growth of franchising in the 1960s was so explosive that it became clear that some regulation was in order. In 1970, California became the first state in the union to adopt a comprehensive law governing the ways businesses could franchise themselves. The franchise law included stipulations that a company must first register with the state before it could franchise itself. The law goes on to require that a business provide a prospective franchisee with a detailed franchise agreement, a company financial statements, and a comprehensive disclosure statement.

The FTC soon joined the regulatory trend and established a set of national guidelines that franchisors must follow. Like the California law, FTC rules require that franchisors provide detailed and accurate financial and disclosure statements to potential franchisees, as well as a franchise agreement, where all the terms of the franchising partnership are to be clearly spelled out. The documents must be provided by the franchisor company to the franchisee either upon the initial meeting, ten days before the signing of the franchise agreement, or ten days before the payment of the franchise fee. Signed into law in 1979, FTC franchising rules are still in effect today. At the bare minimum, make sure that any franchise company you are considering provides these legally mandated documents.

Today, after more than thirty-five years of unparalleled growth, modern franchising is a serious force in the business world. Currently, there are more than three thousand businesses that choose to distribute themselves via franchising. These businesses account for more than $800 billion total sales a year in the United States, according to the latest figures. Franchising's effect on our daily lives is incalculable. Many of the retail outlets you see in your neighborhood, and most of the "fast-food" establishments, are franchises. Automobile service shops, baby-sitting and domestic agencies, all manner of cleaning services, print shops, photographers who provide portraits of your kids' sports team, pet care from puppy training to pet cemeteries, even beauty pageants, are all available for purchase as franchises. Because of franchising, as consumers, we can travel from city to city and recognize many of the same stores, service organizations, and restaurants. In keeping with Ray Kroc's original vision, we can take comfort in knowing what to expect when we walk into or phone these establishments, no matter where in the country, or even the world, we are. To say franchising has changed the very face of society would not be overstating the situation.

Franchising is a mega-trend, and the trend shows every indication of continuing strongly well into the next century. The results of a recent survey conducted by the International Franchising Association show that, by the year 2010, one-half of all retail dollars will be generated by franchises. That's a considerable gain over the one-third share of total retail dollars franchising generates today.

Franchising Meets Working from Home: A Winning Combination

We've talked a little about the remarkable growth of franchising and its effect on the fabric of our lives. Working from home is clearly another economic and social trend that's having as great an impact—with forty-some million Americans now doing some type of income-producing work from home. Several surveys find there are now well over fourteen million full-time home-based businesses in the United States. LINK Resources, a New York–based research firm that specializes in studying the home-based business movement, estimates the number will reach eighteen million in a few years. The past ten years have seen the most dramatic changes and growth. As large corporations and government agencies downsize, millions of displaced American workers have found a new kind of economic security by starting their own businesses from home. The same changing economy that drove many people from their jobs in the first place is actually of great help to most home-based businesses. On the one hand, the change from a manufacturing-based economy to a service-based economy drove many companies to shut their doors in the 1980s. On the other hand, what home-based businesses do best is provide services. The emerging service-based economy is well suited to the home-business phenomenon.

Attitudes toward those working from home have changed radically as well. Gone is the stigma of unprofessionalism once associated with running a business outside of a traditional office situation. In most cases the stigma has been replaced by respect, and sometimes even envy—home-office envy. As more and more of the working population moves from office to home, the notion of running a business from your house is losing its novelty and more and more becoming regarded as a practical and respectable career choice.

Technology has also played an enabling role in the working-from-home movement. Anyone now can have access to powerful computers, easy-to-use and efficient software tools, fax machines, multiline phones, copy machines, pagers, etc. Computer technology, because of its high price tag, was once only available to large corporations. Today, almost anybody can outfit a home office with the same state-of-the-art technologies used by much larger business entities, dramatically leveling the playing field.

Looking at these two trends, working from home and franchising, it seems only natural that one of the largest areas of growth in franchising recently is the home-based franchise. Home-based franchising has several distinct advantages over "storefront" franchises. The overhead is far lower, for starters. Rent for a separate office is not required, and utility bills (with the possible exception of your phone bill) are much lower as well. By running a business from your home, you have greater flexibility to meet your customers' and clients' needs cost-effectively and still earn a good income. Because operating expenses are much lower, home-based franchises generally turn a profit within three months, as opposed to a storefront operation, which takes an average of one full year to begin turning a profit. These advantages benefit not only the franchisee, but the franchisor as well.

Here's an example of the benefits working from home can offer to both franshisors and franchisees. In 1983, Cheryl Dagostaro of San Diego, California, realized that she wasn't the only one who needed to find someone to take care of their pets when they went away on vacation or business travel.

Tired of the commuting and other aspects of her office job, she decided to start a home-based pet-sitting service, and Pet Tenders was born. At first she did all the feeding, walking, and caring for other people's pets herself in the comfort of their own homes. Her business caught on, and she began to hire other tenders as well. Pet Tenders grew from one employee in 1984 to twenty-two today. Cheryl now claims, "I'm never leaving home! With the freedom I have here, the low overhead, the relaxed environment—I could never go back to an outside office situation."

Cheryl's business did so well, she decided to offer her methods for developing a successful pet-sitting service to others as Pet Tenders franchises. She sold her first franchise in 1991. "I provide a proven method for success in this business," says Cheryl. "I've watched a lot of other pet-sitting operations come and go, but I really believe I have the right plan. A good part of that plan involves working from home." Barbara Bokram of Plancentia, California, thought Cheryl had a pretty good plan, too. She bought a Pet Tenders franchise from Cheryl in 1994. "I was looking for a business where I could combine my love of animals with working from home, and I couldn't ask for a better match than Pet Tenders." Being relatively inexperienced in business matters, Barbara really liked the idea of buying a franchise as opposed to starting a business on her own. "Cheryl was there for me in the beginning, helping me get started, and she's still there for me today if I need her," says Barbara. "I feel very fortunate in that everything is turning out the way I hoped it would. I have the flexibility that working from home brings, the support of my franchisor, and a growing business doing what I love."

FRANCHISING TODAY:
WHAT IT IS AND HOW IT WORKS

So just how do you define franchising and what can it mean to you? Let's start with the basics: The franchis*or* is the company that's offering the franchise; the franchis*ee* is the person or company who buys the franchise under strictly defined conditions. One of the most comprehensive, yet succinct, definitions of franchising is from author and franchising consultant Gregory Matusky: "Three elements define a franchise company: (1) use of a trademark or trade name, (2) payment of fees or royalties, and (3) significant control or assistance provided by the franchisor." This definition bears a closer look.

What's in a Name? In Business, Everything!

The use of a company's trademark or trade name is essential to franchising. In business, name recognition means a great deal. Given a choice, would you get your taxes done by H & R Block, or Tiny Tax Service? Whom are you more likely to trust your housecleaning to: Merry Maids or M & M Janitorial? When you buy a franchise, you should expect to buy the good name that the franchisor has worked hard to establish. Opening your own business under an established name with a demonstrated market share and market presence (if you are unfamiliar with these terms, you won't be after reading the Market Check chapter) will save you a significant amount of time and money.

Although, Nothing's Free

In order for you to receive the benefits of using a franchisor's name or trademark, you will have to pay a fee for the right to sell the product or service. The fee might be one or any combination of the following:

- A one-time payment
- An ongoing flat-fee payment
- Ongoing sliding-scale payments
- Ongoing royalties
- Advertising fees

Sometimes, a company will stipulate that you use them exclusively for essential services such as photo developing, printing, or testing. They may also require that you purchase essential tools or merchandise exclusively from them. Fees and payments vary widely in amount and arrangement. Always check that the fee structure is spelled out clearly in the franchise agreement. The amount of the fee triggers requirements for registration with state and federal regulators. Registration is always required if the fee is over $500; in some states, it may be less.

The Franchisor-Franchisee Relationship

Unless the franchisor retains an element of control over the franchise, and, in turn, provides assistance in terms of training and ongoing support, the business is not considered a franchise. This is the third point in Matusky's definition of franchising. It is definitely the most important, and strangely, the one most often overlooked by those considering the purchase of a franchise. Entering into a franchise agreement with a franchisor literally means that you are entering into a long-term relationship with the franchising company.

Although the business will officially be yours, the franchisor will maintain considerable control over the way it is run. This is in your best interest, as well as the franchisor's. A viable franchisor is concerned about the reputation of his or her trademark, or trade name. They will have most likely spent years building a reputation for quality and service that is now associated with their trademark, and they wish to ensure that no one will do anything to sully that reputation. That's why franchisors have established rules and guidelines that their franchisees must follow. The rules and guidelines have proven over time to work well and keep customers satisfied. They often include use of prescribed trade names, marketing procedures, and operational techniques.

In a franchising agreement, following these rules is considered to work to your benefit. They have been tested and proven true, and can save you countless hours of trying to find a system on your own that works consistently. These guidelines also work to your benefit in that they ensure the good name of the company itself. In the franchisor-franchisee relationship, rules and guidelines provide the bond for a win-win relationship. Of course, if you're someone who chafes at rules and proscribed methods of doing things, perhaps franchising isn't for you.

In addition to giving you a formula for the nuts and bolts of running your business, the franchisor should also provide you with significant, ongoing assistance. Assistance can be in the form of advertising, training, technical or other support, and help in getting the best prices on essential products and services. Providing ongoing assistance is in the franchisor's best interest, as well as yours. With assistance, your odds of succeeding in the business and providing the best possible product or service to your customers are greater. Your success adds to the overall success of the franchisor and further galvanizes the good reputation of the trademark or trade name in the public mind.

What Products or Services Are Best Rendered through Franchises?

Modern franchising began as a way for companies to distribute products, and some services, quickly and cost-effectively. Franchising has succeeded remarkably in this regard, and continues to succeed. Products from hamburgers to mailboxes and services from hotel rooms to hair salons have all enjoyed incredible growth through franchising.

Two Kinds of Franchises

There are two kinds of franchising: *Product Franchising* and *Business-Format Franchising*. Large companies such as Coca-Cola, Marriott Corporation, Southland Corporation (7-Eleven) all offer Product Franchising opportunities.

Obviously, you can't run a Coca-Cola bottling operation from your home. Product franchising opportunities almost always require facilities not compatible with a home-based business. Business-Format Franchising, however, is ideally suited to the home-based business. Not surprisingly, of the two, it is Business-Format Franchising that has enjoyed unparalleled growth over the last ten years.

Business-Format Franchising is a straightforward arrangement where the franchisee agrees to purchase the franchisor's trademarks, as well as a predefined system for running the business. What's actually being franchised is a format for doing business, not the production of a product. An important part of the franchise agreement includes a provision that states that the franchisee must stick rather closely to the predefined systems and specifications outlined by the franchisor. This, as we explained, is for your protection as well as the franchisor's. One of the key reasons for considering the purchase of a franchise is that it's already a proven winner. Following the franchisor's guidelines greatly increases your chances of duplicating and continuing that same success.

Business-Format Franchising: Providing Services to a Service-Based Economy

The more you look at the growth of franchising, the more you will realize this growth is due to a confluence of three trends. We've plotted the trend of modern franchising's growth, and we've looked at the working-from-home boom of the last ten years. Now add to that the fundamental shift in our nation's economy from manufacturing based to service based and you have a powerful formula for the success of business-format franchising. Services, not products, are what Business-Format Franchising does best. The services themselves are as wide ranging as the American business landscape. All the franchise opportunities listed at the end of this book are Business-Format Franchises and, by definition, are based on providing some sort of service.

Franchising in Review

Before we get into case histories of people's experiences with running home-based franchises, let's review the key points of exactly what franchising is. See if you can picture yourself in such a relationship.

- Franchising is having your own business, which you are entirely responsible for. You are not someone's employee or field agent. You benefit from your own hard work. You experience the losses and enjoy the gains. You may also sell the business you built up for a profit. There are two kinds of franchising:
1. *Product Franchising*—a franchisor agrees to sell the rights to use a product's name and formula for manufacturing. As the name implies, this type of franchising is concerned with manufacturing and marketing products. McDonald's, Pepsi, and T-Shirts Plus are Product Franchises.

2. *Business-Format Franchising.* a franchisor agrees to sell the rights to use a trademark and a formula for doing business. This type of franchise is concerned with service-oriented businesses. Molly Maid International, Money Mailer, and Decorating Den are all Business-Format Franchises.

- When you buy a franchise, you agree to purchase the rights to use a trade name or trademark and to operate your business in a way prescribed by the franchisor.

- A franchise requires a great deal of hard work and dedication. Franchising is not a get-rich-quick scheme, nor is it a passive income generator.

- Although it is not considered an official partnership, franchising is an ongoing, mutually beneficial relationship between franchisee and franchisor. The franchisor is not legally liable for what the franchisee does, or vice versa.

- Franchising is not a business opportunity nor is it like starting a business from scratch. By purchasing the rights to an established trademark and method of doing business, you have a head start in terms of name recognition, greater business and market knowledge, and a proven method to follow to help you achieve success. You pay for these benefits and you give up a measure of independence. Franchising by definition requires that you follow the franchisor's guidelines.

IS BUYING A HOME-BASED FRANCHISE FOR YOU?

Finding the answer to the above question is, we hope, one of the main reasons you have turned to this book. If you look closely, you will see that it is really a two-part question. The question asks: 1) Is franchising for you? and 2) Is running your franchise from home suited to you? In order to give you some background from which you can find the answers to these questions, let's first consider the following case history:

Case Study #1:
A Crash Course in Home-Based Franchising, the Hard Way!

Nancy (not her real name) is a bright, outgoing energetic twenty-six-year-old living in a popular beach community. She spent much of her twenties dreaming about starting her own business. Visually oriented, Nancy had considerable experience as a graphic designer and had even held an art director's position at a cutting-edge local magazine. While looking through the classified ads in the Business section of the local paper, she came across a small ad for a video franchise opportunity. Intrigued, she called the number listed. A professional-sounding voice told her of the incredible earning potential of a home-based franchise. The franchise consisted of converting people's family photos and editing them together into moving video programs. The voice told her he had been doing it very successfully for years and was now offering franchise opportunities. It sounded good to her. She asked the voice to send her some materials.

The materials were quick in coming. They seemed comprehensive and straightforward. Nancy always liked the idea of getting involved in video, and it was especially of interest to her father, a well-known designer. She called the company, and the voice that answered told her it was essential that she come down to his location in another community, about ninety miles south of her home, to discuss the matter further. Nancy made the trek.

When she got there, she had immediate reservations. The voice had led her to believe that she would be visiting a large, well-funded operation. She found herself standing at the front door of a suburban tract house. She rang the bell. The owner of the voice answered the door in his stocking feet and running shorts. She went in despite her growing doubts. Once inside she got a hard sell on the franchise. She was told that she must act immediately. He showed her the video equipment that she was to use, and then she saw a demonstration program. He quickly presented her with a franchise agreement.

She returned to her home to think over what she'd learned. Although the owner's manner seemed unprofessional, as did his home office, which was a disorganized mess, Nancy thought that the deal itself seemed straightforward enough: a one-time fee that purchased the trademark and all the equipment she needed. She discussed it with her father, who showed the agreement to an attorney. The attorney recommended against the franchise. During this time the owner made nearly daily calls to Nancy pressing her to decide. She asked for a list of other franchisees she could call. He replied that he had over forty satisfied franchisees, although he only gave her two numbers, one of which turned out to be his best friend. Despite her misgivings, she sent in the franchise agreement with a check.

The franchise agreement specified a minimum of two full days of hands-on training. Nancy drove the ninety miles again for her training. After a few hours, however, the owner told her she was a "natural" and promptly declared that she didn't need any further training. She spent the remaining two days trying to figure out how to use the equipment by herself while the owner played basketball with his best friend (interestingly, the same best friend who had given Nancy the glowing reference).

Nancy's video equipment arrived within a few weeks. When she set it up she found one of the VCRs didn't function properly. She called the franchisor to remedy the situation. He became quite agitated: "He actually called me an idiot!" claims Nancy. She now knew she had a problem. To make a long story short, after many calls and much arguing she finally did receive a new VCR that functioned properly. She was now ready to open her business. The problem was, she didn't quite know where to begin. Although the owner had promised extensive assistance in marketing, sales, and lead generation, none, of course, was to be had. His suggestion to find potential customers: "Try the phone book."

Although Nancy was quite good at creating the videos she did free for a few family and friends, she was at a loss as to how to actually market her business. She also felt "bad" about asking for the suggested price for providing the service. As a result, she began to feel overwhelmed. With no support and inadequate training from the franchisor, no experience in marketing, and a "lack of the discipline it takes to work from home," Nancy gave up on making her livelihood from the franchise only four months after receiving her equipment.

In retrospect, Nancy now says that although the franchisor was unhelpful at best, and fraudulent at worst, she was equally at fault for her experience. She has since contacted other franchisees providing the service which she found in the phone book! They have had generally positive experiences with their franchises. In talking with them, she found out that each and every one had had prior extensive experience in video, business management, and marketing before purchasing their franchises. Nancy's advice to anyone thinking about buying a franchise: "Research, research, and more research. Research the franchisor, research your market, and research yourself to make sure you are ready to take on the responsibility of running the kind of business you're considering."

WHAT FRANCHISORS LOOK FOR: FRANCHISOR SURVEYS

Nancy's unsuccessful franchising experience was the result of a number of factors, many of which could have been avoided. The first one is to determine if franchising itself is right for you.

The personality profile a franchisor is looking for should be the same traits you should look for in yourself indicating if franchising is for you. In other words, look at yourself as a candidate in the same way a franchisor would. Look for the personality traits that you have that will help you run a franchise successfully. The best franchisors are quite objective in the way they determine good franchising candidates. You will only benefit from applying the same objectivity in assessing yourself.

To help define just what franchisors are looking for, we went directly to the source. We asked successful franchisors across the country what personality traits, skills, and experiences they look for in a franchisee. We also asked them what characteristics, skills, and talents they find to be helpful to franchisees in achieving franchising success. Here's what they told us.

President: Connie D'Imperio
Company: Color Your Carpet, 1-800-321-6567, 904-272-6567
Founded: 1979
Franchises: 24 franchises in 15 states and 5 countries

"The target market for our carpet-coloring service is upper-end apartment building owners and upscale homeowners, so I look for franchisees who can communicate well on that level. Our coloring process can get quite technical. Excellent math and English skills are essential. In term of general traits, integrity, fastidiousness, and perfectionism are important. Interestingly, I've never granted a franchise to someone who had experience in the carpet-cleaning business. You'll actually find that most franchisors aren't looking for people who have direct experience in their particular industry, especially if the franchise is based on a technical process. I prefer someone with a clean slate who has aptitude. I also don't look for people with huge portfolios or excess capital; they usually aren't as ambitious. I look for people in the middle, with enough capital to be comfortable, but hungry enough to build the business. I look for about a $30,000 to $80,000 income history."

President: Paul Carter
Company: American Leak Detection, 1-800-755-6697
Founded: 1984
Franchises: 100 franchises in 250 offices

"The general impression is that franchisors like people who have always followed a system and are not freethinkers. Our most successful franchisees are entrepreneurial, aggressive, and seek new knowledge about business. We have attracted people who enjoy working outdoors, from home, with spouses. A team environment is encouraged. We look for team players with an entrepreneurial spirit."

Chief Operating Officer: Doug Dwyer
Company: Worldwide Refinishing Systems, 1-800-583-9099 extension 2463
Founded: 1988
Franchises: 400 locations in 20 countries

"Who I'm looking for today is someone that has a desire to express their entrepreneurial spirit. [Someone] that has a vision of building a business, not just being the person that is the business. Earlier we looked for people that were just looking for a business opportunity. In some territories we're still interested in that. In the larger areas we're interested in people who want to build a business, not just someone looking to buy a job. Someone who wants to build a business so once he or she owns something that has a lot of equity built into it for resale."

Manager of Franchise Development: Ray DePouli
Company: Priority Management Systems, 1-800-221-9031
Founded: 1984
Franchises: Over 300 in 17 countries

"In this business, you're selling training. It's conceptual, so the individual has to have some polished skills [which are achieved through training provided by the franchisor]. As far as transferable skills are concerned, the individual first and foremost has to be very persistent as a self-starter, has to have a little bulldog in him. This is what makes a successful business owner; regardless of all the support that's offered them, they've got to pick it up and use it. They're not going to replace the income that they're used to in the first several months. One of the facts behind franchising is that in the first three years, incomes will generally be somewhere below or about equal to the corporate incomes people have been used to. From the third to the fifth year and beyond, incomes far exceed what most individuals earn in corporate America. People have to pay their dues, and they have to realize that up-front. In any franchising [arrangement], if the person is truly independent, it's not good, because that person will not be able to work within the system. The system will be too restrictive for them. We see individuals, as many franchisors do, as people venturing out, possibly for the first time, into their own business. They want the structure, and they want to have some level of comfort that the risk of failure is going to be somewhat minimized."

Director of Administration and Compliance: Katie McLaughlin
Company: Fortune Practice Management, 1-800-628-1052
Founded: 1991
Franchises: 30 nationwide

"We have no set criteria we look for, but there are some things that are important: We look for self-starters who are not afraid of selling or marketing. The franchise fee is fairly high, so we look for people who are well capitalized. Franchisees are calling on doctors and dentists to try and help their practices, so they have to be able to get out there and knock on some doors. We look for people who are resourceful. To be in a franchise situation, you want somebody who has enough of an entrepreneurial spirit to want to run their own business but also realizes that they have to follow some guidelines. A health-care sales and marketing background doesn't hurt. Our business is about helping people improve their lives and businesses, so we look for people who really want to help, who have the attitude that they're not in it just for the money."

FRANCHISING PERSONALITY PROFILE

Some larger, more established franchisors even give a test to determine if you are a good candidate to purchase their franchise. The following informal Franchising Profile Assessor is taken loosely from tests provided to franchisors to help them assess candidates by TIMS Management Systems, Inc., in Tucson, Arizona. TIMS is the foremost psychological test provider for the franchising industry. Although their clients primarily include large, product franchisors, the personality best suited to franchising success is the same for home-based business franchises. TIMS also provides low-cost tests for people who are considering buying a franchise. We suggest that you take a TIMS test. Their tests are professionally analyzed and the results will help provide insights that will be helpful in making the decision to buy a franchise. Their phone number and address are listed in Appendix 2 of this book.

Here, however, are several of the key issues franchise profile tests help you assess and what franchises consider to be the ideal profile.

1. *Dominance.* How dominant are you? Franchisors look for franchisees who rate between 50 and 75 percent in terms of dominance. Moderately dominant personalities are strong willed but understand that their egos must be set aside for the good of the franchising relationship. People who rate from 1 to about 50 percent in dominance generally do not have the drive to see a franchise through rough times, or steer it through conflicts. Those who show a high dominance rate between 75 and 100 percent have the will and drive to establish a franchise but will often chafe at the rules and operating procedures imposed by the franchisor. If you consider yourself a highly dominant person who likes to do things your way, you may be happier in a business opportunity than a franchise.

2. *Influence with People.* Influence, in this case, is described as having an outgoing and enthusiastic nature. High-influence people enjoy meeting people, have a positive outlook, and like to communicate. Again, moderation in this realm is the key to franchising success. It is essential for a successful franchisee to be outgoing, personable, and able to communicate well. If you rate between 50 and 75 percent in this area, that bodes well for your franchising success. Although sales and customer service are important areas that high-influence people excel at, it is also important to be able to keep one's nose to

the grindstone, as it were, and not avoid the less glamorous administrative details of running your franchise. Remember, at least at the beginning, you will probably be solely responsible for every aspect of your business. If you would rather act on your own than follow franchisor rules, sell as opposed to track sales figures, and talk rather than do strategic planning, you may want to consider developing your own business from scratch or buying one of the other kinds of packaged businesses in this book.

3. *Steadiness.* Believe it or not, franchisors prefer franchisees who demonstrate a moderately low steadiness score. Steadiness, as defined by the TIMS tests, deals with traits such as "ability to adapt to change," "sensitivity," and "predictability." If you are uncomfortable with change and prefer predictable routines, you may not react well to the frequent changes thrown at you by the marketplace, and sometimes the franchisor. Also if you often interpret remarks or actions as negative or take them personally, and later find that no offense was actually meant, you may find that you're too sensitive to effectively run a franchise in the hubbub of the business and activities where few people take the time to consider your feelings in their communications with you. If you need to know how everything is going to come out before it takes place, and your peace of mind depends on knowing what each day holds for you before it begins, then you require a significant level of predictability in your life. If this is the case, franchising, or running your own business in general, will not make you happy or fulfilled.

4. *Compliance.* There doesn't seem to be a standard for the Compliance rating. Some franchisors require a high degree of compliance with the rules and systems they outline. Other franchises require a bit more flexibility and the ability to think on your feet. It's up to you to determine how much compliance a franchise you're considering requires. It's also up to you to know exactly how much compliance you're willing to give. Success in the franchise depends upon finding the right balance between complying with the franchisor's requirements and taking enough initiative to assure your own success. If you feel that you are not at all compliant and tend to resent authority, you may wish to consider a business opportunity or starting a business from scratch.

5. *Independence.* How much independence are you comfortable with? This is a crucial question in deciding to become a franchisee. Right now, you may be fed up with your boss, your job, or both. You may justifiably feel that you know how to do things better. But just imagine if it was you who had to make all the decisions. What if there

was no one to tell you what time to be at work, how much or what was expected of you, or how to organize your time? Suppose there was no one around to check the quality of your work? If this situation sounds a little frightening, the structure of a franchise could be helpful, but home-based franchisees must walk a fine line. On one side, the franchisor will generally provide you with an outline of how to run the business, and may set up quotas or standards for performance. On the other side, you will need to structure and manage your own time. Your home can be a mighty distracting place to work. Phone calls, children, your home environment, the kitchen loaded with goodies, the TV in the den, and so forth—all can become powerful distractions from getting your work done.

Also consider this question: Are you used to working closely with others? Co-workers, secretaries, even bosses and supervisors, all share the workday in most salaried situations. Are you ready for the independence of working on your own from home? After a few weeks of working from home, many people find themselves missing those "pesky" co-workers or that overbearing boss. We cannot stress enough the importance of coming to terms with these issues. You must seriously consider the amount of independence you are ready for and create personal and professional support systems for yourself before deciding to operate a franchise.

Checking Your Franchising Personality

Chapter 2 contains a detailed Personality Profile which will help you determine where you fall in terms of Independence, Compliance, Steadiness, Influence, and Dominance. Before working through the Personality Profile, however, read through the following sections in this chapter. You'll find a detailed, easy-to-follow overview of franchising law, problem areas to resolve, and the terms of a basic franchise agreement. This information is intended to give you the background you'll need to negotiate a favorable franchise agreement for yourself and have a more positive home-based experience than Nancy's—perhaps one more like this.

Case Study #2:
A New Franchise Helps Make a Needed Change

Cheryl Trull moved to Birmingham, Alabama, five years ago when her husband, a career steelworker, was transferred. After having spent most of her life in Bucks County, Pennsylvania, a beautiful suburb of Philadelphia, she found the change of regions difficult, to say the least. Trained as an LPN Psychiatric Nurse, Cheryl sought to make inroads into her new environment by finding a job in her field. That's when she got another shock. "In Bucks County," Cheryl discovered, "starting salaries for psyche nurses were about $15 per hour minimum, and that was the early 1980s, when I started out. Down here in Birmingham, there's a great demand for what I do, but I couldn't find anything starting at higher than $6.50 per hour." Cheryl was also raising a family and could only work part-time. "At those income levels, it didn't make sense for me to work at all."

Making the best of her new situation, Cheryl used her move to reinvent herself professionally. "I always dreamed of owning my own business the whole time I was working as a nurse." She read about home-based franchising in *Success* magazine, and the idea appealed to her. The flexible hours, the home-based office, and being her own boss seemed the perfect situation. She even called one or two of the franchise opportunities listed in the magazine. Not being one to jump into things, Cheryl waited almost two years before making her move.

During those two years, she got to know her new community better and continued to research home-based businesses. One franchise opportunity in particular struck her fancy: *Color Your Carpet,* headquartered in Orange Park, Florida. She called the franchisor and immediately felt a rapport. "Connie D'Imperio, the franchisor, described the opportunity straight-out, no heavy sales pitch or unrealistic language. I felt I could trust her," explains Cheryl. The franchise itself consisted of refurbishing carpets with a unique process that actually changed their color, and Cheryl liked that aspect as well: "I've always enjoyed painting, and I like to change things. Perhaps most importantly, I like helping people. With this franchise, I felt I could do all these things." More research into this franchise, as well as a few others who offered similar services, led Cheryl to choose Color Your Carpet.

The going wasn't easy initially. "In the first six months I quit 2,200 times!" said Cheryl. "There wasn't a lot of business, and there was a great deal of competition." One piece of research she hadn't done was how much competition was already established in her market. Cheryl cautions potential franchisees to "always check the phone book to identify what competition you'll have. I didn't realize how many carpet service companies there were in my area." Her first year wasn't a total washout, however. "I did actually make a profit: $181 after deductions!"

Things improved quite a bit her second year. Cheryl kept at it and applied her own personality to building her business. "The franchisor provided some great marketing ideas, but I didn't agree with them. They didn't jibe with my natural way of doing things." Instead of the direct contact recommended by the franchisor, she took out ads and exhibited at local home and garden shows. She also built up a steady stream of referrals through word of mouth. "I basically built my business on word of mouth and from my van.

It's purple with big red lettering! I actually get a lot of business from people who've seen the van."

This year, Cheryl's second year in business, her biggest problem is hiring people to help out with all the business she's getting. "I do all of the carpet coloring and have an assistant help me move the furniture, etc. I get in the truck and go out to the customer. I answer the phones, do the accounting, the billing, and other bookkeeping functions. And I'm a full-time mom." Adds Cheryl, "Sometimes I'm really busy and need help, and sometimes it's still slow and there isn't the income or work to support someone. My husband helps out when he can, and often I can get someone to moonlight, but it's still tough."

Although things are still up and down, in general Cheryl's business is far more stable and generally profitable. "Some days the phone just rings off the hook," exclaims Cheryl. "Just last month I got a major contract with Pizza Hut. My accountant says I'm doing great. My bottom line should be a lot more than $181 this year!"

Is Your Prospective Franchisor Franchising Too Soon?

The tremendous success of franchising has led to a bevy of management-consulting firms specializing in developing franchises. They approach businesses in an effort to convince them to turn their business into a franchise which, of course, these companies will help them do for a substantial fee. While there isn't anything wrong with such business franchising companies per se, if a business decides to franchise too early in its development, there can be problems.

If a business gets franchised before it has had a chance to work out all the kinks involved in making the enterprise successful, that business's franchisees will buy whatever problems remain right along with the company's trademark and know-how. One of the primary benefits of buying a franchise is that the franchisor has already developed a *proven* method of operating the business. This avoids much of the costly trial-and-error process a new business owner must go through. If the business franchises too early in its development, before it has established a proven track record, you and your frachisor will be in the same boat in going through these problems together. Obviously, that's not the kind of franchisor/franchisee relationship you want to have.

The way to avoid this situation is simple: Ask your prospective franchisor how long she was in business before she decided to franchise. If the answer is less than two to five years, approach with caution. If the answer is less than one, consider another franchisor.

FRANCHISING LAW: MAKING SURE YOU'RE IN AGREEMENT

Franchising, like any other area of American business, is subject to a specific body of laws and regulations. These laws and regulations are designed to protect your rights as a franchisee, but unfortunately more often than not, they actually protect the franchisor even more. The following states have their own franchising laws, which are generally more stringent than federal laws, and usually supersede federal law: California, Hawaii, Illinois, Indiana, Maryland, Michigan, Minnesota, New York, North Dakota, Oregon, Rhode Island, South Dakota, Virginia, Washington, Wisconsin. Check with your state attorney general's office to find out more about the franchising laws in your state.

The FTC and the Uniform Franchise Offering Circular

To protect people buying a franchise in states that do not have specific laws regarding franchising, the FTC has established a comprehensive code of regulations, commonly referred to as the "franchise rule." The franchise rule applies to every franchise in the U.S., except where state laws supersede them, as we mentioned above. It stipulates that a franchisor must provide a detailed disclosure statement to any potential franchisee. This required statement is also called the Uniform Franchise Offering Circular (UFOC).

The disclosure statement, offering circular, or "prospectus," as the UFOC is often called, must contain specific information about the franchise and all the information must be accurate and truthful. The information in the statement must include:

- Who the franchisor is
- Persons who are affiliated with the franchisor
- An accurate description of the business
- Background information on the franchisor and principals in the company, including business experience and track record
- The franchisor's financial information
- Information regarding the number of franchises, their failure rate, and their termination rate
- Bankruptcy and litigation histories of the franchisor and principal officers
- The franchise fee (the fee required to purchase the franchise)
- Ongoing fees, royalties, and/or any scheduled continuing expenses that will be paid to the franchisor
- All services or goods that you must purchase, rent, or lease from the franchisor
- All terms of franchisor-provided financing (if any)

- All restrictions on how you are to operate the business
- The details of training programs
- Procedures regarding the renewal, cancellation, or termination of the franchise

If any claims are made by the franchisor regarding potential income, the franchise rule dictates that he or she must provide reasonable proof. It is beyond the scope of this book to outline the many specific franchising laws, especially as they do vary from state to state.

Before entering into a franchise agreement, however, we highly recommend that you familiarize yourself with the basics of federal and state franchising regulations. In Appendix 2 there is a list by region of state agencies that regulate franchises. Contact them for information on the regulations in your state. If you live in a state that does not regulate franchising, any franchise you are considering is regulated by the FTC. Information about the FTC's rules for franchising can be obtained by writing to the Federal Trade Commission, 6th and Pennsylvania Avenue, NW, Washington, DC 20580; calling 202-326-2222; or accessing its Web page at http://www.ftc.gov.

ELEMENTS OF A FRANCHISE AGREEMENT:
KNOWLEDGE IS POWER

The following section will give you an overview of the primary components of an entire franchising agreement. Every franchise agreement is different, so the one presented to you by the franchisor may be quite different from the general outline presented here. What follows, however, is a composite of the main points you should find in a standard franchise agreement. We will explain each area of the agreement, then offer some tips and insights to help you negotiate an agreement that is advantageous to you. Keep in mind that many franchisors, particularly larger ones, are not open to negotiating their franchise agreement. Most have invested a great deal of time and money in the form and content of their agreement. But if you feel the franchise is a sound opportunity and you have a good rapport with the franchisor, if he or she tells you flatly that the agreement is not open for negotiation, don't let that stop you from trying to change what you can. Remember that franchise agreements are written on paper, not engraved in stone.

Use the following information for reference only. And, before making any decision regarding an actual franchising agreement, show it to an attorney and accountant experienced in franchise law and business. You can locate experienced professionals through the organizations listed in Appendix 2.

Grant of Franchise

This is usually the first section of a franchise agreement. Generally it's in the form of an introduction or preamble. The Grant of Franchise defines the nature of the agreement that will be detailed in the following sections.

Tips:
- Don't skip past this part! Often, there will be language that says "I have read this agreement and agree fully with its terms and conditions." Your signature casts the agreement in stone. Make sure that you really have read it and, more importantly, understand it. You'll have to live with it for a long time.
- Do not take this statement lightly. If there is anything in the agreement that's not immediately apparent to you upon signing, this acknowledgment will ensure that you will lose if you try to take the franchisor to court at a later date.

Use of Trademark(s), Patents, and Copyrights

The very concept of franchising is based on a franchisor assigning the rights for use of his or her trademarks and trade names to you. This is the section that spells out the specifics of who owns the patents, trademarks, and trade names (the franchisor) and the ways in which you can use them in your franchise

Tips:
- Make sure you understand the extent of your rights to use the franchisor's trademark and trade name, and try to remove as many restrictions as to their use as possible.
- Find out if you can still use the trademarks and names if the franchisor loses rights to them. (In most cases you will not be able to.)
- Ask whether anyone else in your proposed territory already has rights to use the trademarks, etc. If they do, make sure that this doesn't impinge on your rights of usage.

Defining the Parties

The next section in most franchise agreements defines the relationships of the parties involved. This section stipulates that the franchisor is a distinct and independent entity from you and your business. This means that the franchisor has no legal liability for your actions, nor do you have liability for the franchisor's.

Tip:
- This section will protect you as well as the franchisor. Make sure, however, that indeed you don't have any liability for the frachisor in any way, such as for its debts or other obligations.

Payments

Here the franchise fee will be listed. This section will also define which additional fees, costs, royalties, or any other form of payment are required of you. If these fees are ongoing, a schedule as to their payment will be specified. If fees are based on percentages of your earnings, the formulas will be defined.

Tips:
- The terms of payment should be clearly spelled out in the agreement. Make sure the amount of the franchise fee is spelled out specifically.
- If there is an ongoing royalty fee, make sure you know how much it will be, when it is due, and if it is based on how much you earn (sliding scale).
- If fees are based on what you earn, make sure the percentages of earnings versus payment are clearly spelled out.
- Since start-up is the most cash-intensive period in your business, see if you can add a condition in your contract that will waive or defer royalty payments for the first six months or a year.
- Ensure that the agreement spells out what your franchise fees and royalties will be used for.
- You may also be expected to pay an additional advertising or marketing fee. If your ongoing royalties do not cover advertising, make sure that the additional advertising fee percentage, or formula, is clearly represented and that you understand what it is.

Term of Agreement

Term of agreement language specifies the length of time during which the franchise agreement will be in force.

Tips:
- If, on the one hand, you find the general terms of the franchise agreement to be favorable to you, and you know you will want to be in that business for a long time, try to negotiate a longer term.
- If, on the other hand, you find the agreement's terms not to be so desirable, you may want to try to settle on a shorter term so you can renegotiate a more favorable agreement in the future.

Renewal of Franchise Agreement

Renewal of Franchise clauses specify when, how, and how many times a franchise agreement may be renewed. Almost half of the franchise agreements in force today have a term of ten years, with the second most common term being five years. In rare cases, an agreement will not specify a renewal term. This area was one of the chief concerns franchisees from across the nation brought to the 1995 White House Conference on Small Business. They were upset with franchisors who didn't renew or opened previously exclusive territories to others after the completion of a term during which a franchisor had built a successful business.

> *Tips:*
> - Make sure your agreement contains renewal language, and discuss its terms and conditions with your attorney to make sure you can live with them.
> - If you feel you may be able to negotiate a better agreement in the future, ask the company to include language that specifies that the agreement itself may be changed or renegotiated during a renewal period.

Development and Opening

Development and Opening clauses stipulate how long you have to develop your business and get it open: 90 to 120 days are the average. Generally, you must secure any financing, outfit and set up your place of business, hire any necessary personnel, and otherwise prepare your business for operation within the development and opening period specified in the agreement.

> *Tip:*
> - If you feel that the time period specified is too short, try to lengthen it in the agreement, or delay signing the agreement until you are better positioned to get under way in the specified time.

Territory

There should be a section of your agreement that specifically defines the territory in which you are allowed to operate. Often, franchise fees are determined by the size of the territory you take on. Usually, the larger the territory, the larger the fee.

> *Tips:*
> - Make sure that the franchisor specifically spells out what your geographic territory will be.

- See that your territory, as defined, will be exclusive in that the franchisor will not be allowed to conduct an exact or similar operation within your territory for the duration of the franchise agreement.
- Do not commit to a territory larger than you will comfortably be able to service. This can lead to considerable frustration on your part, and dissatisfaction for the franchisor.
- Conversely, don't settle for a territory too small to be a realistically profitable market for your business.

Advertising

The franchisor will probably include language that stipulates that you use its advertising designs, trademarks, logos, etc., in your advertising. This is generally to your advantage as it will give your business credibility and name recognition (one of the best reasons to get into franchising). There may also be requirements that you submit any advertising designs, flyers, ads, commercials, etc., for the franchisor's approval. (This can be like free advertising consultation; take advantage of it.)

Tips:
- The advertising section of the franchise agreement should also specify exactly what the franchisor's obligations are in terms of providing advertising, especially if there is to be an ongoing advertising fee. Unless these obligations are listed clearly and you understand them thoroughly, you could be expecting more advertising and marketing from your franchisor than they intend to do.
- Look to see if the franchisor offers to assist you in developing advertising specific to your franchise and market. If this is not spelled out in the agreement, try to get the franchisor to include it.
- Make sure that there is enough flexibility in the advertising or marketing plan to allow you to react to the specifics of your market. For example, the agreement might call for an investment of 40 percent of your advertising budget in local television ads. Yet, your particular market might be such that radio or direct mail might be far more effective.

Equipment and Supplies

Many franchise agreements include stipulations that you purchase certain equipment and supplies directly from the franchisor. In the case of many cleaning and inspection types of franchises, the business might be based on unique equipment, techniques, or supplies provided by the franchisor. In most instances, this is to your benefit. You will be able to provide services unavailable from anyone else in your territory.

Tips:
- If the franchise agreement requires that you purchase nonunique equipment or supplies—in other words, equipment and supplies that you can get anywhere—make sure that the prices you are being charged are not inflated.
- Check current market rates on similar items to ensure that you are not being overcharged.

Franchisor-Provided Training and Assistance

Any franchise opportunity should include some sort of training provided by the franchisor. The franchisor may also provide ongoing consultation, training, and marketing assistance. The franchisor will also provide you with a franchise manual. Since this manual contains the essence of the franchisor's business, you will receive it only as a loan; it will not be given to you or sold. The length of time for your possession of this document will be spelled out in this section of the agreement.

Tips:
- Ensure that the length of initial training, the period of ongoing training (if applicable), location of training, and content and nature of the training are specified in the agreement.
- Make sure the specific terms of the training are spelled out (i.e., who pays for travel expenses, who pays for living expenses during training, who pays for training materials, etc.).
- If ongoing training or consultation is provided, make sure that the frequency, nature, and any costs or conditions are clear and that you understand what they are.

Assignment of Franchise

The assignment of franchise clause stipulates who (almost always the franchisor) has the right to grant or assign the franchise and its trademarks. This area of your agreement will also dictate the procedure you must follow if you wish to sell your franchise at a later date. It will also detail how the franchise can be passed on in the unfortunate event of your own passing.

Tips:
- Make sure that you are in full understanding of this area of your franchise agreement. One of the greatest advantages of owning your

own business is the ability to sell it later at a profit, or to pass it on to your heirs. Try to make sure that your agreement allows you to do this.

- If the franchisor stipulates that the franchise may not be assigned without his or her approval, your heirs might not be able to inherit your business in the event of your passing.
- The franchisor may hold the right of first refusal. This means that you must offer the franchise to the franchisor first before you sell it. It also means that the franchisor has first rights to acquire the franchise in the event of your passing. Be aware of this.

Termination of Franchise Agreement

Termination clauses spell out the conditions under which the franchisor may terminate the franchise agreement. This can be an area of great contention in franchise law. In most states, laws still heavily favor the franchisor in regard to the termination of franchise agreements. In many instances a franchisor may terminate a franchise agreement without demonstrating just cause.

Tips:
- Groups of franchisee advocates are lobbying to get Congress to pass national franchise laws that will eliminate a franchisor's right to terminate without cause. Until such a law is passed, try to include language in your franchise agreement that specifies exactly what the causes of termination are, and that termination should be limited to only those causes. Also try into include language that obligates a franchisor to clearly inform you of any cause for termination.
- Since the laws that govern a franschisor's right to termination vary from state to state, check with the agency in your state that regulates franchising (see Appendix 2) to find out what the laws are in your area. If you live in a state that does not govern franchising, refer to the termination rule established by the FTC (see Appendix 2).

NEGOTIATING A FRANCHISE AGREEMENT: SAFEGUARD YOUR RIGHTS

By definition, franchisors have been involved a lot longer than you in the business of franchising and easily have the upper hand in terms of familiarity with the law. Therefore, we strongly recommend that you show any franchising agreement to an attorney experienced in franchise law before you sign it.

There are specific contractual situations you should look out for, however, that some franchisors will try to get you to agree to that greatly tip the legal scale in their favor. This doesn't mean they are being shifty, under-handed, or illegal; it merely means that they are trying to gain an advantage in the relationship, which is common business practice. By being aware of these practices, you can try to make sure unfavorable conditions are not a part of your franchising agreement—or if they are, at least you will know about them and what they mean. The following are some of the most common issues you need to be alert to.

Waiver of Legal Rights

Many franchise agreements will require that the prospective franchisee waive his or her rights under applicable federal or state laws. The reason for the inclusion of these types of clauses is that they tend to relieve the franchisor of liabilities or duties imposed by law. Efforts are being made at both state and federal levels to prohibit the inclusion of these waivers in franchise agreements.

Freedom of Association

A fair number of franchisors actively discourage their franchisees from forming or organizing independent organizations. This might be written into your franchise agreement.

No Fiduciary Duty

Fiduciary duties are an obligation to provide particular factual financial information, and they are common to many business transactions. Some franchising agreements contain wording that reduces or eliminates the franchisor's fiduciary duty to the franchisee. In plain English, this means that the franchisor is not obligated to factually report how a franchisee's franchising fees, advertising fees, royalties, and other fees are being used. Try to get them to spell these out in your agreement.

Encroachment

Encroachment means another franchisee being able to operate in your territory, region, or business area. Try to ensure that the boundaries of your territory are clearly set, and that other franchisees are not allowed to operate within them. At least, be sure that your franchise agreement clearly spells out the terms of any encroachment. Encroachment can take a different form, such as sales being made via informercials or on the Internet.

Sourcing of Supplies

As discussed earlier, many franchise relationships mandate that franchisees purchase supplies, equipment, furniture, or other items from the franchisor or from sources affiliated with or approved by the franchisor. If the prices are inflated, especially if they are grossly inflated, it may be an indication that the franchisor is not acting in good faith. A franchisor should always be oriented to helping you, the franchisee, operate profitably. After all, you are business partners. If the franchisor seeks to make unusual demands on you for his or her profit at your expense, you may wish to consider another franchisor.

Release to Sell

Look for language in your franchise agreement about Release to Sell. In many cases, franchisors require that you obtain their permission before you sell the franchise. This is their right. Make sure, however, that upon sale of the franchise you will be able to realize a profit from all the sweat and hard work you put into the franchise that will make it more desirable for someone to buy. In other words, make sure that you, not just the franchisor, are allowed to make a profit from the sale of your franchise.

Termination without Cause

As discussed earlier, this can be a contentious area of franchising law. Franchisors, justly, reserve the right to terminate a franchise agreement if the franchisee is not living up to his or her terms of the agreement, or if the franchise is not performing as expected. Problems arise, however, when a franchisor terminates an agreement arbitrarily or without cause. To avoid this problem, see the tips on page 61.

Noncompete Clauses

A franchise relationship almost always includes a post-termination covenant that prevents the franchisee from directly competing with the franchisor for a specific length of time after the franchisee has given up the franchise. This means that once you have terminated your relationship with the franchisor, you will not be allowed to open a business that would put you in direct competition with the franchisor for a specified amount of time. In a way, this is fair because in most cases the franchisor will have invested considerable time and resources in training you to run a particular type of business. No franchisor wants to invest in training someone who can become their direct competition. On the other hand, you will have invested a tremendous amount of your own time, hard work, and resources, and you should reasonably expect to profit from this investment as well. It is in your best interest to obtain as short a time as possible in the noncompete covenant of your franchise agreement.

No Private Right of Action

Be aware that as of the writing of this book, current FTC rules on franchising do not grant franchisees a private right of action. This means that you, the franchisee, will have to appeal directly to the federal government for redress if your franchisor violates an FTC rule, or if you have any specific complaints and grievances. In other words, as a franchisee you cannot pursue legal action privately through your own attorneys. So you would be well advised to check with your state attorney general to see whether or not your state grants franchisees the private right of action. If not, negotiate to insert such a right into your agreement.

FIRSTHAND EXPERIENCE: CONVERSATIONS WITH HOME-BASED FRANCHISEES

In the course of writing this book, we interviewed many successful home-based franchisees about their experiences and why they believe they've been successful. The following are a few of their stories. As you read through them, you might want to think about how each franchisee rates in each of the five areas in the Franchise Personality Profile. Then compare your own personality profile with that of the franchisees we've profiled.

A Formula For Success

Case Study #3:
Mike and Cathy King, Wheeling, West Virginia
Bingo Bugle **newspaper, a weekly newspaper for bingo players**

Mike King's long stint as a radio marketing professional and on-air disc jockey had come to an end and it was time to begin looking for the next path to take in his life. The idea of franchising appealed to him, and he also wanted to take advantage of his media background. After researching many possibilities, he came across the *Bingo Bugle* newspaper, a specialty publication that caters to bingo enthusiasts. "I liked that the franchise agreement required very little capital, and although going from radio to newsprint, many of the same marketing principles are the same," explains Mike. He then did extensive checking in his area. He found that bingo was "huge" in his area, and that nobody was filling the void as far as advertising the games available and bringing the bingo community together were concerned. After checking out the franchisor thoroughly, he decided to purchase a franchise. According to Mike, "I liked the support they offered. They provide articles and syndicated columns as an ongoing service. This would put me head and shoulders above anyone else who might try to put out a bingo publication."

The franchising fee was minimal and included three days of training in addition to supplying a steady stream of content for the publication. The franchising agreement also includes a royalty of 10 percent of gross sales. This figure is somewhat high in comparison with most franchise agreements, but Mike says, "As far as I'm concerned, it's worth it for me to pay them a royalty rather try to come up with [content] all by myself." In terms of marketing support, the franchisor also has contacts in both state and county agencies that license bingo games, and he provides Mike with an up-to-date listing of every bingo game in his territory.

In his three years of running the franchise, Mike's success has exceeded his expectations. "The company represented itself fairly and there have been no surprises, other than how quickly I've grown," says Mike. He works an average of twenty-five to thirty hours per month and achieved profitability in one month. This is not the average profile of a new franchisee, but Mike proves it can be done.

Mike sums up his success in franchising with just one word: "Sales!" According to Mike, "If there're no sales, there's no business. Creativity in ad design is helpful, but 80 percent of success is going out there and making the sale." He goes for a very direct, people-oriented approach to getting business. When speaking about the best ways to get business, he gets rather passionate. "Go out and just get the business. I've never been able to sell on the phone. Mailings and other promotions haven't seemed to help either. Prospective customers can't understand the passion you have for the product or service you offer if you're not there, in person, to explain and show it to them."

Finding and consistently tapping resources for information on his industry, customer base, marketing trends, and business in general are the hallmarks of success in any business, and Mike is no exception. Being a people person, Mike's resources are primarily other people. "Overall, working with other publishers is my number-one resource," says Mike. "Number two would be reading as much as possible . . . articles, books, listening to tapes, anything that relates to the business or the market. During the first six months of running the *Bingo Bugle,* I ate, slept, and drank everything having to do with bingo."

One of the most important, if not the most important, reasons people succeed in franchising, or any business, is that they truly enjoy what they do. Their personalities, likes, interests, talents, and skills are uniquely matched to their chosen business. In addition to enjoying the actual nuts-and-bolts operation of a franchise (the Core Function, which we will discuss in greater detail in Chapter 2), it is also important that you feel comfortable with the kind of business you're in. In this case, the kind of business is franchising. Mike sums up the classic advantages of franchising: "I have the freedom to generally operate on my own, but with the support and guidance of the parent company." "The nice thing about my franchising experience," Mike adds, "is that the company doesn't dictate much at all. I've never felt like they were breathing down my neck in any way. I pretty much have creative license to do what I want, but I really do appreciate the support and format for my business."

A Well-Matched Business

Case Study #4:
Bob and Marci Leach, Columbus, OH
American Leak Detection—pinpoint detection of water or sewer leaks
with electronic equipment manufactured by the company

Bob Leach was a U.S. Marine for twelve years. Marci was a homemaker taking care of the kids. When Bob's assignment in the service changed after the Gulf War, he decided he might be more satisfied outside of the Marine Corps. Some checking in local newspapers and other sources revealed a possible new avenue for the Leaches. A franchise from American Leak Detection seemed to offer Bob the kind of work he enjoyed—outdoor activity, problem solving, responding to challenges—and also gave Marci a chance to utilize her prior marketing experience.

"The reason that we chose the company was that they had a much better rating in all the entrepreneur and success-related magazines," explains Marci. After some additional checking into the demand for leak detection services in their area, Bob and Marci bought the franchise. The franchise agreement included a one-time payment for equipment and a sliding-scale monthly royalty percentage. "The initial percentage starts at 10 percent and goes down from there. The more you make, the lower the percentage," explains Marci. The agreement also included ongoing technical and marketing support and an optional six-week training course of which Bob took full advantage.

In their five years of running the business, Bob and Marci are profitable, but "just barely." Yet they both say the franchise has met their expectations in terms of income and workload. They each work about forty to forty-five hours a week. Bob goes out into the field, and Marci focuses on marketing and generating leads. "Ongoing support from the company is 100 percent. Whatever we ask, if they're able to do it, they do it. The support is really tremendous. They even supply us with account leads, which they generate from national trade shows," says Marci. The Leaches live comfortably, are meeting their expectations, and feel fulfilled. This is the very definition of success.

One of the main reasons the Leaches were able to achieve this measure of success was that, despite the hard work and long hours involved, they are always motivated to keep going. The skills they brought with them from previous work and life experiences have helped a great deal. Marci says, "I did marketing for my other job, so that prepared me for this. Bob's technical knowledge—being an aviator taught him how to do things one step at a time—was the most helpful. In this field, that is how you have to do it: one step at a time."

When marketing their business Marci and Bob combine their skills and talents into an effective approach. We've seen this combining of complementary skills work over and over again. Through the years, we've seen that there is no one way to market a business. The best results come from business owners adapting their own unique personalities into a marketing mix that works for them. Some are people oriented and utilize networking, in-person sales calls, and "cold" calling to great effect. Others are more task or process oriented. They prefer marketing through the mail, with ads, on line, etc. Bob and Marci use a combination of approaches. "Our marketing efforts are really a mixture of things. We do Yellow Page ads, direct marketing, we are members of various associations here in town, and encourage word of mouth."

Not only has American Leak Detection been a good choice for the Leaches, they feel that franchising itself is well matched to their needs as well. Marci explains, "One of the reasons we picked a franchise is that we felt we needed the support. In terms of control, the parent company has a very hands-off approach. But then again, we've never stepped over the line either. They don't really dictate how we should do anything, as long as we meet their expectations." Marci's advice for someone considering the purchase of a franchise: "Just do your homework. Make sure you get every piece of information that's out there about the specific company you're looking at. Ask a lot of questions. Franchising is not for everybody. You have to find out if it's right for you."

Semiretired, Totally Satisfied

Case Study #5:
Tony Santell, San Diego, California
AWC Commercial Window Coverings, mobil dry-cleaning services, sales,
installation, and repair of all types of window coverings

Due to downsizing, Tony Santell was forced to retire from his job in the aerospace industry. Too young to stop working, he considered his options. He had some experience in running his own business, a small direct-sales beauty aids distribution service, and liked the idea of going back to work for himself. He was looking for "something that sounded more like a business than a job."

After researching literally hundreds of franchises and multilevel marketing opportunities, he decided on the drape cleaning and installation business. Many franchisor interviews later, he narrowed it down to AWC Commercial Window Coverings. He liked the fact that AWC was willing to give him an exclusive territory of 100 square miles. After looking into the franchise more thoroughly, he decided to buy it.

The franchise agreement included a one-time fee for equipment, a 12 percent service fee, and a 3 percent advertising fee. The agreement also stipulated that Tony must buy the actual cleaning product from the franchisor at a reasonable fee. The franchisor provides all training, national advertising, and brochures and also makes available any other product or equipment Tony needs.

Being responsible for generating business took a little getting used to for Tony. But once he understood what it required from him, he took to it quite naturally. "You have to be able to go out and meet people and talk to people. You don't have to be a high-pressure salesman or anything like that, but you do need to be able to talk to people and explain what you do." He continues to try direct-mail advertising to back up his people-oriented approach, but the results have been mixed. "I still do some mail-out advertising, but when people get my mailers, they just throw them away. Most of the business I've gotten is from knocking on doors."

Like the other successful franchisees we spoke with, Tony likes what he does and is comfortable with the concept of franchising in general. "I like the fact franchising offers a good balance. I have a lot of control, but if I need help the franchisor is there 150 percent." About a year into running the franchise, Tony is happy. "I thought I could get going a little faster, but it's picking up." Being semiretired, Tony appreciates the flexible hours his franchise affords him. He's even thinking of having his son join the business for future growth. Tony's advice for prospective franchise buyers is simple and direct: "Learn the business and learn about the people in your area. If the business is something you like doing, and the people in your area need it, go for it!"

MAKING IT MEANS DOING YOUR HOMEWORK

Let's go back to Case Study #1 and look further at Nancy's franchising experience. The reason she didn't succeed, by her own admission, was that she didn't do her homework. She didn't research the business, she didn't look into who else in her area was already providing a similar service, and she didn't check to see if people in her area were even interested in the service. She definitely didn't check out the franchisor thoroughly. Most important, she didn't investigate her own motivations, interests, and abilities. In the fol-

Advantages and Disadvantages of Home-Based Franchising

The Advantages of Home-Based Franchising

Now that you have an understanding of franchising and how it works, let's review some of the advantages of buying and running a home-based franchise.

- Opening a business with proven name recognition
- You have the franchisor's years of experience in running the business. This can save you countless lost hours and wasted money in trying things that don't work.
- A good franchisor will provide training in how to run, manage, and market the business.
- A good franchisor will provide ongoing support, keeping you abreast of the latest developments in your industry, market trends, etc.
- A good franchisor generally provides wide-ranging regional and national cooperative advertising.
- The collective resources of the franchisor and your fellow franchisees give your business *Fortune* 500 credibility at a fraction of the cost.
- A franchise, by definition, is a proven system.
- You aren't out there on your own. The franchisor has a definite interest in your well-being and profitability. The franchisor can be a valuable resource throughout the life of your business.
- In a good franchise, you will have an exclusive territory, minimizing competition.
- The potential to earn a comfortable, full-time living wage, and often, much more
- Because you are using a proven system, it won't take you nearly as long to turn a profit as when starting a business from scratch.
- Working from home means you'll have more flexibility in your work schedule.
- Working from home also means lower overhead costs.
- A franchise is your own business. You can build equity in your business and sell it later for a profit.
- Although required to follow procedures dictated by the franchisor, you still have plenty of freedom to make your own decisions.

Advantages and Disadvantages
of Home-Based Franchising *(continued)*

The Disadvantages of Home-Based Franchising

Of course, everything has its drawbacks, and home-based franchising is no exception. Consider the following before making your decision to buy a franchise:

- You're obligated to follow someone else's system and procedures. If you are extremely independent or need to have things your way, you may feel oppressed by the many rules of franchising operation.
- On the other hand, if you need a good deal of supervision and direction, the freedom of running your own business may make you uncomfortable.
- Under the majority of franchise agreements you must pay an ongoing royalty or fee to the franchisor for the duration of your business's life.
- You are tied to the fortunes of your franchisor. If the parent company does well, it will help you to do well. If the company has trouble, this will most certainly have an impact on your business.
- Legally, the franchisor still has the advantage. Although there are groups fighting to level the regulatory playing field, franchisors still have the ultimate control over your business, perhaps even to the point of terminating your franchise without having to show cause.
- Working from home you may get distracted by other interests or responsibilities, and it's hard to leave the workday behind.
- You may have to invest more money than you originally thought. Do you have the necessary financial reserves?
- There is a chance that you will fail. Are you prepared to lose the money and time you invest in the business?
- You may not make as much as you expect. Are you ready to do with less for an indefinite period of time?
- You may have to spend long hours for little return, especially in the beginning. Are you ready to work harder than you now do, if necessary?
- Having your own business can be physically and emotionally taxing. Are you up to the challenge?
- Do have the self-discipline and self-motivation to manage your work productively and arrange for the support you need?
- Unlike having a job, there are absolutely no guarantees in having your own business. Are you ready for the uncertainty?
- Having your own business means not having any basic-level employer-provided benefits such as health insurance, unemployment insurance, workers' compensation insurance, or employer's share of Social Security payments. You will be responsible for generating the income to provide these for yourself.

lowing chapter, we're going to outline how you can do the needed homework to know if you're likely to succeed in a particular franchise by specifically assessing four key areas:

- *The Franchise Company.* Is it a solid opportunity, or too good to be true?
- *What You Actually Will Be Doing.* How exactly will you spend most of your time in running the franchise? Is this activity something that's right for you?
- *Your Personal Experience, Skills, and Readiness.* Are you ready to run your own business from home? Do you have the experience, skills, and personality profile to succeed at the franchise you may be considering, or at franchising in general?
- *The Market.* Do people want or need the service or product within the region you propose to operate in?

Chapter 2 will also give you clear guidelines on how to research each of these four key areas. Starting your own business is one of the most exciting and important decisions you will make in your life. Don't rush into anything. Give yourself at least three to six months to properly complete the necessary research before making a decision. If a franchisor is pressuring you to make a decision quickly, take this to be a clear warning sign. It has been the experience of far too many disappointed franchisees that high-pressure sales jobs from franchisors lead to bad experiences. If the franchisor is a solid company offering a solid opportunity, he or she will appreciate your deliberate actions as they know that you are a potential franchisee who is serious about their commitment to success.

2

Testing a Franchise for Fitness, Honesty, and Marketability

PERSISTENCE IS THE KEY to success in franchising. But most people need to experience success 75 percent of the time in order to persist. So to experience enough success to keep yourself motivated to persist in pursuing the franchise of your choice, you must stack the cards in your favor before you even start. You must give yourself as many advantages as possible right from the beginning. And the best way for you to do that is to test out beforehand if the franchise you're considering will be a good "fit" for you, whether the company is an honest and reputable one you can count on, and if there actually is a need you can meet with what you'll be offering. And that's what this chapter is designed to enable you to do—provide you with the tools to carry out three Before-You-Buy Tests: the Fitness Check, the Honesty Check and the Market Check.

While many franchise businesses may "sound" good to you, before you buy use these three tools to identify what you'll *actually* be spending your time *doing* if you buy a particular franchise. You'll know how to assess what you can expect from the franchisor and just how much need there is for what you would be offering. Making sure a franchise passes these three key tests begins with understanding the true nature of any business you're thinking about buying into.

TEST I: THE FRANCHISE FITNESS CHECK

Any business will require you to carry out many different types of activities, from getting customers to servicing them well. But when you get down to the day-to-day running of a business, home-based franchises, like most other kinds of businesses, have one particular type of activity that's at the heart of what the business is all about. We refer to this as the Core Function of a business, and once you buy the business it will become the primary activity you'll be spending your time doing. But unfortunately many times the Core Function, or your role in providing it, is not readily apparent at first in a prepackaged business. Too often people think more about the nature of the business than about the actual functions they'll be spending the majority of their time carrying out once they get down to operating the business.

Many businesses you can buy, for example, will sound glamorous or simple at first, but in actuality carrying out their Core Function may be quite mundane or complicated. Since your Core Function is what you will be spending most of your time doing, however, you should make sure you know what that activity is and that it's something you can truly enjoy or have an affinity for.

What Will You Be Doing?

In researching the key elements of success in home-based franchising, through our interviews and case histories, we found that, in general, successful franchisees had something of a passion or natural proclivity for the actual nuts and bolts involved in carrying out the Core Function of their franchises. Quite simply, successful franchisees like what they do and do it more or less naturally once they've completed the initial learning curve of beginning a new business. On the surface, this may sound rather obvious, but it isn't always. Here are several examples of what we mean.

Ruth was attracted to the idea of running a franchise that involved home decorating. She'd always had an artistic flair and an eye for color, line, style, and form, so she thought a franchise related to home decorating would be ideal for her. After buying the particular franchise she was considering, however, she discovered that the Core Function of her business was selling decorator items from the franchisor's many catalogs. Ruth ended up spending the majority of her time, as she put it, "lugging" sample catalogs to people's homes and giving standardized presentations using sales materials from the franchisor.

Basically Ruth didn't like selling. She liked creating and designing. She had envisioned herself going into people's homes and working with them to design creative alternatives and redecorating their homes. So while the business she bought "sounded" creative, there was no room for her to create new designs; it was about selling existing ones. So, of course, Ruth was disappointed and her business languished.

For Megan, the same home business was ideal. She too liked the idea of home decorating, but she had never had much artistic flair or talent. She was a natural performer, though, and had a great personality and strong communication skills. She loved the chance to spend hours showing people how they could use the items in the franchisor's catalog to brighten up their homes. And, accordingly, her business developed quite well.

Carl loved animals, especially dogs. So he was excited when he heard about a franchise that would help pet owners by tagging and registering their dogs or cats for easy tracking if they got lost or were stolen. This franchise seemed like a great way for him to escape from his stress-filled job driving a delivery truck. His mind danced with pictures of reuniting exuberant pets with their relieved and happy owners. But once he purchased the franchise and got down to the nitty-gritty of building his business, he was most disillusioned.

Instead of working with pets and their owners, Carl was basically selling a service—imprinted metal tags—filling out registration forms, and mailing them to and from the franchisor and his clients. The Core Function of this business was administrative, not interpersonal, in nature. Often he never even saw the pets he was helping to protect. Soon Carl lost interest in this business and negotiated to sell it back to the franchisor.

For José, however, the same franchise was a perfect fit. He, too, loved animals. For years, however, he'd worked processing and filing applications for a credit union. He liked the work but very much wanted to become his own boss, in part so he could have more time to pursue his hobby, breeding and showing champion Skye terriers. He was most satisfied with the franchise and enjoyed selling and processing registrations for other breeders and owners whom he met at dog shows he attended almost every weekend. He also worked out arrangements to sell his new service through other vendors he was already doing business with as a breeder.

Blair had worked for years as a researcher at an investment company, so when he saw an ad for a financial consulting franchise, he felt sure this was his ticket to becoming his own boss. But he, too, failed to consider the Core Function of the business he was buying. While he envisioned himself researching the best investments for his clients and helping them make investment decisions, in actuality, once he bought the business he found he was primarily being asked to gather and send in information from clients to the franchisor, who then prepared a recommended portfolio from its database. In other words, the Core Function of his business was more a matter of recruiting and interviewing clients and organizing and transmitting the information he gathered. While this franchise was a disappointment to Blair, it was perfect for Rene.

Rene wanted to be home with her two toddlers, so she wanted to use her record-keeping skills to start a home business. She found this franchise was an excellent choice for her. The company provided her with leads and she spent her days making phone calls, talking with people, and taking down information. This made it possible for her to set her own schedule and earn a good income without having to leave home.

From these three examples, you can see how vital it can be to explore more than just the general field, concept, or intention of a franchise you're considering. You must look more deeply to discover the Core Function of what *you* will actually be *doing*. Part 1 of the Franchise Fitness Check is designed to help you answer the question "Is This Franchise a Good Fit for You?" Then Part 2 will help you assess "Are You a Good Fit for This Franchise?"

PART 1: IS THIS FRANCHISE A GOOD FIT FOR YOU? DISCOVERING YOUR CORE FUNCTION

Answering the following questions will enable you to identify what a franchise's Core Function is, what your role will be in providing it, and if it's a good "fit" for you. These questions should also help you determine if the actual running of the business and doing the primary day-to-day tasks involved will keep you sufficiently motivated to work long enough and hard enough to succeed.

1. What do you think the Core Function of the business is?

See if you can write a brief description of what you think the Core Function of the business you're considering is. What is at the heart of this business? What is its primary focus, its raison d'être? If you can't describe this simply and clearly to yourself, you need to investigate the business further. Here are several examples:

- To teach children how to use computers
- To provide management consulting to medium-sized companies
- To repair and replace damaged windshields
- To clean out chimneys
- To arrange tours and cruises for associations
- To create high-school video yearbooks

2. What is your role in providing this Core Function?

All businesses, regardless of their goal, require performing some aspects of the six basic functions listed below:

Creating: Someone must create a product or service of some kind.

Problem solving: Someone must analyze and research the best solutions.

Building: Someone must build, manage, collect, store, and maintain the materials involved.

Organizing: Someone must gather, organize, record, file, process, and update the details of administering the business.

Leading: Someone must market, promote, and sell the product or service.

Improving: Someone must listen to and take care of client or customer needs.

As a franchise owner, you will be responsible for running your own business, so you will probably be involved in performing some of all six of these functions. But, your role in carrying out the Core Function of a particular franchise will focus primarily on one (or perhaps two) of these areas. This will be *your* Core Function. It may or may not be the same function as the business itself. For example,

- We just learned that the Core Function of the franchise Ruth bought was to provide decorative items for the home (Creating), but her Core Function was to sell (Leading), not create those items.
- The Core Function of the franchise Carl bought was to help find lost pets (Improving), but his Core Function was to sell and print ID tags for the pets and fill out registration forms (Building and Organizing).
- The Core Function of the company Blair bought was to research the best investments for clients (Problem Solving), but his Core Function in that company was to locate customers, discover their needs, and gather the pertinent information and transmit it to and from the franchisor (Leading).

Look over the following six functions and circle which one (or two) will be your primary focus, the one you will you be spending most of your time performing, *your* role in the franchise you're considering. Then check off (√) the specific activities under that function that you'll be called upon to spend most of your time carrying out.

LEADING
___ administering
___ assigning
___ coordinating
___ delegating
___ initiating

IMPROVING
___ assisting
___ caring
___ collaborating
___ consulting
___ contributing

___ inspiring
___ managing
___ motivating
___ organizing
___ persuading
___ selling
___ supervising

___ counseling
___ encouraging
___ explaining
___ helping
___ listening
___ serving
___ supporting

Organizing
___ arranging
___ cataloging
___ compiling
___ evaluating
___ expediting
___ gathering
___ grouping
___ ordering
___ programming
___ recording
___ tabulating
___ updating

Creating
___ communicating
___ composing
___ designing
___ drawing
___ feeling
___ imaging
___ innovating
___ perceiving
___ performing
___ sensing
___ shaping
___ writing

Building
___ adjusting
___ assembling
___ computing
___ constructing
___ handling
___ maintaining
___ making
___ operating
___ renovating
___ repairing
___ tinkering
___ troubleshooting

Problem Solving
___ analyzing
___ classifying
___ defining
___ diagnosing
___ editing
___ investigating
___ reading
___ reasoning
___ researching
___ solving
___ studying
___ thinking

To find out which activities compose a franchise's Core Function you can:

a. Ask the franchisor what his or her franchisees actually spend most their time doing.

b. Ask existing franchisees what they spend most of their time doing.

3. How much time will you spend performing your Core Function?

As we said, as a franchisee you will probably be spending time doing some of all six of the above functions, but what proportion of your time will you be devoting to each? Put an asterisk (*) beside all the other activities on the above list you will be performing in running the franchise you're considering. Then estimate how many hours in an average day, week, and month these functions will involve. For example:

Leading: How much of your time will be spent promoting the business and finding and selling to clients and customers? Will you need to develop and place ads and other sales materials? Will you be contacting prospects in person? By telemarketing? Giving presentations, demonstrations, or exhibits?

Improving: How much time will be spent working personally helping clients, listening to their needs and concerns, and responding to them?

Organizing: How much of your time will be spent doing paperwork, filling out and processing forms and other administrative tasks?

Building: How much time will you spend purchasing, stocking, fixing, assembling, transporting, carrying or handling essential materials, goods, or inventory?

Problem Solving: How much time will you spend planning, researching, and analyzing information and solving problems for clients and customers?

Creating: How much time will you spend designing or creating a product, report, service, or printed marketing materials like brochures, flyers, etc.?

Doing a Time Analysis

Estimate how much time you will be spending each day, week, and month doing each of these functions:

Daily

___ Leading: i.e., Directing/Marketing/Selling/Promoting

___ Improving: i.e., Helping and Assisting Clients/Other Customer Service

___ Organizing: i.e., Bookkeeping/Paperwork/Processing Information

___ Building: i.e., Assembling/Computing/Constructing/Maintaining

___ Problem Solving: i.e., Planning/Research/Analyzing

___ Creating: i.e., Innovating/Designing/Composing

Weekly

___ Leading: i.e., Directing/Marketing/Selling/Promoting

___ Improving: i.e., Helping and Assisting Clients/Other Customer Service

___ Organizing: i.e., Bookkeeping/Paperwork/Processing Information

___ Building: i.e., Assembling/Transporting/Packing/Constructing/Maintaining

___ Problem Solving: i.e., Planning/Research/Analyzing

___ Creating: i.e., Innovating/Designing/Composing

Monthly

___ Leading: i.e., Directing/Marketing/Selling/Promoting

___ Improving: i.e., Helping and Assisting Clients/Other Customer Service

___ Organizing: i.e., Bookkeeping/Paperwork/Processing Information

___ Building: i.e., Assembling/Computing/Constructing/Maintaining

___ Problem Solving: i.e., Planning/Research/Analyzing

___ Creating: i.e. Innovating/Designing/Composing

3. What functions will the franchisor be providing and what functions, if any, will they carry out for your business?

As we mentioned often, the Core Function of the franchise company and *your* Core Function will be different. Some franchisors are primarily sales and promotion organizations, attracting attention, leads, and contacts for the franchisees to follow up on. Others are primarily administrative arms, processing and shipping orders. Still others actually create the product or service that will be sold or administered by the franchisee. What functions will they be providing for you?

    a. Is the franchisor's Core Function primarily to support you in running your franchise through training, written materials, and consultations? Or do they have other primary functions?

    b. Is the franchisor's Core Function to perform any of the actual functions involved in the running of your franchise? If so, which ones? Will they be doing sales and marketing, creating and shipping products, processing orders, etc.?

    c. Will the franchisor be involved in any other way in the running of your business?

Put a checkmark beside any of the activities on pages 49–50 that the franchisor will be responsible for. The function with the most checks should be a good indication of what the franchisor's Core Function is. Confirm your conclusions with the franchisor and be sure such functional responsibilities are spelled out clearly in your franchise agreement.

4. How will your time be divided among the various key functions you will be spending your time performing?

Now create a pie chart that reflects how much time you will be spending on the various aspects of running the home-based franchise business you're considering. The area that is the most time-consuming *is* the Core Function of your business, even if it wouldn't seem to be the primary nature of the business.

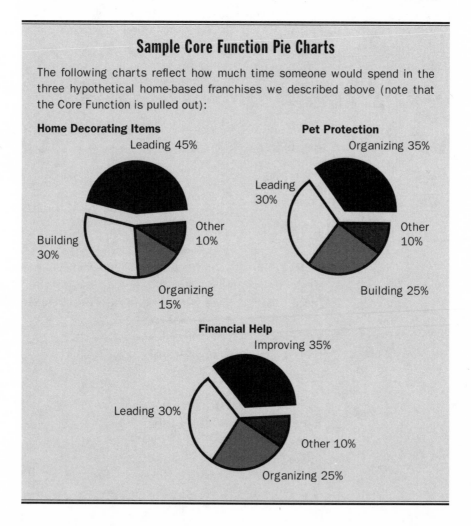

Sample Core Function Pie Charts

The following charts reflect how much time someone would spend in the three hypothetical home-based franchises we described above (note that the Core Function is pulled out):

Home Decorating Items
Leading 45%
Other 10%
Building 30%
Organizing 15%

Pet Protection
Organizing 35%
Leading 30%
Other 10%
Building 25%

Financial Help
Improving 35%
Leading 30%
Other 10%
Organizing 25%

PART 2: ARE YOU A GOOD FIT FOR THIS FRANCHISE? ASSESSING YOUR NEEDS, MOTIVATION, SKILLS, INTERESTS, KNOWLEDGE, AND PERSONALITY

You are the most important element in the success of a franchise you buy. So you need to assess yourself as deeply as you assess the franchisor and your market. What you find may surprise you. Had Nancy from Case History #1 taken the time to assess needs, interests, skills, experience, background, and expectations she might have decided that she wasn't ready to run a business or work from home or she might have chosen a business that was better suited to her. This knowledge would have saved her thousands of dollars and considerable aggravation. Completing this part of the **Franchise Fitness Check** will help in making such an assessment. Use the following questions as a starting point for researching yourself. In answering the following questions, be as impartial as you can. The questions aren't designed to make you right or wrong, but rather to give you the information you need to help you make an informed decision about a very important choice in your life.

Your Needs and Motivation

1. Why do you want to buy a business instead of starting one yourself?
2. What do you want from this business?
   a. Satisfaction
   b. More money
   c. Independence
   d. Flexible schedule
   e. To work less
   f. Other:
3. According to Dr. Tom Hendrickson, president of TIMS Management Systems, a leading authority on personality testing for the franchise industry, "You need to ask yourself some serious questions to determine your potential success." Start with these:
   a. Am I willing to work hard?
   b. How well do I get along with other people?
   c. Do I have good communication skills?
   d. Do I know how to organize?
   e. Do I take pride in whatever I do?
   f. Am I a self-starter?
   g. Do I welcome responsibility?
   h. Am I willing to make decisions?
   i. Am I willing to struggle and make sacrifices?
   j. Can I control my emotions?

  k. Am I self-disciplined?
  l. Do I have enough experience to support my desires?
  m. Am I more of a dreamer than a doer?

Your Interests, Skills, and Experience

This section is designed to assist you in identifying what talents, skills, and experience you bring to the franchise. Begin by making a list of your talents, skills, and experience related to the franchise you're considering. Then read through the lists of activities below and place a checkmark next to those you feel you can do adequately. Place a second checkmark next to the skills you feel you can do well. Then circle the skills you most enjoy using. Now, compare your results below with the activities you found would be involved in the Core Function of the franchise as well as any others you found you would be spending your time doing in the running of the franchise you're considering. Ideally, a franchise that is well suited to you will make heavy use of your strongest, most enjoyed skills and draw little, if at all, on things you don't like or do well.

LEADING
___ administering
___ assigning
___ coordinating
___ delegating
___ initiating
___ inspiring
___ managing
___ motivating
___ organizing
___ persuading
___ selling
___ supervising

IMPROVING
___ assisting
___ caring
___ collaborating
___ consulting
___ contributing
___ counseling
___ encouraging
___ explaining
___ helping
___ listening
___ serving
___ supporting

ORGANIZING
___ arranging
___ cataloging
___ compiling
___ evaluating
___ expediting
___ gathering
___ grouping
___ ordering

CREATING
___ communicating
___ composing
___ designing
___ drawing
___ feeling
___ imaging
___ innovating
___ perceiving

___ programming

___ recording

___ tabulating

___ updating

___ performing

___ sensing

___ shaping

___ writing

BUILDING

___ adjusting

___ assembling

___ computing

___ constructing

___ handling

___ maintaining

___ making

___ operating

___ renovating

___ repairing

___ tinkering

___ troubleshooting

PROBLEM SOLVING

___ analyzing

___ classifying

___ defining

___ diagnosing

___ editing

___ investigating

___ reading

___ reasoning

___ researching

___ solving

___ studying

___ thinking

Your Knowledge of Business and Franchising

According to almost every franchisor we spoke with, one of the single greatest reasons people fail in franchising is their lack of general business knowledge. Answer the following questions to find out how much business knowledge you currently have. Each one of these questions represents an important aspect of running a franchise, including business terminology franchisors will most likely expect you to be familiar with. If you are unfamiliar with any terms, concepts, or procedures, you will need to make a point of becoming familiar with them since your business success may depend on it. It is beyond the scope of this book to give you an overview of all the principles of running a home business, so we recommend the Resources listed in Appendix 7.

1. Can you develop and write a business plan?
2. Can you develop and write a marketing plan?
3. What is a UFOC?
4. What is a financial statement?
5. What are projected earnings?
6. What is a profit and loss statement?
7. What is the most effective way to market the business you're thinking of buying?
8. What licenses, permits, etc., will you need? Where can you get them?

9. Will you need to pay sales tax?
10. What is the difference between accounts payable and accounts receivable?
11. What is the difference between gross and net income?
12. Are there any zoning restrictions pertinent to running a home business where you live?
13. What business insurance do you need for this business?
14. What is market research?
15. Will you be incorporating, running a sole proprietorship, forming a partnership, or going public?
14. Will you be selling wholesale, retail, or distributing?
15. How costly will insurance be, particularly liability insurance?

Your Personality Profile

The following questions will help you gain an understanding of your own personality and the personality traits that might help, or hinder, you in franchising. If there are areas you are weak in, that doesn't mean you can't succeed in a franchise or that there is no hope in trying. Being weak in an area will only mean that you have to develop those aspects of yourself in order to increase your chances of success.

A. Independence
Rate yourself in regard to your work from 1 to 100 percent in the following areas, with 1 being "not at all" and 100 being "absolutely":

_____ 1. Do you like the idea of being your own boss?
_____ 2. Do you like getting and using someone else's suggestions?
_____ 3. Do you generally like following a set of guidelines and seeing them through?
_____ 4. Are you good at managing your time?
_____ 5. Are you good at setting goals?
_____ 6. Are you good at meeting goals?
_____ 7. How well do you like working alone?
_____ 8. Do you feel working with others gets in your way?
_____ 9. How productive are you working alone?
_____10. Do you hate being told what to do?
_____11. Are you strong willed?
_____12. How much do you enjoy starting major projects from scratch?
_____13. Do you enjoy actually following through and completing a project once it is started?
_____14. Do you respond well to close supervision?
_____15. Is it hard to distract you?

_____16. Does it take a lot to get you frustrated?
_____17. Do you rise to the challenge of adversity?
_____18. Can you keep yourself consistently motivated?
        Total ÷ 18 = _____.

Add up the points you've given yourself for each of the above questions, then divide the total by 18. According to most franchisors, those scoring between 50 percent and 75 percent for independence make the best candidates for successful franchisees. A very high independence score indicates that you may be too independent to feel comfortable in the franchisor-franchisee relationship. You may want to consider buying a business opportunity or starting your own business. If you scored under 50 percent, you may not be sufficiently goal oriented and self-motivated at this time to start and operate a home-based franchise.

| 1 | 25 | 50 | 75 | 100 |

B. Compliance

Rate yourself in regard to your work from 1 to 100 percent in the following areas, with 1 being "not at all" and 100 being "absolutely":

_____ 1. How tactful are you?
_____ 2. Are you able to get past anger over injustices?
_____ 3. Is it important to you to maintain good relationships with people?
_____ 4. Do you care about how you are perceived by others?
_____ 5. Do you put other people's desires ahead of your own?
_____ 6. How accepting are you when someone else "wins"?
_____ 7. Rate your attention to detail.
_____ 8. Are you conservative in your actions (not politics)?
_____ 9. Are you cautious?
_____10. Do like to be told what to do?
_____11. Do you feel more secure when someone else sets the agenda for you?
_____12. When confronted with a stressful situation, do you turn to others for advice and guidance?
_____13. Are you comfortable working within a system?
_____14. How true is the following statement for you: "I don't have to call the shots all the time. I get satisfaction from the process of actually doing a task."

_____15. How true is the following time-honored cliché for you: "It doesn't matter if I win or lose; it's how I play the game." Total ÷ 15 =_____.

Add up the percentage points you've given yourself for each of the above questions, then divide the total by 15. Franchisors' opinions vary on how much compliance they find is good in a franchisee. On the one hand, non-technological, service-based franchisors believe that a compliance rating of 40 percent to 75 percent will serve a franchisee well. A lower compliance rating indicates that the franchisee is more likely to be able to solve problems, think on his or her feet, and act more decisively. On the other hand, franchisors of technologically oriented businesses or businesses that involve a sophisticated set of procedures find that a higher compliance, rating 50 to 75 percent or higher, helps their franchisees succeed. A higher compliance rating generally means a greater attention to detail and a greater thoroughness in understanding complicated equipment and procedures.

| 1 | 25 | 50 | 75 | 100 |

C. Steadiness

Rate yourself in regard to your work from 1 to 100 percent in the following areas, with 1 being "not at all" and 100 being "absolutely":

_____ 1. How flexible are you?

_____ 2. Do you often feel hurt?

_____ 3. Are you generally calm?

_____ 4. Do you have difficulty coping with change?

_____ 5. Are you a "low-key" person?

_____ 6. Do you prefer to really think things out before making a change?

_____ 7. Are you comfortable with routine?

_____ 8. Are you often offended by what goes on in the business world?

_____ 9. Do you like to go to the same restaurants and stores?

_____10. How important is following a strict daily routine?

_____11. Are you frequently nervous or anxious?

_____12. Are you a sincere person?

_____13. Do you like knowing how something is going to turn out beforehand?

_____14. Do you like the idea of having your own business so you can set up a system that will allow the business to run itself?

_____15. Do you get nervous when money is low?

_____16. Do you quit easily when something is not working out?
_____17. Are you easy to talk to?
_____18. Do you like to follow trends?
       Total ÷ 18 = _____.

Add up the percentage points you've given yourself for each of the above questions, then divide the total by 18. Surprisingly, franchisors prefer franchisees who score fairly low in the steadiness category, about 25 to 50 percent. Although the "stick-toitiveness" of high-compliance people is desirable, the downside can often be fatal to a franchise. High-steadiness folks, whose comfort level hinges on predictable routine, generally have a difficult time dealing with and reacting to the constant changes of the marketplace.

| 1 | 25 | 50 | 75 | 100 |

D. Influence
Rate yourself in regard to your work from 1 to 100 percent in the following areas, with 1 being "not all" and 100 being "absolutely":

_____ 1. Are you an outgoing person?
_____ 2. How enthusiastic are you, in general?
_____ 3. Do you enjoy meeting new people?
_____ 4. Do you enjoy being in the spotlight?
_____ 5. Is it important for you to be popular?
_____ 6. Do you have a great many friends?
_____ 7. Do you sometimes feel directionless?
_____ 8. Would you rather talk to customers or associates than do the actual work of your business?
_____ 9. Do people generally trust you?
_____10. Rate your sales skills (1 = very poor; 100 = outstanding).
_____11. Do you generally win arguments?
_____12. Do you find more people agree with you than disagree with you?
_____13. Do you get a strong sense of personal worth from how well you do in the world?
_____14. Do you care about what people think of you?
_____15. Do you communicate well?
_____16. Do you frequently feel misunderstood?
_____17. Do you actually enjoy sales and customer service?
_____18. Are you a "warm" person?
       Total ÷18 = _____.

Add up the percentage points you've given yourself for each of the above questions, then divide the total by 18. If your score is between 50 and 75 percent, you are a good candidate for franchising, according to what franchisors look for in terms of influence. According to Kirk Shivell and Kent Banning, authors of the book *Running a Successful Franchise*, "Most franchisors feel that, although sales, promotion, public relations, and customer service are essential skills in franchising, the disadvantages and the lack of independent direction in the high-influence person are too much of a trade-off."

| 1 | 25 | 50 | 75 | 100 |

If you scored extremely high in the influence domain, you may want to consider a business with sales or public relations as its Core Function. A home-based franchise, unless it is highly sales oriented, may not be fulfilling enough to motivate you to make it successful. If your score was low, you may not have the people skills at this point to market a franchise and deal with the politics of keeping customers satisfied.

E. Dominance

Rate yourself in regard to your work from 1 to 100 percent in the following areas, with 1 being "not at all" and 100 being "absolutely":

_____ 1. Do you have very high standards?

_____ 2. Are you often critical of those who do not meet your standards?

_____ 3. Do like to make your own rules?

_____ 4. How true is the following statement for you: "I really don't care what others think when I know I'm right about something."

_____ 5. Would you rather do things yourself because you know they will be done correctly?

_____ 6. Do you think of compromise as something negative, as in "I won't compromise myself."

_____ 7. Is one of the reasons you are considering buying a franchise so that you finally won't have do what someone else says?

_____ 8. Do you have frequent conflicts with co-workers or superiors?

_____ 9. Once your mind is made up, do you have difficulty changing it?

_____10. How important is it for you to be right?

_____11. Do you sometimes feel threatened in work-related matters?

_____12. How true is the following statement for you: "I won't play politics just to get ahead."

_____13. Is assistance from others unimportant or not needed?

_____14. Do you like the idea of independence of decision making that self-employment brings?

_____15. Do you feel that in business "too many cooks spoil the broth"?

_____16. Do you feel that, until now, others have hampered your progress?

_____17. Are you easily bored with routines?

_____18. Are you always looking for new challenges?

Total ÷ 18 = _____.

Add up the percentage points you've given yourself for each of the above questions, then divide the total by 18. If your score is between 50 percent and 75 percent in the dominance domain, you will have the best chance of success in franchising according to franchisors. A low score in dominance usually indicates that you will not have the self-confidence or vision to compete. Too high a dominance rating indicates that you may resent the rules imposed by the franchisor. In this case your entrepreneurial spirit will be better served by buying a business opportunity or starting your own business.

| 1 | 25 | 50 | 75 | 100 |

TEST II: THE HONESTY CHECK
CHECKING THE INTEGRITY OF THE
FRANCHISING COMPANY

Before signing a franchise agreement, it is absolutely essential that you research the integrity of the franchisor or parent company. Most franchises are offered by solid, reputable companies and are authentic opportunities. Yet, as with everything else, the buyer must beware. The following series of questions and work sheets will help you determine not only if a franchise company is aboveboard but also if it will give you the kind of support you need.

The Honesty Check allows you to cut right to the make-or-break issues for a company you are considering. It provides you with the right questions to ask to find out if the company is representing itself honestly and openly. It will also tell you what areas of the company you need to investigate, how to do such research, and how to ensure that what you've been told checks out.

What Must a Franchisor Disclose to You in a Prospectus or Offering Circular?*

1. Information identifying the franchisor and any predecessors and describing their business experience
2. Information identifying and describing the business experience of each of the franchisor's officers, directors, and management personnel responsible for franchise services, training, and other aspects of the franchise program
3. A description of the lawsuits (if any) in which the franchisor and its officers, directors, and management personnel have been involved
4. Information about any previous bankruptcies (if any) in which the franchisor and its officers, directors, and/or management personnel have been involved
5. Information about the initial franchise fee and other initial payments that are required to obtain the franchise
6. A description of the continuing (royalty) payments franchisees are required to make after the franchise opens
7. Information about any restrictions on the quality of goods and services used in the franchise and where they may be purchased, including restrictions requiring purchases from the franchisor or its affiliates
8. A description of any assistance available from the franchisor or its affiliates in financing the purchase of the franchise
9. A description of restrictions on the goods or services franchisees are permitted to sell
10. A description of any restrictions on the customers with whom franchisees may deal
11. A description of any territorial protection that will be granted to the franchisee
12. A description of the conditions under which the franchise may be repurchased or refused renewal by the franchisor, transferred to a third party by the franchisee, and terminated or modified by either party
13. A description of the training programs provided to the franchisees
14. A description of the involvement of any celebrities or public figures in the franchise
15. A description of any assistance in selecting a site for the franchise that will be provided by the franchisor
16. Statistical information about the present number of franchises, the number of franchises projected for the future, the number of franchises terminated, the number the franchisor has decided not to renew, and the number repurchased in the past

17. The financial statements of the franchisors
18. A description of the extent to which franchisees must personally participate in the operation of the franchise
19. A complete statement of the basis for any earnings claims made to the franchisee, including the percentage of existing franchises that have actually achieved the results that are claimed
20. A list of the names and addresses of other franchisees

*From the **Franchise Opportunities Handbook,** published by the U.S. Department of Commerce Minority Business Development Agency.*

Franchising Red Flags

There's nothing worse than having wasted your time, with the possible exception of having wasted your money. If in your initial negotiations with a franchisor, he or she says or does any of the following, hold everything. These are almost sure signs of a bad deal. Beware of any of the following:

- The franchisor does not give you a copy of the legally mandated disclosure statement *the first time you meet.*
- The franchisor pressures you to sign the franchise agreement.
- The franchisor discourages you from showing the franchise agreement to an attorney.
- The franchisor tells you you don't need to read the contract.
- You are promised big profits for a very small amount of work.
- You are not provided with a list of current franchisees, or you receive a suspiciously short list.
- The franchisor is new to the business, but not new to franchising.
- The franchisor is new to the business *and* new to franchising.
- The franchisor spends more money and time recruiting franchises than running the actual business.
- From your first meeting you feel the franchisor is somehow shifty or untrustworthy. Trust your own feelings; they are often dead-on in these kinds of situations.

PART 1: THE PARENT COMPANY: WHO ARE THEY?

Any viable and honest franchisor will check you out thoroughly. It's only good business. They will expect and welcome you to do the same. Franchising is a partnership, so it's vital that your partner be compatible; and, most important, make sure he or she is who they say they are. Finding answers to the following questions will give you a pretty good idea about where the parent company stands in terms of stability, honesty, and fair dealing:

1. How many years has the parent company been in business?
2. How many franchise outlets are in operation?
3. Who is the company's management team? What are their experience, background, education, and track records? Poor or inexperienced management is one of the key reasons businesses fail!
4. How does the company's own financial statement look?
5. How many of their franchise outlets have failed? Why have they failed?
6. Can the franchisor give you a reasonable indication of what you may expect to earn monthly, yearly—after three years, five years? Upon what are these figures based?
7. Does the franchisor have benchmark earnings figures for an average franchise in a territory similar to what yours will be?
8. Is the franchisor a large or small company?
9. How deeply, if at all, has the company checked you out? The more deeply a company researches you, the more they care about the success of your enterprise.
10. Is the company well respected in its field? What do competitors, associates, trade organizations, and publications have to say about the company?
11. How long has the company been in franchising? How did the company distribute its products or services before deciding to sell franchises?
12. Is the company a leader in their industry? What is their percentage of market share?
13. What is the company's net worth? Do they have the cash reserves to make it through a crisis?

PART 2: DOES THE NAME ON THE DOOR MATCH WHAT HAPPENS ON THE FLOOR?

If no red flags are raised in your first phone conversations or meetings, and the franchisor seems to be a straightforward business with a good reputation, it is now time to investigate the inner workings of the company. Finding answers to the following questions will go a long way toward helping you determine the "cleanliness" of the company you are considering:

1. What is the company's record of complaints?
2. What is the company's record of consent orders?

3. Are there any lawsuits or official complaints pending with any of the following regulatory organizations?
   a. Better Business Bureau
   b. state, county, and city consumer protection offices
   c. city/state/federal agencies specific to the company's industry (e.g. day-care franchise—state department of child services)
   d. Federal Trade Commission
4. Are there any complaints lodged or pending with any professional organizations related to the company's industry?
5. Has the company provided you with a list of other franchisees, etc.?
6. Are the past and existing franchisees and their customers you talk with satisfied?
7. Is the list of franchisees, etc., "highlighted," or do all the parent company's franchisees appear on the list? If they don't, why not?
8. How do past or existing franchisees answer the following questions?
   a. What did/do you dislike about the parent company?
   b. In what ways, if any, were you disappointed by the company?
   c. Did the parent company support and assist you as they said they would?
   d. Did you receive the training you were promised?
   e. Did the parent company give you any assistance in marketing?
   c. Did the franchise perform as you were told it would?
   d. Do you regret buying this business?
9. Will the parent company supply you with references?
10. Can you freely check the company's references?
11. Will the parent company provide you with a business plan?
12. What are your own feelings and impressions about the following?
    a. Do you feel that you're being dealt with honestly?
    b. Are statements made by the company consistent?
    c. How do you feel about the business in general?
    d. Do you like the parent company?
    e. Are you scared?
    f. Are you excited?
    g. Are you raring to go?
    h. Do you feel trepidatious?
    i. Do you feel confident?
    j. What are your reservations?

Be as honest as possible with yourself when answering the above questions. Often, we ignore our feelings, or dismiss them as irrelevant. Generally this is a big mistake. Our feelings almost always give us clues to the fundamental nature of the things that concern us.

PART 3: WHY YOU FEEL THE WAY YOU DO

As you assess your feelings about the company you are considering, it's important to determine why you are feeling the way you do. Don't just take your feelings at their surface value. What desires of your own could be coloring the way you feel? What nonverbal signals could you be picking up from the franchisor that are causing you to feel the way you do. For example:

- If you are not feeling confident, figure out why.
    Are you unsure of your own abilities?
    Are you threatened by the unknown?
    Is the franchise opportunity itself or its Core Function somehow dampening your confidence?
- Examine your positive feelings, too:
    If you're raring to go, look into why you're so raring to go.
    Do the franchise company, its products, and its Core Function excite you?
    Are you more motivated by leaving your current situation behind?
    Does it all sound too good to be true? If so, it probably is.

Again, we can't overemphasize the importance of your feelings. Long and careful thought and consideration will lead to some very fruitful insights.

TEST III: THE MARKET CHECK
DISCOVERING IF THE BUSINESS WILL BE VIABLE FOR YOU

Once you've discovered a franchise opportunity that passes your tests for Fitness and Honesty, and you've determined that your personality is a goal match for the Core Function of the business and for being in your own business. You can't go wrong, right? Wrong! There's one other area crucial to any business that you must also research and consider thoroughly: the market.

The market? Of course we're not referring to the place where you buy your groceries; rather, the "market" we're referring to is the potential buyers of your prospective business's products or services. Who is your market? That is, who knows they need what you'll be offering and will be willing and able to pay for it? How much do they need it? How eager will they be to buy it? The better you can answer such questions, the greater your success in business will be. Doing the following Market Check before you invest in a franchise will help you answer these key questions: Is there a market? Is it saturated? Can you reach and tap into the market and how do you know if you have a viable market?

No Market

Market in Some Communities

Market for Some People

Market for You

PART 1: IS THERE A MARKET FOR YOUR INTENDED BUSINESS?

Just because others have found a market for a business does not mean you will. Each community or part of the country has different needs, customs, and resources. What sells fabulously on the East Coast may flop on the West Coast. What sells great in a rural area may hold no interest for people in a large metro area or a suburb. Some communities already could have an over-abundance of other such services, whereas others are starving for such a service.

To help you determine if there even *is* a market for your prospective business that you can reach, answer the following questions:

1. Do you use or buy the product or service the franchise offers?
2. Do you know people who do? How many?
3. Do people you know express a desire for the product or service?
4. How do you see people using it?
5. What kind of people do you see using it?
6. Is there a market in your community or proposed territory?
7. Is there a market in outlying areas?

To answer these questions, you will need to do some investigation. There are two ways to gather the information you need: (1) You can communicate directly with potential customers and those already in the business you are considering; or (2) you can check out the market by reading statistics and other published figures, looking at census results, or going to the library and looking up any published market research for your area of business. We suggest doing both whenever possible.

Discovering whether there would be a market for you in a particular business also depends on you. Will your aptitudes, talents, skills, personality, and current contacts (friends, clubs and organizations, current business contacts) help you find customers? How familiar are you with the market you propose to enter? If you remember, José had a built-in market for his pet registry. He spent every week at dog shows where most people were willing and eager to spend money on their pets. He also had long-standing relationships with vendors who could sell for him. Carl had no such advantages in tapping a market for his registry. Here are a few questions to help you find out how easy or difficult finding a market for a particular business would be *for you:*

1. Do you know people right now who need or want the products or services your franchise will offer?
2. Do you know anyone who is currently offering the same or similar products or services? How busy are they? Might they need someone to take their overload?
3. Do you yourself need or want the product?
4. Is the product or service something you can believe in or get excited about?

PART 2: IS THE MARKET SATURATED?

Market saturation is a term that's used to describe how much competition there is for any product or service you will be offering. If there are already a lot of people providing the same or similar products or services to your market, unless there is an even larger need for these things, your market may be saturated. Most franchise agreements give you a territory protected from competition in terms of other franchisees of the same franchisor, but that doesn't mean there aren't a great many other businesses similar to yours that are already saturating your intended territory.

To find out if your proposed market is already saturated, or close to saturated, answer the following:

1. How many people do you know personally who are already offering the same services as you will be?
2. Call ten friends or associates and ask them if they know anybody who is providing the products or services you intend to provide.

3. Look through your local newspaper thoroughly for ads either offering similar services to the ones you will be offering or ads offering "jobs" for companies selling similar services.

4. Look through your local Yellow Pages to see how many businesses similar to yours are already in operation.

5. Check with your local chamber of commerce and ask for a complete member listing. Look for any businesses similar to yours.

PART 3: CAN YOU TAP THIS MARKET?

If it seems that, indeed, there is a need for what you'll be offering, it's time to do some further investigation. You need to discover how well you are positioned to tap into what need there is and how you can best go about reaching those who need you. Here are the questions you need to answer:

- Do you feel comfortable asking friends, family, colleagues, and associates to buy from you?
- Do you belong to any professional associations that might be of help to you in selling your product or service?
- Do you belong to any civic organizations that might be of help in selling your products or service?
- Do you have any current expertise in the product or service provided by the franchise you are considering?
- Do you have any direct experience with the industry from which the products or services originate in the franchise you are considering?
- Do you have any hobbies or interests that can lead to desirable contacts for your proposed franchise in terms of sales?
- Do you have any current business contacts that might lead to possible sales or expanded industry knowledge?
- Are there any professional organizations in your area that cater to the market your business will serve?
- Are there local or regional trade publications that cover your proposed business area or appeal to your prospective customer base?
- If your business will be based on providing services to other businesses, how many of those businesses are listed in your local phone book?
- Does your prospective business cater to men more than women, or vice versa?

- Does your prospective business cater to older, younger, or both age groups?
- Who is your target customer?

Again, the more specifically you can answer that last question, the more information you will be able to find out regarding how many prospective customers you have (the size of your market), what their likes and dislikes are (the psychographic profile), and their age, sex, income levels, etc. (demographics).

PART 4: HOW DO YOU KNOW IF YOU HAVE A VIABLE MARKET?

If there are enough people in your market whom you can reach and who fit the psychographic and demographic profiles of your target customer, you have a viable market. Gloria, for example, wanted to buy a commercial cleaning franchise. In talking with the franchisor, she figured she needed to find ten customers a week to reach her income goals. There were plenty of businesses who needed cleaning services, but most of those she contacted were already using a service they were satisfied with. There were twenty other commercial cleaning services listed in her local Yellow Pages. Last year there had been twenty-five. That didn't look good. But through her research she learned that a new regional mall would be opening in a nearby area, two new strip malls were near completion, and a couple of office buildings were under construction. While the other services would undoubtedly solicit this new business, she at least felt she would have a chance to succeed in this business, especially since her brother-in-law was a real estate agent. She was right. She's been able to achieve her goals for ten steady customers each week within the year.

If your research, like Gloria's, indicates that there are not enough potential customers in your territory who would respond to your product or service, you do not have a viable market. But what, exactly, constitutes "enough" potential customers? Again, like Gloria, to find the answer, you need to do some homework first:

1. You need to determine the pricing for the product or service you propose to offer. In franchising, your franchisor may have already determined the pricing. But in many cases, you will have to do it yourself. Different markets, territories, and regional economies make it difficult for franchisors to establish standardized pricing. Local competi-

tion, costs of doing business, and differing perceptions of value result in your needing to devote time and thought to your pricing. Finding the right prices is key to your success in business. If your pricing structure doesn't allow you to make the income you need to live the lifestyle you want, it doesn't matter how good your market is, or how well you market your business. Your prices themselves will never allow you to succeed. On the other hand, if you overcharge, unless you can offer something awfully special, it will be virtually impossible for you to compete with others in your market and you won't attract enough business to get your franchise off the ground.

Let's consider the elements you need to consider in pricing. The basic formula for establishing a price for a *product* is:

Material Costs + Labor + Overhead + Profit = Price

- Your material costs include items you acquire from the franchisor as well as things you purchase independently. Packaging costs may be accounted for here.
- Your labor cost is what you pay yourself or someone else. Include fringe benefits in calculating your labor costs.
- Overhead must encompass both your cost of *being* in business as well as the costs of *doing* business. The costs of being in business are usually fixed; you pay for such things as a business license, insurance, and equipment whether you sell anything or not. The costs of doing business are variable and include such things as what you spend on marketing, supplies, and transportation.
- Profit is an amount calculated over and above your costs. Remember, one of your costs is the value of your labor.

The basic formula for pricing services is:

Labor Cost + Overhead + Direct Costs + Profit = Price per Hour or per Job

- Direct costs are ones you incur as a direct result of providing your service. For example, if you are providing cleaning services, the cost of cleaning supplies is a direct cost. If you are providing accounting and financial services or pet-sitting, the cost of driving to your customer's office or home is a direct cost. Other examples of direct costs are telephone calls, postage, printing charges that are specific to a job. In some businesses, it's customary to bill these items directly to the customer, thus they do not have to be calculated in the job or hourly price.

- You may charge for your services on an hourly basis, but many businesses find it to their advantage to price on a per-job basis. Customers often feel more comfortable knowing what the total cost will be rather than be subject to the uncertainty of the hourly charges mounting as the clock ticks. Guidance from your franchisor and your own experience will enable you to determine how much time you can expect to devote to a job and thus enable you to come out financially by pricing by the job.

2. After you've determined your pricing, you need to calculate your break-even point. How much in products or services must you sell in order to cover your cost of being in business and your living expenses? For example, let's say that figure is $8,000. How many sales do you need to make to earn $8,000? How many hours or jobs do you need to bill? Are there enough potential customers in your proposed market to generate that many sales each month? If you don't have enough potential customers to cover this most basic monthly income level, you do not have a viable market.

3. You may be willing to accept less in terms of money to cover living expenses in the beginning. But will you be willing to just get by over time? Are there enough potential customers in your market to enable you to grow to the point of achieving your personal income goals? If not, you may have a market that's viable to cover your basic expenses and keep you afloat, but if the potential for real success isn't there, do you really want go through all the hard work of having your own business?

This is a simplification of the complex issues involved in pricing and determining market feasibility. We present these ideas as a way to get you to start thinking about what you will need to do to complete your market test and know what it will take to actually succeed in a particular franchise. For a more detailed presentation of price setting, we suggest you refer to the chapter "Pricing: Determining What to Charge" in our book *Working From Home,* and *Priced to Sell* by Herman Holz, and the other resources listed at the back of this book.

If you have determined that there is no real market for the product or service in the territory outlined in the franchise agreement, it is pointless to undertake the business. You would do well to look for another kind of franchise or to research another territory, if that's feasible. Do not succumb to pressure from the franchisor to buy the franchise anyway, despite what looks like a bad market. Numbers don't lie. There are plenty of other kinds of businesses, including other franchises and business opportunities for you to consider.

ONE FINAL CHECK

Once you've checked out everything and a franchise has passed the test as a reputable, marketable company that's suited to your personality, interests, skills, and background, there's one final test you should do before you buy.

Ask yourself if you already have most of the information, knowledge, background, and resources to do this business yourself without the structure of a franchise organization. Could you obtain whatever added information, knowledge, background, and resources you need on your own through books, courses, private consultations, and the like? If so, you don't need to buy a franchise to do what you want to do. If not, go for the franchise.

After investigating rug cleaning franchises, for example, Tom Coventry decided he didn't need a franchise to start his own rug cleaning service. He read a variety of books, attended several seminars, got free training from suppliers, paid for several consultations from a colleague, and took off on his own. Although there was a cost involved in gaining all this expertise, it was considerably less than the price of the franchise.

He told us, "It was definitely a learn-as-you-go proposition." He admits he made mistakes along the way, and it took him more than six months to work out a system for cleaning that he could count on. He ended up trying various products and had to buy several different pieces of equipment before he found what would work best for him. "But," he says, "now I own my own company free and clear and I get to keep all the money I make."

James McAllister decided differently. An ex-UCLA football star, McAllister wanted to open his own rug cleaning business after graduation, but he knew he needed help to get started. He bought a franchise and considers the franchisor to be his business partner. They taught him their system, supply him with all the equipment and cleaning products, provide ongoing assistance in marketing and promotion, and have been available over the years with advice and support whenever it was needed. James not only believes he was able to get under way more quickly than if he had tried to do it alone, but he's also not certain he would ever have done it if he'd had to do it alone. "I'm proud to own my own business," he says. "It's something I always dreamed of doing."

So, weigh the options and decide which route is best for you.

3

Could Multilevel Marketing
Interest You?

YOU'VE PROBABLY HEARD the offers: "If you're not making at least $500 dollars a day, we need to talk!" or, "No buying, no selling, make $100,000 per month!" This is the language that surrounds, and in some sense, plagues the multilevel marketing (MLM) industry. This kind of advertising, by no means confined to MLM, is not used by the majority of companies offering legitimate business opportunities. The following chapter will give you an overview of what MLM is, how it works, and how to identify the scams from viable, potentially profitable, and satisfying business opportunities.

A BRIEF HISTORY OF MULTILEVEL MARKETING
AND ITS DEVELOPMENT

It is generally agreed that what is called multilevel marketing began in California in 1945. Lee Mytinger, a former cemetery plot salesman, and William Casselberry, a psychologist, decided on a new way to market their company, California Vitamins. The company manufactured and sold vitamin supplements made from watercress, parsley, yeast, and other ingredients. The best-selling product was called Nutrilite, for which they renamed the company.

Mytinger and Casselberry developed a unique way of distributing and selling their tablets and capsules. They set up a system whereby their products were sold to distributors at a 35 percent discount. What made their plan unique was that almost anyone could be a Nutrilite distributor after using the product for thirty days. Housewives, doctors, construction workers, teachers—everyone was encouraged to sell Nutrilite. Another unique aspect of Nutrilite's sales approach was that distributors were encouraged to work from their homes, and indeed, most sales were generated from the home. Working from home was not fashionable at the time. In addition to the profits distributors made on sales, they also received monthly bonuses of up to 25 percent, based on how much they sold. The plan didn't stop there: when a Nutrilite distributor got 25 people to purchase a month's supply of Nutrilite, he or she was "promoted" to the level of sponsor. Many of the distributors' customers became distributors themselves. As a sponsor, customers and distributors bought directly from her or him. The sponsor then earned the usual 35 percent profit on sales, as well as 25 percent of the sales his or her distributors made. When the sponsor and his or her distributors lined up 150 total customers, the sponsor was promoted again to key agent. This promotion earned the key agent the ability to make an additional 2 percent on the sales of every one of the sponsors working in his or her organization who also became key agents. Sound confusing? Maybe so, but this unique sales concept caught on.

Throughout the late 1940s and '50s, hundreds of companies were founded on Nutrilite's network marketing concept. Because of the different levels (i.e., distributor, sponsor, key agent in Nutrilite's case) inherent in these systems, the concept soon became known as multilevel marketing, or MLM.

In the late 1950s, two of the giants of modern MLM were founded: Amway and Shaklee. Shaklee, like Nutrilite, used the MLM concept to move a family of vitamin and nutritional supplements. Amway's main products consisted of household cleaning products. Soon thereafter Mary Kay Cosmetics came into being. These MLM-based companies have grown into mega-businesses, and have become household names.

Of the entire group of MLM companies started in the 1950s, Amway, founded in 1959, has become the largest and in many ways the most powerful. Founded in the homes of two Nutrilite distributors, Rich Devos and Jay Van Andel, Amway grew so quickly that it bought Nutrilite outright in 1972. Amway's success, and its problems, mirror the MLM movement in general. From its humble beginnings, Amway now has distributors in over forty countries, well over two million distributors, and annual sales that exceed $4.5 billion dollars.

As MLM grew, so did the number of scammers and disreputable operators. False claims of earning potential, bogus products, and illegally high "entrance fees" were some of the many problems. Because MLM is structured like illegal "pyramid" schemes, it held, and stills holds, a real attraction for con artists. The problem became so rampant that the FTC (Federal Trade Commission) put a large number of these operators out of business in the 1970s and '80s. Many others, some of them the biggest names in MLM, like NuSkin and Herbalife, were forced to substantially change the way their businesses were organized.

Today, MLM is something of a reformed industry. Many MLM companies are toning down their pitches and restricting what their distributors can say. The industry is also taking great pains to regulate itself. The DSA (Direct Selling Association) is the largest industry-based group whose mission it is to set a clear ethical standard. Membership in the DSA is open to companies only, not distributors. Each one of their member companies must agree to follow a comprehensive code of ethics. The MLMIA (Multilevel Marketing International Association) is an organization for both MLM companies and distributors as well as suppliers and the industry. They meet regularly with regulators, attorneys general, and securities regulators to help the industry stay clear of unethical practices.

MLM: OPPORTUNITY OR PYRAMID SCHEME?

Pyramid power may have been a fad in the 1970s, but the power of an illegal pyramid scheme is enough to turn an honest MLM recruiter's blood cold and bring federal and state regulators' to a boil. In researching MLM, you will see the term *pyramid scheme* pop up again and again in most of the articles and books you read. That's why it makes MLM recruiters mad with frustration. They can't seem to escape that term.

Let us start out by saying that the great majority of MLM opportunities *are not* pyramid schemes. The MLM industry as a whole goes to great lengths to expose any unscrupulous company. Yet, the problem persists. What exactly is a pyramid scheme? The Better Business Bureau in its pamphlet *Tips on Multi-Level Marketing* says, "'Pyramid' schemes . . . concentrate mainly on the quick profits to be earned by recruiting others to invest who, in turn, will recruit others, and so on. The merchandise or service to be sold is largely ignored, and little or no mention is made regarding a market for the products. Pyramid scheme participants attempt to recoup their investments in products by recruiting from the ever-decreasing number of potential investors in a given area."

So, to know if an MLM company is really just a front for a pyramid scheme, you can check to see if most of the money you earn will be generated by bringing people into your organization as opposed to selling products. If a company's primary emphasis is on collecting initiation fees, demonstration kits, dues, or any other kind of fee not derived from the sale of products, it is most likely to be a pyramid scheme. Quoted in *Kiplinger's Personal Finance* magazine in November 1991, Larry Hodapp, senior attorney with the FTC, says that an MLM crosses the line into an illegal pyramid scheme "when money is coming in from the recruitment of people, not the sale of products."

Notably, one of the highest-profile cases was brought against Amway itself. Begun in the mid-seventies, the case was resolved in 1979 after much litigation. The FTC ultimately found that Amway was not running a pyramid scheme because the company offered a viable product line upon which company income was based. (One of the outcomes of this suit is that Amway publishes financial data about distributor income that is unique in this industry.) Other companies have not fared as well.

Another kind of pyramid scheme to be aware of is one in which the company claims, "All you have to do is buy and use the products yourself, and recruit others to do the same," says Sidney Schwartz, a noted expert on MLM. The outcomes of cases brought against NuSkin and Herbalife both included specific restrictions against the paying of commissions on products purchased by distributors for their own personal use. In attorney Jeffrey Babner's book, *MLM: The Definitive Guide,* he quotes Doris Wood of the Multilevel Marketing International Association as saying "Remember . . . when looking at any MLM opportunity: The focus of the marketing program would be to promote retail sales to nonparticipants."

MLM IN THE NINETIES

Much like franchising, multilevel marketing has seen a tremendous amount of growth in the last few years. After some rough times in the late seventies and eighties, national and statewide regulations helped establish the legitimacy of the industry. According to the Direct Selling Association, the trade organization for the direct-selling industry, which includes MLM, the number of people involved in direct selling, which is principally MLM, rose a whopping 53 percent from 1990 to 1995—an increase from 4.7 million people to over 7.2 million. Based on DSA figures, direct selling accounts for 3 percent of all retail-level sales, nationally. Sources no less than the *New York Times* have recently had articles about MLM, portraying it as a viable opportunity for those seeking a second career. People from all walks of life—recently downsized white collar executives, former construction workers, struggling professionals and other small-business owners, homemakers, current and former military personnel, to name just a few—turn to MLM as either a way out of economic hard times or as a way to augment stagnant incomes, make ends meet, or make retirement more comfortable.

Direct-Selling Distributors in the U.S.

Multilevel Marketing Estimated to Be 65 to 70 Percent of Direct-Selling Industry

Millions

Source: Direct Selling Association

According to Richard Poe, author of the influential *Wave 3: The New Era in Network Marketing*, MLM (also known as Network Marketing) is now a fully matured industry. In his book, Poe defines today's MLM climate as *Wave 3*. By this he refers to the three distinct periods in MLM's development: Wave 1 being the pioneering of the industry, Wave 2 being the next stage—one of growth and development, and now, Wave 3. Wave 3 companies, says Poe, use technology and the latest business principles: "Wave 3 companies use computers, management systems, and cutting-edge telecommunications to make life as easy as possible for distributors," explains Poe. "For decades, network marketers have been promising financial freedom . . . with the advent of Wave 3, that promise has been fully realized." No one accuses Mr. Poe of lack of passion. Whether his optimism will prove warranted remains to be seen.

The attraction MLM has for so many people is its relatively low start-up costs and incredibly high earning potential. With total sales last year of $16.5 billion in the U.S. alone, there is indeed money to be made. Yet, it's important to realize all published indications are that over 90 percent of those involved in MLM earn not much more than a thousand dollars a year. So don't be tempted to think of MLM as an easy guaranteed route to fortunes, or even a good living. But why is there so great a discrepancy? A close look at the facts and fallacies of MLM will go a long way toward helping us explain both its promise and its limitations.

WHAT IS MULTILEVEL MARKETING?

Multilevel marketing, like franchising, was conceived as a system of distribution of products and services. Oftentimes, new products, especially those aimed at the retail market, are very hard to get onto store shelves. Power has shifted from manufacturers like Proctor & Gamble and Beatrice Foods to the large retail chains. Retailers charge "slotting allowances" to companies seeking to get new products onto store shelves. Then costly national advertising is necessary to get consumers to buy the new products. As a result, most new products disappear from store shelves within a matter of months. MLM is a less expensive way for new companies to get their products out to a large number of people quickly, bypassing normal channels of distribution. This is a classic piece of American ingenuity and optimism. New companies figured that if they couldn't get their products into stores through traditional distribution channels, they would turn their problem into an advantage. "Not available in stores" has been an MLM selling point almost since its inception, and it is still a powerful advertising slogan today.

Because of problems MLM has had, while working to clean up and professionalize their industry, many MLM companies will state that they are not multilevel marketing companies. Instead, they will describe themselves as direct-sales organizations, network marketing companies, or marketing companies. All three of these terms are accurate descriptions of MLM companies. All MLM companies are part of the direct-selling industry, but not all direct-selling companies use MLM as a means of distributing products. We'll discuss this further below.

How Does MLM Work?

The basic concept of MLM is a simple one. When you accept an MLM opportunity, you essentially take on two responsibilities, both of which can lead to income for you. When you embark on an MLM business, you become a distributor for the parent company's products and/or services. The distributorship aspect of MLM can seem a little confusing at first. Traditionally, in standard business operations, a distributor buys a product from a wholesaler, then sells the product to a retailer at a profit, who in turn sells to the ultimate consumer. In MLM, you often do buy the product from the parent company, but you do not sell to a retailer. Your sales are directly to the public—friends, family, associates, etc. This kind of approach is almost always the case when you start out. You buy from the company and sell to your customers (the consumer) at a profit.

Your first priority in MLM is that you must sell something. This is usually a consumable product or family of products such as a line of vitamins, chemical-free cosmetics, or services such as insurance, travel, or telephone service. Always make sure, though, that an MLM company promotes the importance of its products or services and emphasizes your role in the sale of its products or services to consumers who are not participating in the company. Companies who don't offer much in the way of product or place little emphasis on selling their products, relying instead on your membership fees as their primary source of income, come dangerously close to or cross the line of being an illegal pyramid scheme, as we discussed above.

The second responsibility in an MLM company is recruitment. What makes MLM different from franchising and business opportunities is its emphasis on building the size of the organization through recruiting other distributors. In addition to selling the actual products, you will be encouraged, though not required, to recruit people into the sales organization. You yourself will probably have been recruited into the organization by someone else. The person who recruits you is considered your sponsor, and you will be part of what's called his or her "downline" organization. Your sponsor is part of what's called your "upline" organization. The people you bring in to help sell the product or service become part of your downline. This is where MLM starts to resemble more of a traditional distributorship. You provide products to your organization, which is similar to providing products to a retailer who in turn sells directly to the end consumer. You will receive a percentage of each sale that every person in your downline organization makes, which, again, is similar to the profit made by a traditional distributor, but not quite. As you recruit more and more people, you are "promoted" to higher levels in the organization. As the people in your downline become promoted as well, your position rises accordingly. With each new level comes the opportunity to earn money from the efforts of those in your downline organization. Taken at face value, this is a win-win situation that puts cash in your pocket, while exponentially increasing the distribution of the MLM company's product line and providing income for those you've recruited.

MLM, Part of the Direct-Selling Industry

Direct selling is often mentioned in the same breath as multilevel marketing, and rightly so. Direct selling has been around for a very long time and is a traditional way to distribute and sell products and services. The Yankee ped-dler selling goods from his wagon was a direct seller. Direct selling does not include heavy emphasis on the recruiting of others into an organization or building a downline. It is the straightforward act of selling a product or ser-vice away from a store location directly to a consumer and receiving a profit from the sale.

In direct sales, you are a distributor only. You receive no commissions or overrides from anyone else's sale other than your own. The benefit of direct selling is that the percentage of profit made from each sale is generally higher than in the other plans we will discuss. Other benefits include simplified busi-ness operations—you don't have to sign up, motivate, and maintain a down-line—and a fairly high assurance that the parent company is not offering a pyramid scheme.

Avon, the largest direct-selling company for a time experimented using MLM. Some leading direct-sales-only companies are listed at the end of Chapter 9.

Party Plans

Party plans, as they are known today, are a popular way of direct selling. They were the brainchild of Brownie Wise and Earl Tupper of—yes, you guessed it—Tupperware renown. In 1946 Brownie and Earl accurately read the change of the national focus after World War II ended, from global con-cerns to home and family. Earl developed a line of high-quality, plastic-based household products and Brownie figured out an innovative way to sell them: the party plan.

Party plans themselves are different in detail from company to com-pany, but their organizing principles are the same. Someone is enticed, usu-ally with an offer of free products, to "host" a party. It is the host's job to invite party attendees and ensure a turnout. The person who actually sells the product or service is the demonstrator. The demonstrator presents the products to the attendees of the party and takes orders directly from them. He or she earns a commission or percentage of the total sales of each party.

Demonstrators are also encouraged to sign up other demonstrators, often the hosts of the parties at which they demonstrate. As a demonstrator, you will receive either commissions or "bonuses," based on the sales success of those whom you recruit. Many companies who use party plans also have levels you can work through, with each new level bringing with it additional commissions, bonuses, perks, etc.

Act II Jewelry, Longaberger (baskets), Mary Kay Cosmetics, and Tupper-ware make extensive use of the party plan method.

Network Marketing / MLM

Network marketing and *multilevel marketing* are two terms used interchangeably to describe the same thing. As we have done throughout the book, for clarity's sake, we'll call these MLM plans. MLM compensation or business plans are usually based on a series of levels. Each company's plan specifies how much commission or what percentage you will receive for each direct sale of a product or service you make yourself. The plan will also outline how much you will make for each sale made by your downline (your organization of recruits), according to whatever "level" you and they are on. MLM compensation plans can be *very* complex, even convoluted. Many people don't take the time to fully understand how they work, or figure out what their earnings could realistically be.

As an example of a typical MLM compensation plan, we've shown the Mary Kay Cosmetics compensation plan, based on 1994 published materials. Remember, the compensation is cumulative as you work up through the levels.

Qualification Levels (ranked lowest to highest)

Beauty Consultant: 40 to 50 percent markup on direct sales. This means that you buy from Mary Kay at a 40 to 50 percent discount and mark up the price accordingly to your buyer. If you place an order for $300 to $499, you qualify for the 40 percent discount, $500 to $799 for a 45 percent discount, and $800 or more for a 50 percent discount.

Star Recruiter: 4 percent commission on wholesale orders placed by your recruits. You must have three or four active recruits to qualify for this level.

Team Leader: 8 to 12 percent commission on personal recruits. You must have five or more active recruits to qualify for this level.

Team Manager: up to 12 percent commission on personal recruits. You will also receive a car or cash and a $50 to $300 performance bonus, based on recruiting and time put in as a team manager. To qualify for this level, you and your downline in combination must produce at least $3,600 in orders a month for a period of four consecutive months, and you must qualify for auto insurance to get the car.

Director-in-Qualification: You receive all team manager benefits. To qualify, you must be a team manager, have twelve active recruits in the month prior to submitting your "commitment" card, and leadership profile.

Sales Director: You will receive up to 12 percent in commission from sales of personal recruits, 9 to 13 percent on unit sales, $300 to $3,500 bonus, life and disability insurance, and a car of some kind, most notably the eye-catching Mary Kay Pink Cadillac.

Compensation can vary dramatically from company to company. For example, long-distance telephone service is a popular MLM product right now. Commissions for sale of telephone service vary from company to company—from 2 to 9 percent for selling the service to a consumer, with total possible commissions and overrides from your downline ranging from 8 to 12 percent.

A compensation plan for an MLM covers:

- How much of a volume discount you get for purchasing the product
- How "deep" and "wide" your downline organization can be:
  "Matrix" plans, for example, dictate a specific structure, or matrix, to which your downline must conform—that is, allowing you to have a specific number of people on a specific number of levels. An example would be three people on the first level, nine on the second level, twenty-seven on the third, eighty-one on the fourth, continuing down to the number of levels on which the company will pay commissions.
  Some plans dictate a specific structure yet have no limits on width. A stairstep plan has no limit on depth.
- How commissions and bonuses are paid out on the various levels and when different product volumes are reached
- Companies establish requirements for attaining different levels in the commission structure and any changes that take place in your relation to your upline and downline. In a "breakaway" type of compensation plan, for example, when a downline group reaches a certain size they "break away" from you and the method of calculating your commission changes. This is where things can get complicated but where those who earn very large incomes from MLM usually derive their sizable earnings.

You can see how complex an MLM compensation plan can be, and the above is by no means the most complicated. In most cases an MLM is not just one of these three general plans. Often MLM companies are flexible enough for you to mix and match what you're most comfortable with; i.e., direct selling, recruiting, and/or party plan demonstrations. If you have any questions about a company's plan (and unless you are whiz with numbers and systems, you will), ask your recruiter (sponsor), upline, or the company itself to provide the detailed explanations you need to be certain of just how, when, and in what way you will be compensated. Have them go through each level with you, and make them use actual, realistic sales figures as you go. In this way you will have a more realistic idea of what to expect, and you will see how the sales, commissions, bonuses, and other aspects of the compensation plan will actually pan out for you.

Using Talent Creatively in MLMing—How to Cross-Dress for Success

Case Study #1:

Jeff Sumner/Pam Teflon, Tupperware

One of the most innovative and creative people we interviewed for this book is Jeff Sumner of Los Angeles. By applying his own unique talents and ingenuity, along with more than a little fortitude, Jeff has combined his passion for acting, writing, and stand-up comedy with the very down-to-earth necessity of earning a steady living. This combination has brought him not only financial rewards but also the fame and recognition he's always dreamed of.

If you attend one of Jeff's Tupperware parties, which have become all the rage with the Hollywood crowd in trendy Los Angeles, you might be a bit confused at first. The invitation you receive says that someone named Jeff Sumner will be giving a Tupperware demonstration, so when you arrive, you may wonder who the tall, trashy blond woman is with the big hair and trailer park attitude talking in front of the room about the essential meaning of plastic? And the answer is, that's Pam Teflon, Jeff's alter ego!

How Jeff Sumner became Pam Teflon is a classic example of the power of combining personal talent with innovative marketing and good, old American ingenuity. "As an actor and writer here in L.A., I've had my share of day jobs," explains Jeff. "Someone told me about being a Tupperware demonstrator—how the hours were flexible and how you could make some okay money—but, boy was I skeptical. I hated the idea of selling." However, he wasn't so skeptical as not to try it. He received training in the product line and how to organize parties and demonstrate the product. "It was actually kind of nice knowing I had a big company behind me," admits Jeff. His first few parties were nondescript, and it began to seem like just another in a long line of routine jobs. Then he was hit by an inspiration. "In writing and acting, I've always been attracted to outrageous characters. I decided to try integrating this idea into my Tupperware demonstrations," says Jeff. So he created the character Pam Teflon, Tupperware Demonstrator Extraordinaire. Pam is a wisecracking, tough-talking, big-haired blonde with a pickup truck full of attitude. She also "has a husband named Marvin, and two kids, Allen and Sue," according to Jeff.

You might think that doing Tupperware parties in full drag would be enough to capture people's attention, if not their desire to store leftovers more efficiently, but Jeff didn't stop there. "I turn each party into a kind of play, or performance piece. Part scripted, part improvisation, each performance is designed to feature a different product." How do people react to Pam Teflon? Well, it seems there's money in "them thar high heels." Jeff is one of Tupperware's top executive managers (their highest level) in the country and he made more than $160,000 last year, his first year in the business.

"One of the most incredible things about this experience is that it has actually helped my acting and writing career," says Jeff. "I've been on television, had features done on me in magazines and newspapers. Producers and directors are actually calling me to get invited to my parties!" Jeff advises anyone considering an MLM opportunity to look for a company that will allow flexibility in the way their products or services are presented. Jeff started out being extremely skeptical and with a marked distaste for selling, but "because Tupperware was so flexible and allowed me to be creative, it's worked out really well for everybody."

What Kind of Goods and Services Are Sold through MLMs?

In the beginning, MLM companies provided, for the most part, cosmetics, jewelry, cookware, and cleaning products. Today, anything from motel rooms to children's toys, and telephone services to water-treatment technology is being sold through MLM systems.

1995 Percentages of MLM Sales by Major Product Groups

Personal-care products (cosmetics, jewelry, skin care, vitamins, etc.)	51.1%
Home/family-care products (cleaning products, cookware, cutlery, etc.)	27.2%
Services/miscellaneous	16.8%
Leisure/educational products (books, toys, games, etc.)	4.7%

(Source: Direct Selling Association, Washington, D.C.)

As MLM continues to grow, even more products and services will be distributed through MLM channels.

MLM AS A HOME-BASED BUSINESS

Almost from the very beginning in the early 1950s, MLM companies recognized that the home was an effective environment from which to work and sell products. Of the $16.5 billion dollars in MLM sales last year, 72.1 percent were made from the home. MLM opportunities typically involve a very low investment, especially when compared with franchises and business opportunities.

Space requirements for working in MLM are minimal. You will generally not be required to maintain a large inventory of merchandise, so storage space is not usually a major concern. Many MLM companies even do the majority of the paperwork to keep track of your sales, the sales of your downline, and the payment of the appropriate commissions, so space used for file storage and general work space can be kept to a minimum as well.

One of the main advantages of working from home is the very personal nature of MLM selling and recruiting. According to the DSA, nearly 73 percent of all sales last year were made in individual, one-to-one situations. Storefronts and offices are not conducive to developing the personal, individualized kinds of relationships the MLM system thrives on. Your home is the perfect place to work the phone, have meetings, hold sales parties, and gather for other events. If these activities don't take place in your home, they most probably will occur in the home of a customer.

MLM operations, more so than franchising or business opportunities, seldom, if ever, benefit from renting space in a storefront, office, or warehouse. People who buy into an MLM actually prefer the "homey" nature of its products and services. Prospective customers enjoy getting to know their salesperson personally. They also respond to the group spirit of buying merchandise at home-based MLM parties and events.

Working from home is also effective in recruiting others into your downline organization. Potential recruits also will want to get to know you and the nature and personality of the products you represent. By meeting with people in your home or theirs, you are inviting them to share a personal side of yourself. It shows you are open and trusting. It conveys the notion that you have nothing to hide. It also shows your prospective recruits that it will be possible for them to work out of their homes, too. An office or storefront location will actually work against you in this regard.

Most people get involved in MLM on a part-time basis. This is a very important fact to consider. In 1995, 91.6 percent of people working in MLM worked part-time, fewer than thirty hours a week. An office or other business location with its high overhead costs is a poor choice in terms of money you invest in your business. Working from home, on the other hand, gives you flexibility to work when you wish, with no additional investment in costly office space. Do not be tempted to think, however, that MLM is a source of "passive" income. As with any business, you will need to invest time and energy and work hard if you want to make more than a few dollars here and there.

MLM Case Study #2:
An MLM Horror Story—How to Lose Friends and Influence

A two-career couple we'll call Jane and George both had good jobs, but in the midst of putting two kids through college, they were struggling to make ends meet. When they were recruited for a new MLM that was selling health and fitness products, they were intrigued by the potential for "passive" income and impressed by the contingent of nationally known spokespersons who were endorsing the program on video and in the media. The gentleman who was recruiting them to be in his downline was retired and was investing his savings in building a successful downline. He took Jane and George to dinner at a lovely restaurant and talked about how within two years this business would enable him to move to Hawaii and live happily every after on his MLM earnings.

That sounded so good to Jane and George, and their enthusiasm grew even stronger after attending a hotel-style meeting with hundreds of other interested people who listened to many speakers describing the new Mercedes convertibles and Rolex watches they had purchased since joining the MLM. It seemed as though lots of people were becoming rich overnight. Since Jane and George had been interested in health and fitness for many years and most of their friends were also fitness devotees, this opportunity sounded like a godsend.

They were told they wouldn't have to buy a lot of product up-front since the parent company would ship all orders, but they were urged to stockpile product anyway to use in getting customers and recruits onboard immediately. So they invested the few thousand dollars they could scrape together in starter products and an array of training videos and promotional tapes to use when showing others the products and the business opportunity.

They quickly signed up ten or fifteen professionals like themselves who knew and trusted them. In the meantime, their interest in the products started to cool as they began developing several negative symptoms. Their friends also began complaining about unpleasant physical symptoms, but they were complaining even more vehemently about not being able to sell any of the products. Although Jane and George had no experience in sales themselves, as their "downline" grew more and more discouraged, they started holding motivational training sessions in their home. Unfortunately these gatherings turned into gripe sessions about all the money their friends were losing and the many excuses they kept hearing from others about why they couldn't get involved.

Meanwhile Jane and George were running wildly from evening meeting to evening meeting, trying to shore up the sagging spirits of their downline and simultaneously urging other friends to get involved. Six months later they were totally exhausted. They'd lost several friends and many thousands of dollars. At that point, they'd received one check from the company—for $1.60.

Then came the final blow. Public news scandals about the company began breaking. The national sports figures and leading medical authorities who had endorsed the products on the videos and in the media were claiming they had never agreed to have their names used. The nutritional research underpinning the projects was attacked and called into question. The company filed for bankruptcy. People who had purchased new homes with large mortgages were going into foreclosure. Jane and George were mortified. They wrote their few remaining downline friends a letter of sincere apology and to this day remain humiliated by their brief MLM experience.

"We were really taken in," Jane laments. "We heard what we wanted to hear. It all sounded so good. I guess you could say we got stars in our eyes." Jack advises, "From the beginning, I was always somewhat doubtful a company could grow so fast without toppling over. But it goes to show that even if you read praiseworthy clippings in major newsmagazines you've got to listen to your own reservations and give yourself time to test them out."

Some might say that this story also illustrates that Darwin's theory of the survival of the fittest applies to business as well as biology. Fortunately, most MLMs don't become such public debacles, but most start-up MLMs do fail within a few years. Just keep Jane and George's story in mind when you're looking for an MLM, franchise, or business opportunity. A company doesn't have to be a scam or fraud to be a bad idea or a colossal failure. So, don't be tempted to jump onto a glamorous-looking bandwagon until you know that a company is actually on sound financial ground with a truly viable product. Don't take what you hear at face value. Try products out yourself for some time before you leap into urging others to buy them and join you in selling them. Doris Wood of the Multi-Level Marketing International Association advises investing no more money in products than you can personally consume in sixty days. "That still provides you with some to sell to friends and family."

Play the devil's advocate. Try to find the holes in any pitch you hear. Question those involved and pay close attention to their answers. If anything seems inconsistent or poorly thought out, be wary. Realize that, like Jane and George, you can't accurately evaluate whether or not a company's business plan makes business sense unless you yourself have an understanding of basic business principles and practices. So, educate yourself before you buy in—especially before you risk your reputation by convincing others to follow in your footsteps!

What Kind of People Get Involved in MLM?

A better question might be: What kind of people live in America? Once the realm of homemakers, MLM now attracts a wide variety of people for a great number of reasons. Corporate downsizing, defense cutbacks, a generally slow-growing economy, the increasing cost of goods and services, health care, college tuition, retirement worries—and a slew of other, sometimes very personal, reasons have made MLM an attractive option for many people across the demographic spectrum.

Ann Nunnally had worked as a chemical engineer for ten years when she decided to quit her job to raise a family. A few years and two kids later, she started to look around for something to do part-time that would bring in some additional income. After checking her options, she chose an MLM distributorship that specializes in children's educational books and materials. Her fifteen-hour workweek and downline organization of about twenty people bring her about $5,000 a year gross, which is exactly the national average. "I'm happy with my business because I love the books we sell and the company itself is very responsive and supportive," says Ann.

Ann does indeed represent the national average in terms of income, yet there are more than a few people with similar backgrounds who have achieved much greater numbers. Profiled in a recent article in the *Wall Street Journal,* Paula Cook-Ehrlich worked as an airline industry executive until five years ago, when she became a distributor for NuSkin, a maker of personal-care and nutritional products. She's now a "Blue Diamond" (remember, each step in the MLM hierarchy has a name that varies from company to company), NuSkin's highest sales level. At her $704,000-a-year income level, Ms. Ehrlich now says, "After five and a half years I'm living a lifestyle people couldn't imagine!"

Historically, women have had a greater involvement than men in MLM. This is still true today. Of the 6.3 million total salespeople involved in MLM, 76 percent are women. Yet this figure is somewhat misleading. There has been a sharp increase in the number of men getting involved in the industry. In 1992 men represented 10 percent of the MLM sales force. The figure for 1994 (the latest available) indicates that the number of men in MLM has doubled in just two years. Many of these men have come from the ranks of white collar corporate America. The influx of white collar workers and professionals, both male and female, into MLM constitutes one of the industry's fastest-growing segments.

Part-Time or Full-Time?

For most people, a multilevel marketing opportunity is a part-time venture. Although it is possible for some people to make a comfortable full-time living from MLM, over 90% work on a part-time basis. Amway, the largest MLM company, is one of the few MLMs to report the earnings of its distributors. From time to time, other companies, as part of court cases, have had to report their distributors' earnings, and at the time they paralleled those of Amway distributors. So we take the Amway figures to be representative. The average gross income of active Amway distributors is about $1,056 a year. *That's $88 per month.* Another indication that this average is on target is that if one divides the dollar size of the industry ($16.5 billion) by the number of direct-selling distributors (7.2 million), it comes to $2,292 per distributor.

Because of the low income involved, many people combine an MLM business with another business or career. We found an excellent example of this in a recent article in the *Wall Street Journal.* Among others, the article profiled Dr. Lewis Kulik, who sells Calmplex 2000, a Rexall herbal product, to patients who experience anxiety about visiting a dentist. Dr. Kulik found a complementary product to sell via MLM and uses his dental practice as a source of not only potential buyers but potential recruits as well. While we don't recommend that doctors and lawyers go out and recruit patients and clients, Dr. Kulick's example shows how people can tie an MLM in with a full-time career.

Part-Time, First and Foremost

Based on all our interviews and research, it seems that the safest way to consider an MLM distributorship, initially at least, is on a part-time basis. Again, the average monthly gross income of an active Amway distributor is only $88. Average incomes of distributors are simply too overwhelmingly low to expect that you could support yourself on a full-time basis until proven otherwise. Although companies aggressively recruit by using claims of financial independence and luxurious incomes, only 3 in 1,000 active distributors actually earn gross incomes over $70,000. Of course you may be one of the few, but you would be ill-advised to quit or pass up a well-paying job, or make other irreversible sacrifices, in the hope that you could be one of the few who achieve big-time MLM success. A rule of thumb in the industry is to wait until your part-time income surpasses that of your full-time job; then decide whether to devote yourself full-time to MLM.

Mixing MLM with Other Careers

Because of its low-overhead and low-inventory requirements, you can run an active MLM enterprise concurrently with a job or ongoing temporary work. A word of friendly advice, however: Don't aggressively go after your immediate co-workers and colleagues to get them to buy your products or join your downline. We've heard countless horror stories about people who have alienated their co-workers, bosses, subordinates, neighbors, fellow church

members, and even their own family members by aggressively selling or recruiting for their MLM. A casual mention once to assess interest would be
about the tolerable limit. So keep your MLM activities separate from your
current job or career and you will generally be more secure in both activities.

However, when considering an MLM company, try to find something
that is somewhat similar to or has commonality with your current job, profession, or interests. If you are in a service field, such as accounting, insurance, customer service, the legal profession, or a computer-related industry,
for example, you will probably find greater success in an MLM company that
provides a service related to your field such as tax preparation, long-distance
telephone service, life insurance, etc. Without having a genuine feel for a
product or service you will find it difficult to generate the kind of passion required to effectively sell it and build your downline. Or if you are staying
home to provide care for your children, you might want to find an MLM
company that somehow relates to children, children's issues, or education.
You will have a definite head start in these areas by keeping your MLM focus
related to the other major priorities in your life. If you can't find something
appealing that is related to children try, for example, to find a company that
offers a product or service that caters to parents' or family interests. This way
you can have a strong start by utilizing the network of friends and contacts
you already have, which is one reason why such a large percentage of people
in MLM sell vitamins, skin-care products, and jewelry. Sellers are familiar
with the products and most people use them.

Be careful, however, to make sure that none of the MLM company poli-
cies will prevent you from participating fully while pursuing your other line
of work. A self-employed newsletter publisher found himself in an unexpected dilemma. He was recruited into a company and advanced rapidly up
the MLM ladder. He was earning over $2,000 a month after developing a
downline that was ten levels deep and crisscrossed the nation in thirty-five
states. Having arrived at this level, he was told he was considered to be in a
leadership position and thus eligible for a special bonus "paid only to those
who were totally committed and not involved in any capacity in any other
MLMs." Since his own newsletter was marketed in a manner that could be
defined as a multilevel program and he had disclosed this to the company,
they told him he either had to close his newsletter business or risk termination as well as lose his eligibility for the special bonus pool he had earned.

MLM AND THE INTERNET

The tremendous growth of the Internet over the last few years has had a considerable impact on multilevel marketing as well. Because of its overwhelm-

ing popularity and unique capacity to communicate on an intimate basis, the net has become a favored tool of many in the MLM business.

Distributors now use the Internet to advertise their products and services. MLMers also use the net to recruit new people for their downlines. This second aspect has added a significant new wrinkle to the MLM landscape. In the past, someone's downline was primarily confined to the immediate region where he or she lived or had strong existing contacts. Traditional recruiting required face-to-face contact or knowing the person you were contacting by phone or at least having an introduction in some way. With the proliferation of MLM or special-interest groups on popular services such as CompuServe and America Online, people can network and form intimate "communities" across states, countries, even continents.

If the Internet is unfamiliar territory for you, there are a great many excellent books that will give you the information you need to become cyber surfers. And once you get on line, you could find an entire new community of people who will be more than happy to assist you in getting around on the information superhighway.

The World Wide Web, the fastest growing part of the Internet, allows MLMers to create a worldwide presence for their businesses. They create sites on the Web that advertise their products and services, solicit recruits, provide industry information, as well as provide "links" to other relevant Web sites.

Another way MLMers are using the Net to grow their businesses is E-mail (electronic mail). For example, if you had a site on the World Wide Web for your MLM business, you would include a link to your E-mail address (essentially an electronic mailbox that people send messages to). Anybody who views your site can place an order for a product, request information, or send a message of any sort whatsoever to your E-mail address simply by using his or her mouse and clicking on the prescribed link. MLMers exchange and post their E-mail addresses on message boards and while interacting on various forums as well.

Of course with every advance come a few retreats, and the Internet is no exception. The Net has spawned a new generation of cyber scammers in the MLM and biz op world. We strongly advise you to apply all the criteria outlined for testing in the following chapter for Fitness, Honesty, and Market before getting financially involved with any MLM opportunity you come across on the Internet or elsewhere.

MLM IN REVIEW

Before presenting more case stories of people's experiences with multilevel marketing, let's review the key points of exactly what multilevel marketing is:

- Multilevel marketing (MLM) is also known as network marketing and is a way of compensating people for direct selling.
- MLM is an alternative way for companies to distribute products and services to buyers.
- MLM companies offer an extremely wide range of products and services and are not limited to cosmetics, food supplements, housewares, and cleaning products.
- MLM is based on two components. The first is selling a product, product line, or service for which you receive a commission. The second is building an organization of recruits who also sell the products or services and sign up other recruits as well. You receive a percentage of the sales of each recruit in your organization and a percentage of the sales of each of their recruits to the extent the compensation plan allows.
- MLM companies offer a series or levels of rank you can attain according to how much sales volume the active recruits you bring in to the organization produce.
- The Federal Trade Commission has held that MLM is not an illegal pyramid scheme because it is focused primarily on selling products and services, not headhunting.
- An MLM distributorship is your own business. You do not "work" for the parent company, nor are you its agent.
- Having an MLM distributorship is compatible with working from home.
- According to statistics, over 91 percent of MLMers work part-time.
- MLM usually requires low start-up costs, generally less than $300.
- MLM is based on selling. It is primarily a sales and sales-management function.

FIRSTHAND EXPERIENCE: CONVERSATIONS WITH HOME-BASED MULTILEVEL MARKETERS

These conversations represent a cross section of people working in MLM. With just one exception, everyone profiled has been with his or her company for less than a year. This seems to be the average, according to our informal survey. Everyone we talked to here has had positive experiences in MLM. A few are earning above-average incomes. The attitudes, experiences, and achievements of these folks are presented to be informative and instructive. A very interesting exercise for you might be to see how each of these MLMers rates in each of the areas of the MLM Personality Profile you can fill out in the following chapter. Then check your own personality profile with the MLMer being interviewed.

Working from Home Works for Her

MLM Case Study #3:
Robin Droppa, Rexall Showcase International

Robin Droppa started her professional life as a representative for a prestigious office furniture manufacturer. She was very successful. After about ten years, she decided to take some time off to raise a family. Soon after the birth of her first child, she got the itch to get back into some kind of paying work and so began to look around for opportunities. "I was specifically looking for a home-based business, and I stumbled onto a network marketing on-line forum," explains Robin.

At first she didn't know what network marketing was. When Robin found out that it is also known as multilevel marketing, she was skeptical. "I had a very negative impression of the whole industry. But I saw the people talking [on the forum], did some research, and decided 'if these people can make money . . . I probably can, too,'" says Robin. So she went looking for MLM opportunities, and after many phone calls and a lot of careful checking, she decided on Rexall, a nutritional supplement and consumer health products company. She liked Rexall's name recognition, their honest, no-hype approach, and the fact that they were very accessible. "I had a list of questions. They answered them. My sponsor was immediately available to me. We talked for hours before I actually took the dive."

Robin went on to become a successful Rexall distributor working approximately forty hours a week. Robin attributes some of her success to the assistance she received from Rexall, especially early on. According to Robin, "For the first three to five months I probably spoke to my upline daily. The company has a phenomenal free support system—it's all through (800) numbers." Reasonably priced training materials were also helpful. "Rexall publishes training and support materials that are all sold at cost." For Robin, it all comes down to support. "The company is really behind me in helping me support my customers, as well. Whatever questions or concerns I have, they're right there. Rexall is a very, very customer-service and distributor-service–oriented company."

Another advantage Robin looked for and found with Rexall is exclusivity of products. It is generally much easier to sell a product through MLM that cannot be bought anywhere else. Robin explains, "The major products I offer are exclusive to Rexall. We sell very specific formulas that are unique and patented. There's a tremendous advantage to that. The product lines address a dynamic and growing marketplace."

Like franchising, MLM as an industry has several aspects that make it unique. If you find a product line or service you can be passionate about selling, consider if you will be comfortable in the MLM industry itself before making your decision. After initial reservations, which included her awareness of the "tremendous abuses of MLM by unscrupulous companies out there" and her personal knowledge of others who have had negative experiences, Robin found that MLM offered her some real advantages, too. "MLM is a business in a box. Everything's done for you—the graphic [design] work, the planning. You have to be a unique person to come up with an independent business idea, an independent business plan, then make it happen. Try to do that while raising a six-month-old. It's impossible!"

Robin believes that certain kinds of people do better in MLM than others. She looks for certain personality traits in those she recruits. To succeed in MLM, Robin says, "You need to have self-confidence, you need to be outgoing. You need to be a people person." Basic business and selling experience are also helpful, in her estimation. "It helps to have some selling or marketing experience in your past. I think basic selling skills are very effective in this business. You also have to have a plan, or at least the ability to plan. If you work at home and you don't want to get out of bed, you're not going to. You have to be self-directed and self-motivated."

Part-Time MLMer, Full-Time Mom

MLM Case Study #4:
Jennifer Harper, Ohio
Workshops of Gerald E. Henn

Jennifer Harper is brand-new to MLM. She's had an interesting background, having worked as a mechanical engineer for seven years, then quitting when her daughter turned eighteen months old. She then started a business around knitting personalized children's sweaters from her home. Always the engineer, she used a knitting machine and a computer. Recently, she was invited to a workshop party. She wasn't able to attend, so she invited the host over to her house for a demonstration. "The more she [the party host] talked and the more she showed the products . . . I just loved them. I thought 'I could do that.'" said Jennifer. Although the initial idea was a "stretch" for her, Jennifer decided to research MLM.

"I started reading up on it quite a bit. I ordered every book at the public library that they had on MLM. I got some magazine articles, just to see the pros and cons," explains Jennifer. Based on what she found out about MLM, she decided to get involved. She quickly found a company to her liking and has been working about ten to fifteen hours per week at her business.

Support from her sponsor and the company as a whole has been very important to Jennifer. "When you sign on and order the product kit, the training videos and manuals come with it. The videos were excellent. In fact, I borrowed them from my upline sponsor before I ever signed a contract." In addition to the training materials, her sponsor has also been quite helpful in other ways. "My sponsor was happy to give me any resources she had. She even let me know what her income was and what her upline's income was." That kind of open disclosure was exhibited by the company as well. "The company was very up-front about how much money it was possible for me to make, and how much hard work was required to make that money."

Multilevel marketing, as we've stated, offers distinct advantages and disadvantages. One of its advantages is the measure of freedom it offers to distributors. Jennifer has found that this matches her personality quite well. "I'm very self-motivated, so the advantage to me is that I can work as hard as I want to." One of the lesser mentioned positives of MLM is the satisfaction that you can get from helping others start their own businesses, which is inherent in building a downline. Jennifer recognizes how this not only helps her be more satisfied but also actually helps her grow her business—a win-win situation. In summing up her own perceptions of MLM, Jennifer provides one of the better definitions of what makes MLM unique: "I've found that MLM is not like being an employee without any say-so in how the business is run. Nor is it like being totally on my own without anyone to turn to. MLM, to me, is right in the middle of these two extremes. There's help if I want it, and if I don't want it, I can act in a completely independent manner."

Jennifer has seen the downside of this independence. "One of the major problems I've seen is motivation. If you're not highly motivated yourself, there's no one else there to motivate you. There's no boss there to breathe down your neck and say you have to work harder." She's found that the parent company doesn't pressure its distributors to achieve standout results. She believes this is because the majority of distributors are mothers with children who are working in order to earn extra income without having to leave their homes.

In her brief experience in MLM Jennifer has only come across one drawback: She's been occasionally let down by her downline in terms of their living up to her expectations, and sometimes not even coming through on their obligations. "I have been disappointed in some of the people. Not those that work directly for the parent company, but the ones you try to get to do shows for you [recruits] who say they will, then never call you back."

On the whole, though, MLM has exceeded Jennifer's expectations. Her success was apparent right away. "The company tells you that you should be able to make back your initial investment within your first five shows. I made mine back after the first four. I was very encouraged by that." She's found that the parent company's other claims have actually been quite accurate. "The information the company represented to me in terms of what income I could expect and how much effort was required was really true. Because I have met these expectations so quickly, I now have confidence in passing that down to the people I try to recruit."

Other traits Jennifer finds helpful are her organizational skills and her surprisingly thick skin. "You have to be willing to hear 'no,' which I sure wasn't used to hearing. That's why I never pictured myself in sales because I hated it when people said 'no' to me."

Jennifer finds her MLM business meets her needs on a number of levels, but primarily she likes the flexible hours and the fact that she can work from home. "I have two kids, and they're very little. I just don't have a lot of time to devote to a business. What works for me in MLM is that I don't have spend a great deal of time in order to generate a little income."

How to Really Succeed in MLM with Ten Years of Trying

MLM Case History #5:
Steve and Ginnie Bretzke, Watkins

Steve and Ginnie Bretzke are full-time MLM professionals. They have been distributing for their present company, Watkins, of Winona, Wisconsin, for over five years. They belong to a small but extremely outgoing group of people who have been involved in MLM for over ten years and have made comfortable lives for themselves. Steve's approach and philosophy can be seen as an almost textbook example of how to succeed in MLM.

He started out as an electrical engineer. Herbalife, a company that primarily offers weight-loss products, was his first experience in MLM. "The money is what interested me, at first," says Steve. "It was my first exposure to big-money multilevel talk, and that's what sold me." It didn't take long, however, before Steve figured out that actually making that kind of money was going to take hard work, time, and dedication. "I'd lose 80 percent of my customers every other month because those people weren't prepared to really use the product as part of an overall weight-reduction program," explains Steve. "I had to rebuild the majority of my customer base every month." The reason for this was the nature of the product he was selling. Weight loss, like everything else, takes consistent effort. People abandoned Steve's products as quickly and as often as they abandoned their diets.

Learning from his experiences with Herbalife, Steve understood that it was the product line, not the promised income figures, that was most important to MLM success. "It always has to come down to the product line," explains Steve. "Not necessarily a product line that changes your life, grows hair on your head, or anything—just a group of products that make sense in the market and can compete at the retail price level. Otherwise, it doesn't work." A strong product line and a strong demand are what attracted him to

Watkins. "I look for a company, like Watkins, that has products that have a wide appeal, something like 80 percent. There are other good companies that have very good products that are probably worth the price, but the demand for those high-end products is pretty small. Let's say you had a $150 skin-care system. There are people who would buy a $150 skin-care system, but the percentage is not very large. I look for a product line that can appeal to the masses, that representatives would buy, that customers would buy."

Steve believes that after researching a company's product line and demand, the next step is to find out all you can about the company. He's right. In multilevel marketing, companies fail with great regularity in their first year of business. Steve advises, "Look for a company that's been around for a while, at least three to five years." People need to know that they're not going to get rich overnight. It's going to take three, five, ten years to build a good income. That's why it's essential that you feel good about the company you're working with and that you know they're going to be around that long."

Steve feels he has found such a partner in Watkins. Watkins offers basic bookkeeping support and genealogy reports (reports on purchases made by your downline). The company also provides product-training videos, audio-tapes, and written materials on how to sell. They also lend support in helping distributors build a downline organization. Watkins actually offers two kinds of businesses. Buyers have the choice of becoming strictly distributors in the classic sense. That is, they can opt to simply sell Watkins at a profit without recruiting a downline. The company also offers a true multilevel distributorship that does allow for the building of a downline organization. Steve chose the latter.

The only disadvantage in his Watkins business Steve sees is one of perception. "We're a 128-year-old company. People remember their mothers telling them about door-to-door Watkins salesmen. This isn't a problem when making sales; it actually helps. But it does become a problem in recruiting. People are a little confused at first. They think they'll have to go door-to-door, or something"

Five years into their Watkins distributorship, by all accounts, the Bretzkes have been very successful. They earn a yearly income greater than 99 percent of all MLM distributors. When asked if his experience has met his initial expectations, Steve's answer is predictable: "The business has far exceeded my expectations. When I got in five years ago, my expectations were realistic at that time. There's no question it's far exceeded anything that I could have imagined. If Watkins is guilty of anything it's underselling itself. Thankfully, I've done very well—I'm the second-largest distributor in the company. I think I had realistic expectations, but I also planned to go out and really work hard, and I did."

Steve believes the core of success has been hard work, consistency, and knowing more than a little about human nature. Steve explains, "I know that selling and recruiting are just dealing with human nature. The toughest challenge in this business, because this industry is somewhat misunderstood, is getting people in your downline to believe in it, and believe in it to the point that they're willing to go tell their friends and build the business." He also believes in the company and in the validity of the opportunity it offers: "It's very easy to recruit someone if you believe in what you're doing. It's very hard if you're not sure it's legitimate or not. That's probably our biggest challenge—to get people to believe in themselves and in the company and the industry." Another important component of his success, and the success of others he's seen, is open-mindedness and willingness to learn. Communication skills also play a crucial role in MLM success, although Steve believes these can be learned: "I've seen some people who are better at that to start with. Others benefit from spending a little time honing their communication skills."

One of the chief advantages in MLM that Steve sees is that people can achieve up to a level they're comfortable with. In franchising, the franchisor almost always has a specific set of expectations in terms of earnings or sales that a franchisee must fulfill. If these expectations are not met, the franchisee may be relieved of his or her franchise. In MLM, these expectations rarely exist. "There are many people who succeed up to what they want, and that may be a couple of hundred dollars a month. That's all the time they're going to put into it and in their own way they've been successful. There are people who have the drive to go beyond that. In MLM your definition of success is really up to you."

Steve brings up an important point—a point we will discuss at length in the following chapter, "Testing an MLM for Fitness, Honesty, and Marketability." Steve credits his engineering experience with helping him really understand how various MLM compensation systems work. "I was able to work through the numbers in the compensation plan and was able to really understand what would happen if I built this business over time. And many people out there, they have no idea how these plans work. They're joining based on hearing someone talk about how much money they're making, but they don't have a clue as to how that can actually happen."

Steve likes MLM's flexibility in terms of marketing and selling as well. "I think marketing is very much an individual thing that's based on each person's personality. Some people that are very outgoing do very well with direct-selling-type techniques . . . party plans, talking to friends at church, etc. Some people need to be more indirect, because they're not comfortable directly approaching someone. I've worked a lot better indirectly, because, being an engineer, I haven't really been the social type that's able to just start talking about my business. For me, effective ways to market have been advertising, for the most part, and on line, and so forth. On line is a safe way to interact. It's like being part of a big group of people, but they can't see you and you can take all the time you want to try and figure out what to say."

In giving advice to potential recruits, Steve always tell them: "Before you can be successful in MLM in any substantial way, you have to believe in yourself. I've been successful because I've had my mettle tested time and time again. Each time I'm tested, it has deepened my resolve and added to my conviction. The worst thing you can do is believe someone else when they question your resolve or intentions."

MAKING IT MEANS DOING YOUR HOMEWORK

In reviewing the stories of people who have been successful in multilevel marketing, it's clear that the more carefully you look into what you're getting yourself into before you buy, the more satisfied you'll be with whatever decisions you make. That means doing your homework: researching the company, talking to others who have been involved both happily and not so happily, and checking to see if you are in a position to contact people who are interested in and willing to pay for what you'll be offering. Most important, assess yourself and your own motivations, skills, interests, and abilities. In the following chapter, we're going to outline how you can do the needed homework to know if you can succeed in MLM, specifically by assessing four key areas:

- *The Company.* Is it a solid opportunity, or too good to be true?
- *What You'll Actually Be Doing.* How exactly will you spend most of your time in running the MLM? Is this activity something that's right for you?
- *Your Personal Experience, Skills, and Readiness.* Are you ready to run your own business from home? Do you have the experience, skills, and personality profile to succeed in an MLM you're considering, or in MLM in general?
- *The Market.* Do people want or need the service or product within the region you propose to operate in?

Starting your own business is one of the most exciting and important decisions you will make in your life. Don't rush into anything. Give yourself time to properly complete the necessary homework before making a decision. Research shows that those who spend six to nine months doing research and preparation are more likely to succeed. If a friend or associate is pressuring you to make a decision quickly, take this to be a clear warning sign. It has been the experience of far too many disappointed people that high-pressure sales jobs from MLMers lead to bad experiences for everyone. If the MLM is a solid company offering a solid opportunity, those you'll be working with will appreciate your careful consideration before acting because they know that's what makes you someone who will be serious about your commitment to success if you decide to proceed.

The Advantages of MLM

Let's sum up the advantages of an MLM distributorship business:

- Low cost to start up means that if the business fails you haven't risked as much money as you would have had you invested in or bought a franchise or business opportunity.
- High earning potential, though only relatively few people reach a six-figure income.
- MLM distributorships are designed to be run from your home. Working at home and MLM are extremely compatible.
- You can have a satisfactory MLM distributorship on a part-time basis.
- You can successfully run a part-time MLM distributorship in addition to having a job or another business.
- The MLM parent company generally provides the marketing and promotional materials you will need.
- In many cases, the MLM company provides bookkeeping, sales tracking, and other business-related services.
- Your downline organization could eventually provide you with some "passive" income.
- Reputable MLM companies stand by their products and assist with customer support and/or complaints.
- MLM companies usually provide extensive low-cost training and motivational materials such as videotapes, audiotapes, books, and special events like rallies, etc.
- You can learn selling and people-management skills usable later in your career.
- You may find a community of people in your MLM company that satisfies your social and business aspirations.

The Disadvantages of MLM

The multilevel marketing industry to this day is still fraught with controversy, mixed messages, and inaccurate or incomplete information. MLM distributors are sometimes hostile and defensive when questioned about MLM. Sidney Schwartz believes this comes about as a result of "a combination of a number of interrelated factors. One is that MLM companies, lacking traditional means of controlling and motivating their workers, have turned to instilling in distributors a near-evangelical belief in the product and in their mission as promoters of the American Dream. Another is that the continued existence of MLM relies on the constant recruitment of large numbers of people to replace those who drop out, so competition is fierce. There's also the public's generally negative perception of MLM, which serves to fuel the MLMers' view of themselves as a select but misunderstood and persecuted minority. I've never seen any other type of business where those who are involved must expend so much time and energy justifying and defending the business itself rather than selling their products. When I was working in retail I would sometimes have to justify to a customer why he or she should buy from my store rather than a competitor's, but I never had to justify the concept of 'retailing.'"

Great efforts have been made by the industry itself and groups like the Direct Selling Association and the Multi Level Marketing International Association to polish MLM's image, but problems persist. Please consider the following points carefully before you consider going into MLM on a full-time, or even part-time, basis:

- Despite the longevity of industry leaders such as Amway, Shaklee, Mary Kay Cosmetics, and others, a great many MLM companies only stay in business for a few years.
- MLM's reputation, justified or not, often makes it difficult to recruit people into your downline.
- Keeping your downline motivated to stay active selling and recruiting is sometimes more difficult than recruiting them in the first place.
- MLM companies do not offer exclusive territories. In fact, the very nature of MLM distribution is based on recruiting as many people as possible. Some people feel this can quickly lead to a saturated market for the products you offer.
- The average gross income of an active Amway MLM distributor, based on Amway published figures, was $88 per month in 1995.
- Despite the claims, actual average incomes derived from MLM distributorships are so low that for most people they are not viable as full-time opportunities.
- MLM contracts are not as formalized as those in franchising and therefore can lead to more disputes and other problems.

- You may experience some unpleasant changes in your relationships with friends, family, and associates. By attempting to sell and recruit those closest to you, you may be perceived as pesky, pushy, or worse.
- MLMs tend to market themselves with inflated offers and misleading promises. It is sometimes difficult to find out what you can realistically expect.
- It is harder to research an MLM company before becoming involved, especially since some MLM companies even deny they are an MLM.
- There is generally less support in terms of business planning, market analysis, and other business-planning functions.
- Many MLM companies use highly emotional appeals to address people's fears and dreams. Such approaches purposely obscure the company's actual structure.
- Rules of termination are far less clear than in franchising.
- The structure of MLM companies makes the industry hard for state and federal agencies to regulate.
- The complex "matrixes" used to calculate the commissions you will earn from your downline are often complicated, convoluted, and just plain hard to understand.
- Most people won't get to the point of generating much "passive" income.
- Not everyone can generate the "passion" MLM uniquely requires for successful sales and recruitment. As a result, the turnover rate of distributors exceeds 100 percent a year.
- You must feel comfortable knowing that the overwhelming number of people you recruit will end up spending more money than they earn.

4

Testing an MLM for Fitness, Honesty, and Marketability

To do anything well, you need to have some level of personal interest in or passion for it. In this chapter, you'll find an array of detailed tests and work sheets to help you find the kind of MLM opportunity, if any, you can believe in and feel passionately about. Nearly every person we interviewed for this book, and every source we checked, basically said the same thing when it came down to analyzing the fundamental key for MLM success: You have to believe in the products or services you're selling and in the company you represent.

The following three tools, the Fitness Check, the Honesty Check, and the Market Check, will help you test how well suited a particular MLM you're considering is to your needs, so that you can make the best decisions as to whether you could feel strong and confident about pursuing an MLM as a business.

TEST I: THE MLM FITNESS CHECK

As in franchising, any kind of business, including an MLM, has one key activity that's at the heart of a business, or what we call its Core Function, so to speak. In some cases, that activity isn't readily apparent when you first begin to look at the business. Many people get excited, for example, about the idea of MLM or a particular product or service, like nutrition or children's toys, without considering what they will actually be spending the majority of their time doing in the running of an MLM distributorship. Because this "main activity," is what you will actually be spending most of your time doing, you need to be certain to know exactly what the Core Function of any business you buy is and if it's an activity you actually enjoy or have an affinity for.

What Will You Be Doing?

Unlike other businesses, however, which have many possible Core Functions, the Core Function of all MLM businesses, no matter what field they're in, is selling—selling a product and/or selling people on the idea of becoming distributors in your downline. This is understandable if you think back on the history of MLM we have just reviewed in the previous chapter. While franchises were developed as a way to quickly duplicate successful businesses in various locations throughout the country and even internationally, MLM was developed as an alternative distribution system, an alternative way to sell products and services.

So, when it comes to knowing what you will be doing, while the nature of the products or services you will be offering is important, it's secondary to the fact that no matter what it is, you will primarily be selling it and/or convincing others to join you in selling it. This means that no matter how much you believe in the product or service and enjoy being involved in an industry like high-tech telecommunications or all-natural, environmentally friendly cleaning products, unless you sincerely enjoy meeting people, communicating the value of the products and services, and convincing them to buy what you're offering, you will not be satisfied with an MLM business.

Marnie learned this the hard way. In the throes of graduate school, she was complaining about barely being able to make ends meet each month when a friend told her about a weight-loss drink she was selling. The friend convinced Marnie to try out this drink with the promise that if she liked it, she could make some extra income selling it on campus to fellow students. Marnie liked the diet drink "okay," and she did loose a few pounds, but best of all, she liked the fact that her friend was making over $1,000 a month from this diet program. So within the month, she signed up for the MLM. Her friend had convinced her she could "make lots of money at this," because as she put it, "This product sells itself."

Having never sold anything before, Marnie was relieved that the product would sell itself, but she felt particularly confident that, being an education major, she could teach people how to use the product to lose weight. In fact, she even envisioned herself holding weight-loss classes for the people who bought the product.

Unfortunately, as with most products, this one didn't sell itself. Lots of people were interested, and most of them would try the sample packets. But few bought and of those who did, most didn't reorder. To compound the problem, there was really no role for her to teach people about weight loss. There were ample videos and written materials about the product, which Marnie was supposed to purchase and pass out. But her sponsor told her that if people wanted to talk about specifics of diet and nutrition she wasn't supposed to provide anything that might be construed as medical advice. "Whatever they ask," she was advised, "just tell them you don't know about that, but that the product works for you and you believe it could work for them too."

Worst of all, it turned out, Marnie's sponsor was making 90 percent of her $1,000 a month not on sales of the diet drink but from a percentage of the sales from her downline, who were also primarily selling it as a business opportunity to other people they knew who were using it themselves. "This," Marnie concluded, "was a real waste of my time."

Dean had an experience that was completely the opposite, however. He'd been selling things since grade school when he sold more candy for an annual Little League fund-raiser than anyone else in his district. So, when a co-worker at the fast-food restaurant where he worked after school told him about an MLM opportunity selling water filtration systems, Dean was excited. Before long, he had recruited a downline of other guys, all of whom were selling and servicing filtration systems to restaurants.

From these two examples, you can see how vital it can be to realize that an MLM is primarily about selling and not just get excited about the field, concept, or intention of the product the MLM sells. In other words, if you don't enjoy and have an aptitude for selling or aren't willing to learn the skill, you won't like MLM, no matter how much you like the product—because that's what you will need to be *doing* if you want to succeed.

The following Fitness Check will help you explore whether you are or could do well at the selling activities MLM involves, what other, if any, activities a particular MLM will require you to carry out, as well as your own motivations, interests, strengths, and weaknesses. Part 1 of the MLM Fitness Check is designed to help you answer the question "Is This MLM a Good Fit for You?" Then Part 2 will help you assess "Are You a Good Fit for This MLM?"

PART 1: IS THIS MLM A GOOD FIT FOR YOU? ANALYZING THE CORE SALES FUNCTION

As we said, our research shows that successful MLMers have a passion for, a faith in, and an enthusiasm about the products they represent and an aptitude, willingness, and passion for selling them. They are enthusiastic, people oriented, sales savvy, and not easily frustrated. This doesn't mean that you have to be a superslick salesperson to succeed at MLM. On the contrary, most people enjoying MLM success are down-to-earth folks who are selling a product they honestly believe will help people.

The following will help you determine if the MLM's core sales function is an activity that you will enjoy sufficiently to do well at it.

1. How do you feel about the product or service?

One reason Marnie was so unhappy with her MLM experience was that she had very little passion for the product. She described the diet drink as "okay." If you are going to convince other people to buy or sell an MLM product or service you will need to feel much more strongly about it than "okay." Products and services don't sell themselves; people do. A person's personal excitement and enthusiasm is what ignites the desire that makes buying something contagious. No matter how promising or appealing the sales pitch or materials make an MLM seem, you need to have the firsthand experience of knowing that its products or services produce the results you were promised and will be promising.

So, we suggest giving yourself a considerable period of time to try out and use any MLM product or service before you decide to sell it. Does it deliver for you or are there problems in using it you didn't expect? For example, can you find better products or services for less money at your local drug or grocery store? Does it have unexpected side effects? What, if any, complaints do you or others have? Consider some of the common complaints you might encounter like "It tastes nasty," "It got corroded in just a few months," "I installed it and it didn't work," "It gave me a stomachache," "I got a rash," "It dried out too fast," "It broke," "It costs too much."

Can you overcome these problems? Your reputation and ability to sell, resell, or get others to sell will depend on it.

2. How do you feel about selling?

Since selling is the Core Function of any MLM, you need to honestly assess how you feel in general about selling. We recommend doing an initial check of your feelings. Which of the following statements, for example, best describes you:

a. I love to sell. It's one of my favorite activities.

b. Selling is okay as long as I feel good about what I'm selling.

c. I'll do it if I have to.

d. I don't particularly like to sell.

e. Selling scares me.

f. I'd rather have a root canal than sell.

If your initial response is (a) or (b), your feelings about selling shouldn't deter you from getting involved in an MLM if it checks out positively in other regards. If your answer is (c) or (d), take a more careful look at the next question and see if it alters the way you feel about selling. If your answer is (e) or (f), even after weighing the issues raised in the next question, you need to ask if you're willing to overcome your fear and dislike of selling so that you can get involved in an MLM. It can be done. But chances are it will not be a quick or easy process.

For Suzanne, whose Mary Kay experience you will read about later in this chapter, overcoming her fear of selling was a major part of the pride and self-esteem she gained over the months and years of becoming a successful distributor. But as she is the first to admit, it was a painful and difficult experience. "I thought I'd die more than once before I discovered I could not only do this well but I could enjoy it."

3. What is the nature of the Core Sales Function?

While selling is the core function of all MLMs, there are, as we discussed in the previous chapter, a variety of differences in the nature of MLM sales functions. Some companies, like Mary Kay, put greater emphasis on direct sales to customers, while others place more emphasis on downline development. And, of course, you will need to decide what balance you personally want to place on these two MLM selling functions and weigh how much you could expect to earn if you limited yourself more or less to selling products or services.

In some companies you really can't make much money if you only sell products or services. To make any substantial money in most companies you have to build a downline. But then, you'll be operating more like a sales manager and it's difficult to develop good salespeople if you yourself don't have some personal sales skills and experience. So you will need to be, or become, strong in most of the leading functions listed below whichever MLM sales role you take. Also be aware that in addition to most of the Leading Functions, building a downline will also involve many Improving Functions. So talk to others in any upline you're considering and (√) check off which of the following activities they spend most of their time doing:

LEADING
___ administering
___ assigning
___ coordinating
___ delegating
___ initiating
___ inspiring
___ managing
___ motivating
___ organizing
___ persuading
___ selling
___ supervising

IMPROVING
___ assisting
___ caring
___ collaborating
___ consulting
___ contributing
___ counseling
___ encouraging
___ explaining
___ helping
___ listening
___ serving
___ supporting

In addition, how you or those in your downline will be expected to go about selling the MLM product or service can vary greatly too. Some companies allow great leeway to do sales person to person, by phone, at group meetings, house parties, or expos, or through print advertising. Other companies preclude you from doing anything but person-to-person selling, while still others prefer sticking with group sales. What do you feel most comfortable with?

Some people hate to do cold calling but would enjoy presenting or demonstrating a product at an expo or party where people will buy afterward. Others are mortified at the thought of selling anything to family, friends, or others they know but wouldn't mind recruiting strangers into a business opportunity.

If there are forms of selling you could enjoy and others you would hate, be sure that the company you're considering allows or provides ways of selling that are compatible with your preferences. For example, Steve Bretzke mentioned that he isn't comfortable selling directly but does well placing small advertisements. While he can do that within the Watkins system, he couldn't in others. So, again, talk with your potential sponsor about what is and isn't allowed and identify which of the following types of selling activities you would be called to draw upon most:

LEADING
___ coordinating
___ demonstrating
___ entertaining
___ initiating
___ inspiring
___ motivating
___ organizing
___ performing

___ persuading
___ presenting to a group
___ selling by phone
___ selling in person
___ supervising
___ writing sales copy
___ on-line marketing

4. How much time will you spend selling versus doing other activities?

As we mentioned, in addition to your Core Function, in running most businesses you will also be doing some or all six of the functions listed below. Sometimes this is true in MLM, too. In addition to selling, for example, in some companies you may be teaching parents about children's toys, installing water systems, or giving facials. You may be placing orders, stocking inventory, delivering or distributing products, and doing detailed record keeping. Increasingly, however, many MLM companies are streamlining their operations through technology so that you virtually won't have to do anything but sell, or sometimes just sign people up.

In some companies, for example, you won't ever stock or even touch a product you sell. Everything will be shipped by the company. Even reorders in many cases are automated and charged automatically by the MLM company. And, although we *always* recommend keeping your own records for tax and legal purposes, in most companies now, all upline and downline records are kept electronically by the MLM company.

So, in evaluating an MLM, find out what proportion of your time you will be devoting to selling versus the other aspects of running a business. Ask your MLM company, your sponsor, and other people in your upline the following questions to get a clearer picture of how much time you will spend doing what:

1. Are you always "on," constantly looking for a sale?
2. Do you have the product or catalog with you constantly so you are always ready to sell?
3. Will you be stocking inventory? How much?
4. Do you look at social functions as opportunities to sell?
5. How much time do you spend working with customers doing activities other than selling? Who handles customer complaints, returns, etc.?
6. Will you need to organize parties, presentations, and other sales events?
7. How will reorders be handled? Will they be automatic or will you need to stay in touch with customers to stimulate reorders.

8. How much ongoing training is available through the upline or the company? What training, if any, will you need to be doing for your downline.
9. What type of record keeping will you need to do? Will you need to produce marketing materials (brochures, flyers, etc.)?
10. How much total time do you spend doing the above?

Check off any of the activities you will be doing among the six functions commonly carried out in any business:

LEADING
___ administering
___ assigning
___ coordinating
___ delegating
___ initiating
___ inspiring
___ managing
___ motivating
___ organizing
___ persuading
___ selling
___ supervising

IMPROVING
___ assisting
___ caring
___ collaborating
___ consulting
___ contributing
___ counseling
___ encouraging
___ explaining
___ helping
___ listening
___ serving
___ supporting

ORGANIZING
___ arranging
___ cataloging
___ compiling
___ evaluating
___ expediting
___ gathering
___ grouping
___ ordering
___ programming
___ recording
___ tabulating
___ updating

CREATING
___ communicating
___ composing
___ designing
___ drawing
___ feeling
___ imaging
___ innovating
___ perceiving
___ performing
___ sensing
___ shaping
___ writing

BUILDING
___ adjusting
___ assembling
___ computing

PROBLEM SOLVING
___ analyzing
___ classifying
___ defining

___ constructing   ___ diagnosing
___ handling   ___ editing
___ maintaining   ___ investigating
___ making   ___ reading
___ operating   ___ reasoning
___ renovating   ___ researching
___ repairing   ___ solving
___ tinkering   ___ studying
___ troubleshooting   ___ thinking

5. What proportion of your time will you be devoting to the various activities your business will involve?

From the above analysis, create a list of the activities you will be performing and how many hours in an average day, week, and month you will spend:

Time Analysis

Daily
___ Leading: i.e., directing/marketing/selling/promoting
___ Improving: i.e., assisting clients/other customer service
___ Organizing: i.e., bookkeeping/paperwork/processing information
___ Building: i.e., assembling/computing/constructing/maintaining
___ Problem Solving: i.e., planning/research/analyzing
___ Creating: i.e., innovating/designing/composing

Weekly
___ Leading: i.e., directing/marketing/selling/promoting
___ Improving: i.e., helping and assisting clients/other customer service
___ Organizing: i.e., bookkeeping/paperwork/processing information
___ Building: i.e., assembling/computing/constructing/maintaining
___ Problem Solving: i.e., planning/research/analyzing
___ Creating: i.e., innovating/designing/composing

Monthly
___ Leading: i.e., directing/marketing/selling/promoting
___ Improving: i.e., helping and assisting clients/other customer service
___ Organizing: i.e., bookkeeping/paperwork/processing information
___ Building: i.e., assembling/computing/constructing/maintaining
___ Problem Solving: i.e., planning/research/analyzing
___ Creating: i.e., innovating/designing/composing

6. What is the Core Function of the MLM company? What will they be providing?

If you recall, Jane and George hoped they would be providing counseling and assistance to people in how to live more healthfully. As it turned out, that was not the Core Function of their MLM company. Their Core Function was to sell the health products and services for the company. But like most MLMs these days, their MLM was also responsible for most of the administrative and record-keeping functions, and all the shipping and promotions of the company. They did not want Jane and George to ship any products or do any media promotions. So, be sure to find out just what role the MLM company will play in your business. Find the answer to the following questions:

- a. What activities will the MLM perform in the actual running of your distributorship? (They will almost always be manufacturing or otherwise selecting or creating the products or services you will be selling.)
- b. Will the MLM assist you in getting customers by generating leads?
- c. Will the MLM assist you in signing up recruits for your distributorship?
- d. Will the MLM be taking and shipping all orders?
- e. Will the MLM be offering ongoing training or training materials for downlines?
- f. Will the MLM be doing national advertising, marketing, and promotions?
- g. What role will the MLM play in finance, sales, and record keeping?
- h. How will you be informed about these transactions and how can you verify them?

7. What functions will your upline provide you with?

Many of the people we talked with mentioned the tremendous amount of assistance they were receiving from their upline. Answer the following questions regarding any upline you are considering and find out if you will be expected to do any of the following for your downline as well.

- a. Will the upline perform any tasks in the actual running of your distributorship?
- b. Will the upline assist you in getting customers for your distributorship?
- c. Will the upline assist you in signing up recruits for your distributorship?

PART 2: ARE YOU A GOOD FIT FOR THIS MLM?
ASSESSING YOUR NEEDS, MOTIVATION, SKILLS,
INTERESTS, KNOWLEDGE, AND PERSONALITY

As with franchising, the most important element in the success of a multilevel marketing business is *you*. MLM companies know this more than anyone. Almost every company we checked offers an extensive array of motivational videos, audiocassettes, rallies, and meetings that are designed to increase your selling abilities, keep you motivated, and educate you on every aspect of the company, its products, and plans for the future.

So, truly knowing yourself can save you thousands of dollars and many hours of wasted time. Had Marnie spent more time assessing her own motivations, experience, and background, for example, she would have realized that selling was neither her interest nor her forte. She would have realized that she wasn't that interested in the product either. These two insights could have saved her the time, money, and headaches of a negative MLM experience.

Completing this part of the **MLM Fitness Check** will help to make such an assessment. Use the following questions as a starting point for assessing yourself. In answering the following questions, be as objective as you can. The questions aren't designed to make you feel right or wrong, but rather to give you the information you need to help you make an informed decision about whether an MLM is a wise choice for you. This part of the **Fitness Check** will help you analyze your motivations, assess your experience and skills, and examine your expectations.

Your Needs and Motivation

1. Would you want to be an MLM distributor instead of starting a business of your own from scratch?
2. What do you want from this business?
   a. satisfaction
   b. additional Income
   c. riches
   d. independence
   e. flexible schedule
3. As Dr. Gini Graham Scott, an internationally known speaker, author, and MLM expert, writes in her book *Get Rich through Multi-Level Selling,* to be successful in MLM sales "you have to develop the qualities that contribute [to success]." The following list contains some of Dr. Scott's criteria for success as well as those of many other

experts. See how many of the following qualities you currently possess. Check the statements that are true for you:

a. I am a positive person.
b. I am quite persistent.
c. I am not easily discouraged.
d. I am very good at setting goals for myself.
e. I am enthusiastic about what I believe in.
f. I am focused on my goals.
g. I like people.
h. I communicate well.
i. I can budget my time well.
j. I am always looking for ways to improve myself.
k. I can take "no" for an answer without taking it personally.
l. I like to take the initiative.
m. I am a good listener.
n. I am self-motivated.
o. I can motivate others.
p. I believe in my abilities.
q. I understand people.
r. People understand me.

Your Interests, Skills, and Experience

1. What talents and skills do you bring to the distributorship?
   a. List your talents:
   b. List your skills:
   c. How many of the above will help you in selling and performing the other duties involved in the distributorship?
2. Do you have any experience in selling or performing these duties, or in the market or field in which the MLM operates?
3. Review the activities listed below and place a checkmark next to those you feel you can do adequately. Place a second checkmark next to the skills you feel you can do well. Then circle the skills you most enjoy using. Now, compare the results you get below with the activities you found would be involved in the MLM you're considering. If most of your skills and interests lie outside Leading, and secondarily Improving, you must face the fact that MLM is not your best choice for starting a home-based business.

LEADING	IMPROVING
___ administering	___ assisting
___ assigning	___ caring

___ coordinating

___ delegating

___ initiating

___ inspiring

___ managing

___ motivating

___ organizing

___ persuading

___ selling

___ supervising

___ collaborating

___ consulting

___ contributing

___ counseling

___ encouraging

___ explaining

___ helping

___ listening

___ serving

___ supporting

ORGANIZING

___ arranging

___ cataloging

___ compiling

___ evaluating

___ expediting

___ gathering

___ grouping

___ ordering

___ programming

___ recording

___ tabulating

___ updating

CREATING

___ communicating

___ composing

___ designing

___ drawing

___ feeling

___ imaging

___ innovating

___ perceiving

___ performing

___ sensing

___ shaping

___ writing

BUILDING

___ adjusting

___ assembling

___ computing

___ constructing

___ handling

___ maintaining

___ making

___ operating

___ renovating

___ repairing

___ tinkering

___ troubleshooting

PROBLEM SOLVING

___ analyzing

___ classifying

___ defining

___ diagnosing

___ editing

___ investigating

___ reading

___ reasoning

___ researching

___ solving

___ studying

___ thinking

Your Knowledge of Business and MLM

A frequent cause of people's frustration with MLM is their lack of general business knowledge as it applies to MLM. An MLM distributorship is most definitely a business. The more you treat it that way, the greater your chances of success.

Answer the following questions to find out how much business knowledge you currently have. Each one of these questions represents an important aspect of running an MLM business and includes the terms used in MLM. If you are unfamiliar with any terms, concepts, or procedures, make it a point to become familiar with them. Your business success may depend on it, especially if your goal is to become one of the elite full-time, high-earning MLM superstars.

It is beyond the scope of this book to give you an overview of specific business principles, but the Resources listed in Appendices 3 and 7 should help you gain the additional knowledge and information you need.

Answer the following questions to test your basic business acumen:

1. Do you understand the MLM's compensation plan? Could you explain it to others so they could understand it, too?
2. Is the opportunity you are considering primarily a Direct Sales situation, a Party Plan, or an MLM/Network Marketing distributorship?
3. What is a financial statement?
4. What are projected earnings?
5. What is an override?
6. Will you be responsible for collecting sales tax?
7. What is the most effective way to market the distributorship you're thinking of getting involved in?
8. What licenses, permits, etc., will you need? Where can you get them?
9. If you must collect sales tax, which state agency oversees sales tax?
10. What's a debit? How about a credit?
11. What is the difference between gross and net?
12. Do you understand margin and markup?
13. Are there any zoning restrictions pertinent to running a home business in your locale?
14. What are the business' insurance requirements?
15. What is market research?
16. How much do you know about inventory control?

Your MLM Personality Profile

The following questions will help you gain an understanding of your own personality as it relates to MLM. Your personality traits can help or hinder you in MLM. The general model for the following test was loosely based on a joint research project undertaken by the Drake P³, the Network Institute, Inc., and *Upline*™, a journal for network marketing leaders, as well as other research by industry leaders.

If there are areas you find yourself weak in, that doesn't mean you could never succeed in MLM or that there is no hope in trying. Weak areas only mean that you should work to improve these aspects of yourself to increase your chances of success.

A. Leadership

Thinking about how you work, rate yourself from 1 to 100 percent in the following areas, with 1 being "not at all" and 100 being "absolutely":

____*160*____ 1. How much do you like to control situations?

_____ 2. Are you an extroverted person?

_____ 3. Do people perceive you as powerful?

_____ 4. Would you consider yourself a nonconformist?

_____ 5. Do you find yourself leading most conversations?

_____ 6. Would you consider yourself a dominant person?

_____ 7. Do you chafe at following rules and structures?

_____ 8. Would you consider yourself a bold person?

_____ 9. How persistent are you?

_____10. Do you enjoy challenges?

_____11. Are you good at analyzing situations?

_____12. How organized are you?

_____13. Are you a risk taker?

_____14. Are you convincing in your conversations?

_____15. Do you delegate tasks to others easily?

_____16. Would you consider yourself influential?

_____17. How competitive are you?

_____18. Are you perceptive in your assessment of other people?

_____19. How sensitive are you to other people's concerns, feelings, etc.?

_____20. Do you have a large circle of friends?

_____21. Would you consider yourself to be congenial?

_____22. Are you generally trusting of others?

_____23. How optimistic are you?

_____24. Would you consider yourself friendly?

_____25. Are you eager to please?

_____26. Are you a good communicator?

Add up the percentages you gave in rating yourself for each of the above questions, then divide the total by 26. If you scored between 75 and 100 percent, you have the leadership qualities necessary for MLM success. According to John Milton Fogg, editor of *Upline*™ and noted MLM author, and Mike Cooper, president of the Network Institute, in their article "Do You Have The Right Stuff?" published in the book *Multi-level Marketing, The Definitive Guide,* "A networking [MLM] leader is a dominant and controlling person, outgoing—an extrovert. He or she balances that outward expression of power with a degree of patience well above that possessed by the average man or woman." If you rate lower than 75 percent, don't let it discourage you if your desire is to succeed in an MLM. Most people are not born with these skills. They can be developed. Fogg and Cooper go on to state that developing what they define as leadership skills "will put you right on track to becoming a high-performance top producer and high-income earner in network marketing, if you wish to."

1	25	50	75	100

B. Motivation
Thinking about how you work, rate yourself from 1 to 100 percent in the following areas, with 1 being "not at all" and 100 being "absolutely":

_____ 1. Do you need to interact with people to stay happy?
_____ 2. Do you enjoy meeting new people?
_____ 3. Are you a team player?
_____ 4. Is your public image important to you?
_____ 5. Is prestige important to you?
_____ 6. Do you need to feel you belong somewhere?
_____ 7. Do you need acceptance?
_____ 8. How important is it to be recognized for what you do?
_____ 9. Do you enjoy opportunities to innovate?
_____ 10. Do you need to be rewarded for what you do?
_____ 11. Are you a high-energy person?
_____ 12. Are you easily bored?
_____ 13. Do you need to be given challenges?
_____ 14. Are you quickly frustrated with routine?
_____ 15. Are you sometimes bored by details?
_____ 16. Do you need to know your life is headed somewhere?

Staying motivated is the key to MLM success. The industry itself has some powerful built-in motivators. The question is: Will you be motivated by them? Typical MLM motivators are the promise of money, advancement, recognition, and group support. Add up the ratings you gave yourself for each of the above. Then divide the total by 16. If your score is 75 percent or better, you will definitely respond to the built-in motivators in MLM.

1	25	50	75	100

C. Decision-Making/Assessment

In regard to your work, rate yourself from 1 to 100 percent in the following areas, with 1 being "not at all" and 100 being "absolutely":

_____ 1. Can you "read" other people?

_____ 2. Do you have a strong sense of intuition?

_____ 3. Do you trust your intuition?

_____ 4. Can you predict how people will react?

_____ 5. Are you logical?

_____ 6. How analytical are you?

_____ 7. How empathetic are you?

_____ 8. Do you consider your feelings when making a decision?

_____ 9. Do you often go by "gut feeling"?

_____10. Are you a caring person?

_____11. Do you generally understand people?

_____12. Are you a good judge of character?

_____13. Can you quickly find what motivates someone?

_____14. Do you make decisions quickly?

_____15. Are the decisions you make usually right?

_____16. Are you perceptive?

_____17. Are you "tuned in" to the environments you find yourself in?

_____18. Are you observant?

MLM is a people-oriented business. The more you understand people, their feelings, their motivations, their actions, the more effective you will be in MLM. Your ability to make decisions about others and assess their needs and desires must be highly developed, according to most MLM experts. Add up the ratings you've given yourself in the above questions. Divide the total by 18. If you scored 75 percent or higher, you have the natural intuition and people skills to do well in MLM's many sales and recruitment situations. You also have the logical and analytical capabilities to back up your more intuitive predilections. If you scored substantially below 75 percent, you may wish to think about developing these abilities in yourself or consider another type of business activity.

1	25	50	75	100

Personal MLM Disqualifiers

The above checks will help you decide if you **could** do well as an MLM. But even if you **could** succeed, the following list is designed to help you decide if you should screen yourself out of MLM.

____ 1. You dislike selling.

____ 2. You don't know how to sell and don't want to learn how.

____ 3. You don't like supervising others.

____ 4. You find it discouraging, or irritating, to be around others who get discouraged or have difficulty achieving their goals.

____ 5. You don't like to do any of the following:
- attend a lot of meetings
- talk on the phone
- network on line

____ 6. You don't like having to keep your mood upbeat and positive for others regardless of how you feel.

____ 7. You're uncomfortable leading most people to think they could be their own boss.

____ 8. You don't really want to use the product yourself.

____ 9. You would be easily discouraged by encountering people who don't like MLM or direct selling.

____ 10. You want to start making a full-time income quickly.

____ 11. You have little tolerance for listening and accommodating other people's problems and excuses.

____ 12. You don't like people calling you at home.

MLM Red Flags

As we've said before, there's nothing worse than wasting your time, with the possible exception of wasting your money. If in your initial negotiations with an MLM company or upline they say or do any of the following, stop everything. These are surefire signs of trouble. Look for any of the following:

- The company or upline requires you to purchase any inventory. You should be able to get started with a kit costing less than $100 and never more than $500.
- The company or upline exerts pressure on you to purchase inventory or pay a high fee of some kind.
- The company does not specifically agree to repurchase any of your unsold inventory.

- Sale of products is downplayed or seems nonexistent (a pyramid scam for sure!).
- You are promised big profits for a very low amount of hours.
- The MLM company is new to the product, but not new to MLM.
- The company or upline doesn't provide you with sales history figures, current and projected earnings.
- The person representing the company will not give you the name of the company until after you've listened to their sales pitch.
- From your first meeting, you feel the upline or person representing the company is shifty or untrustworthy. (Trust your own feelings; they are often dead-on in these kinds of situations.)

TEST II: THE MLM HONESTY CHECK
EVALUATING THE INTEGRITY OF THE MLM COMPANY

You can save yourself hundreds, and sometimes thousands, of dollars and untold hours of aggravation by thoroughly checking out an MLM company before getting involved. The following Honesty Check allows you to cut right to the bottom line of the company you are considering. It will give you the right questions to ask to find out if the company is representing itself honestly and openly, and to find out if their claims of income are realistic, or bogus. The Honesty Check will also tell you what areas of the company to research, how to do the research, and concrete steps to ensure that what they've told you checks out.

PART 1: THE PARENT COMPANY—WHO ARE THEY?

A conscientious sponsor will check you out to some extent by at least interviewing you. You, however, will benefit greatly if you check the company out to the highest degree you are able. MLM is a partnership (not in the technical sense) among the company, your upline, and yourself. Make sure your partners are compatible, and, most important, make sure they are who they say they are.

According to Corey Augenstein, publisher of *Down-Line News*, over 85 percent of MLM companies go out of business in their first five years, most in the first eighteen months. This is an important statistic to keep in mind when researching a company. If they have gone into business within the last eighteen months, you may want to look elsewhere. According to Richard Poe, you may do better "to value stability over novelty" when choosing a company. However, not everyone agrees. Doris Wood, founder of the industry trade association, the Multi Level Marketing International Association, states, "If everybody waited until a company was three years old or even three months old, no new companies would get started. The people who take a chance have a great amount to gain."

Dr. Charles King, University of Illinois professor of marketing, advises that you look for five criteria in an MLM:

1. A well-established and developed distribution network
2. Programs and provisions for international expansion (to avoid saturation)
3. Extensive distributor support
4. Product diversification (more products means you will have more to sell to different people and different products to sell to established customers when they tire of the original products)
5. Prospecting videos and comprehensive training programs.

The conditions that Dr. King spells out pretty much exclude the smallest companies and most start-ups.

Finding answers to the following will give you a pretty good idea about where the company stands in terms of stability, honesty, and fair dealing:

1. How many years has the parent company been in business? (In MLM, the longer the better.)
2. How many distributors operate in your area? In total? Most companies will not provide this information, but there's no harm in asking.
3. Ask for a detailed breakdown of the company's management team. Poor or inexperienced management is one of the key reasons businesses fail!
4. Ask for the company's own financial statements (however, a privately held company is not required to publish them).
5. Contact a credit reporting agency and ask for a full credit report on the company. Your banker may be of assistance.
6. Richard Poe, in *Wave 3: The New Era of Network Marketing*, suggests, ". . . ask the company for the names and phone numbers of its attorney, banker, and accountant. If the company has nothing to hide, it will grant this request without fuss." He also suggests that you obtain a litigation history for "$60.00 to $80.00 from Prentice Hall Legal and Financial Service" (see Appendix 3). Dunn and Bradstreet also can provide this information.
7. How many of their distributors fail each year? Ask why they fail. (Learn from other people's mistakes.)

8. Is the company giving dramatically optimistic indications of what you may expect to earn monthly, yearly, after three years, five years? Find out what such figures are based on. In MLM, these kinds of projections are extremely difficult to make, even for the most conservative and reputable companies. Keep in mind that projections are usually best-case scenarios, based on the most favorable elements of chance.

9. Does the MLM company have benchmark earning figures for an average distributorship? A company cannot legally provide a high projected income without providing the average.

10. Is the MLM a large company or a smaller one? A small MLM company, even a company that operates only locally, is not necessarily an indication of a bad risk. Some of the largest companies (NuSkin, Herbalife, Amway, for example) have experienced the greatest legal problems.

11. How thoroughly, if at all, does your sponsor check you out? The more a sponsor wants to know about you, the more he or she probably cares about your success.

12. Is the company well respected in its field? Ask competitors, associates, trade organizations, and publications. Is the company a member of an industry association? The Direct Selling Association has standards for membership.

13. How long has the company been in MLM? Did the company distribute its products or services through traditional channels before deciding to offer distributorships? This is important to ask. Some companies, such as Watkins and Rexall Showcase International, were in business many years before successfully converting their distribution to MLM. Other household-name companies, like Avon, have sought to make the transition to MLM with mixed results.

14. Is the company a leader in its industry? What is its percentage of market share in MLM? In overall retail?

15. How financially stable is the company? If it's a public company, you will be able to learn about net worth and cash reserves, but most MLM companies are held privately and this information will probably not be given to you, even though you ask. What can be a clue to a company's financial stability is whether it pays commissions on time and ships products promptly without lengthy back orders. Back orders can indicate very fast growth of a company but they can also indicate a company that is not well managed or is behind on paying its suppliers.

16. Check for complaints and whether they were satisfied with the agencies listed in Appendix 1.

PART 2: DOES THE NAME ON THE DOOR MATCH WHAT HAPPENS ON THE FLOOR?

If no red flags come up in your initial phone conversations or meetings, and the MLM seems to be a straightforward business in terms of its reputation and track record, it is now time to do some research on the inner workings of the company. Finding answers to the following questions will go a long way in helping you determine the integrity of the company you are considering and the veracity of its claims:

1. What is the company's record of complaints?
2. What is the company's record of consent orders?
3. Are there any lawsuits or official complaints pending with any regulatory organizations?
   a. Better Business Bureau
   b. state, county, and city consumer protection offices
   c. attorney general's office
   d. city/state/federal agencies specific to the company's industry
   e. Small Business Administration
4. Are there any complaints lodged or pending with any professional organizations related to the company's industry (DSA 202-293-5760, MLMIA, 714-622-0300)?
5. Has the sponsor provided you with a list of the names of people in his or her upline?
6. How does the company generate the majority of its income: product sales or membership fees paid by distributors? If more money is generated by fees, steer clear.
7. Does the company sell motivational "tools" such as videotapes, audiotapes, books, etc., for a profit? How much of a profit? If prices seem unusually high, be wary. At current prices, cost is about one dollar for audiotapes and four for videotapes.
8. How hard do they push the sale of such "tools" versus sales of their actual products or services.
9. How much of the company's total income is derived from the sale of "tools?" (If more than 25 percent, watch out!)
10. If you can, identify and talk with past and current customers and distributors (we suggest you make an effort to do so). Are or were they satisfied with the products they've received?
11. Are or were distributors satisfied with the service they've received? Some questions to ask:
    a. "What did/do you dislike about the parent company?"
    b. "In what ways, if any, were you disappointed?"

   c. "Did you get the support and assistance you were told you would get?"
   d. "Did you receive the training you were promised?"
   e. "Did the company/upline give you any assistance in marketing?"
   f. "Did you get the results you were told you would?"
   g. "Do you regret entering this business?"
12. Will the parent company supply you with its references?
13. Can you freely check the company's references?
14. Will the parent company provide you with a business plan? (Its own or one for you?)
15. Check your own feelings and impressions:
   a. Do you feel that you're being dealt with honestly?
   b. Are statements made by the company/upline consistent?
   c. How do you feel about the business in general?
   d. Do you like the parent company?
   e. Do feel good about their product line? Are their prices competitive with those of other similar products, or do they seem inflated?
   f. Do you feel good about their customer service policy?
   g. Does the company seem organized, consistent, and focused?
   h. Are you scared?
   i. Are you excited?
   j. Are you raring to go?
   k. Do you have trepidation?
   l. Do you feel confident?
   m. What are your reservations?

Be as honest as possible with yourself when answering the above questions. Often we ignore our feelings, or dismiss them as irrelevant. This is generally a big mistake. Our feelings give us clues to the most fundamental issues of our lives and the things that concern us.

PART 3: WHY YOU FEEL THE WAY YOU DO

As you assess your feelings about the MLM you're considering it's important to determine why you're feeling the way you do. Don't just take your feelings at their surface value. What desires of your own could be coloring the way you feel? What nonverbal signals could you be picking up from the MLM company, your potential sponsor, others in the upline, and so forth, that are causing you to feel the way you do. For example,

- If you aren't feeling confident, figure out why.

  Are you unsure of your own abilities?

  Are you threatened by the unknown?

  Is the MLM opportunity itself, or the Core Function, somehow dampening your confidence?
- Examine your positive feelings, too:

  If you're raring to go, look into why you're so raring to go.

  Do the MLM company, its products, and the Core Function excite you?

  Are you more motivated by leaving your current situation behind? Or are you getting swept up in the hype or excitement of the moment?

Again, we can't express the importance of your feelings and emotions enough. Careful thought and consideration can lead you to helpful insights.

TEST III: THE MARKET CHECK
DISCOVERING IF THE MLM BUSINESS WILL BE VIABLE FOR YOU

If you discover an MLM opportunity that passes your Fitness and Honesty tests and you've determined that your personality, background, and experience are suited to the Core Selling Function of the MLM business, it's time to test out whether the market is large enough to generate the income you want.

Even though others may be successfully selling this MLM's products or services, you will need to find out if there are potential buyers you can reach with this business's products or services. So, the better you can define and describe who these buyers will be, the greater your success in MLM will be and the easier it will be to involve others in your downline.

So, here's a rule of thumb: If you can't find ready-made buyers, your downline will probably have difficulty, too.

PART 1: IS THERE A MARKET FOR YOU IN THIS MLM?

Just because others are doing well in an MLM does not mean you can too. Each community or part of the country has different needs, customs, and resources. What sells fabulously on the East Coast may flop on the West Coast. What sells great in a rural area may hold no interest for people in a large metropolitan area or a suburb. Some communities may have too many MLMs and distributors in your product category; others may have little competition. To help you determine if there even *is* a market for your prospective MLM business that you can reach, answer the following questions:

1. Do you use or buy the product or service the MLM offers?
2. Do you know other people who do? How many?
3. Do people you know express a desire for the product or service?
4. How do you see people using the product or service?
5. What kinds of people do you see using it?
6. Is there a market in your community?
7. Is there a market in outlying or other areas?

PART 2: IS THE MARKET SATURATED?

As we mentioned before, market saturation refers to how much competition there is for the product or service you will be offering. If there are a lot of people already providing the same or similar products or services to your market, it could be saturated. Unlike franchising, MLM does not generally offer protected, exclusive territories. Quite the opposite; one of the main drawbacks of MLM is that a market can get saturated quickly. (Another way to think about this is that with no territorial restrictions, you can enter into new markets and move your business.)

Think about it: Part of your business will be to recruit people to work in your downline. If you recruit people in your local area, these people will be selling the same products as you and recruiting others from the same human resource pool as you. You'll be recruiting your own competition. Therefore, saturation can be a particular problem in MLM. Hundreds of distributors may already be trying to reach, sell, or recruit for the MLM you're thinking of in the same milieu you're planning to enter. Or, there may already be so many similar products on the market that people aren't interested in hearing about one more. Marnie found this to be true in selling her MLM diet drink: "There are a million diet products, and lots of people just didn't want to hear about it."

To find out if your proposed market is already saturated, or close to saturated, answer the following:

1. How many people do you know who are selling the same products as you will be?
2. Call ten friends or associates and ask them if they know anybody who is selling for the MLM you are considering. Keep track of the numbers.

3. Ask the same ten friends and associates how many people they know who are selling similar products or services. Keep track of the number.

4. Look through your local newspaper thoroughly for ads either selling products similar to the ones you will be offering or offering "jobs" for companies selling similar products.

PART 3: CAN YOU TAP THIS MARKET?

If it seems that, indeed, there is a need for what you'll be offering, it's time to do some further investigation. You need to discover how well you are positioned to tap into this need and how you can best go about reaching people with this need. Here are the questions for you to answer:

- Do you feel comfortable asking friends, family, and associates to buy from you or work with you?
- Do you belong to any business or civic groups, or other organizations whose members might want your products or be potential recruits for your downline?
- Do you have any direct experience with the product or service provided by the MLM you are considering?
- Do you have any direct experience with the industry from which the products or services originate in the MLM you are considering?
- Do you have any hobbies or interests that can lead to desirable contacts for your proposed MLM?
- Do you have any current business contacts that might lead to new business or expand your industry knowledge?
- Are there any professional organizations in your area that cater to the market your MLM will serve?
- Are there local or regional trade publications that cover your proposed business area or appeal to your prospective customer base?
- If your business will be based on providing services to other businesses, how many of those businesses are listed in your local phone book or are members of a national trade association?
- Does your prospective MLM cater to men more than women, or vice versa?
- Does your prospective MLM cater to particular age groups that you can relate to?
- Who is your target customer and, if you plan to have a downline, whom do you intend to recruit?

Again, the more specifically you can answer that last question, the more information you will be able to find out regarding how many prospective customers you and your downline could have (the size of your market), what their likes and dislikes are (the psychographic profile), and their age, sex, income level, etc. (demographics).

Here's an example of how this process worked effectively for an MLMer. Coreen is an actress. When a friend at church introduced her to a health drink called KM, she was skeptical at first, but her hectic schedule working multiple part-time jobs left her feeling more exhausted every day, so she decided to try the product. She really liked the results. "I felt so energized that I started telling everyone about it and, of course, they wanted to try it, too."

Coreen's friend urged her to join her downline to sell KM herself. Again, she was skeptical, but the start-up costs were low so she could recoup her money just with people she knew who were already interested. But before deciding to sign up, she talked with people in her acting class about KM. Most had never heard of it before but were interested.

"Within a month, I had so many people buying KM from me that I began cutting back my part-time jobs and started recruiting other actors and actresses to be in my downline," she told us. Her boyfriend joined her business and before long they were making more money at KM than their collective jobs, so they decided to put all their efforts into their KM business. "It's perfect for us, and people like us because we can make money and still have the flexibility to go out for acting jobs when we get the chance."

PART 4: HOW DO YOU KNOW IF YOU HAVE A VIABLE MARKET?

If there are enough people you can reach in your market who fit the profile of your target customer, you have a viable market. But what, exactly, constitutes "enough" potential customers? Again, to find the answer, you need to do some homework first:

1. You need to analyze the compensation plan for the MLM you are considering. These can be complex, so be sure to ask all the questions you need to in order to understand it.

2. Take special note of the amount you can earn by directly selling to customers. This is indicated by the discount you get on the retail prices. These vary significantly from company to company and within products in the same company. Some companies offer discounts on retail as low as 10 and 15 percent. Others offer discounts as high as 60 percent. Keep in mind that the difference between what

you buy something at and sell it for must cover your cost of being in business, which in MLM includes marketing materials, samples, and meeting and training costs. There's obviously more incentive for you (and for those you recruit) to make sales to customers when the margin between what is paid for a product and what it is sold for is high than when it is low. Take into account how much you will need to sell and what you will make on the sales of your downline to determine how large your downline will need to become to hit your income goals.

3. This means defining how much you will need to earn a month to make your efforts worthwhile. It may be money for some of life's extras, an amount to enable you to make ends meet, or you may aspire to earning a living wage or more. Let's say you want to bring in an additional $1,000 a month. How many sales will you or your downline need to make to bring in this extra $1,000? How many hours will be required of you all to generate that much sales activity? And most important, is there enough potential demand for the product on an ongoing basis to enable you to make enough sales each month? If you want to earn enough to support yourself on a full-time basis, what level of sales activity will it take? If the product is something that people may buy once but not order again or infrequently or that most people give up on after a month or two, you do not have a viable market or product.

In Coreen's case, she knew fifty or sixty other actors whom she could tap to join her downline. No one else was tapping this pool of prospective people. So she was well positioned and did have a viable market. But, returning again to Marnie's situation, although there were lots of students on her college campus, there were lots of diet programs in the area and many other people already selling similar-sounding diet programs. Of course, her product was "different"—they all are—nonetheless her market was already virtually saturated and to compete in such a busy market, she would have had to work many more hours than she had available as a full-time graduate student with a teaching assistant position. For her, it wasn't worth the effort.

So if there aren't enough prospective customers in the circles you can function effectively in to reach your income goals, look for another MLM, franchise, or biz op, or consider starting your own business for which there is a market.

ONE FINAL CHECK

Once you've found an MLM that passes all the tests as a reputable, marketable company that suits your personality, background, interests, skills, and contacts, do this one final test before you buy.

Ask yourself, is this what you want to do or are you doing this because what you really want to do isn't working out or doesn't seem possible?

Klara was a publicist. After being laid off from her job, she decided to start a PR firm of her own. It had long been her dream to have her own firm and work from home in the Grand Teton area of Wyoming. The layoff provided her with the opportunity and the severance package to act on that dream. She lined up several clients and moved to Wyoming. At first things went pretty well, but then the economy hit a downturn and her business slowed. She began to panic as her client list shrank.

Then a new friend told her about MLM and suggested she join her downline. She would be selling telephone services by phone, and all the paperwork would be handled by the MLM company. Her friend was quite excited about the potential of this opportunity but had been in the MLM herself only about two months. Klara began thinking of the MLM as the best way to save her business and her dream. It didn't take long for her to realize, however, that joining the MLM wasn't going to be a quick fix for her bank balance. She discovered that making sales and building a successful MLM downline was going to take as much work and effort as rebuilding her PR firm would take. Of the two, she preferred to concentrate on her PR firm, since it had long been her dream and she already had many years of experience and contacts in the field.

"Starting an MLM meant building a brand-new business and I already had a business," Karla says. "By refocusing full-time on my PR firm I've been able to get it going again. It was hard, yes, but starting a new business would have been even harder for me and I only wanted to do it as a stopgap measure."

Suzanne, a newly single mother, made an entirely different choice. "After my husband left me with two toddlers, I became severely depressed. I hadn't been in the job market for more than five years and I really didn't want to put my daughters in day care," she remembers. Although she had some child support and a year of alimony during which she was to find work, she had to move in with her mother and still needed more income. When she learned that her mother's friend was a Mary Kay distributor and wanted to talk to her about becoming one too, she was skeptical. "I thought I'd hate selling, but I discovered that I could 'sell' by giving free facials and demonstrating my products in other women's homes." That appealed to her. "I feel like Mary Kay saved my life. It provided me with so much training and emotional support and I started making a little income almost immediately." Now she says that Mary Kay is like a second family and that she considers herself to have become a confident, successful businesswoman.

No longer living with her mother who still helps out by baby-sitting her daughters, Suzanne boasts that "if anyone had told me at the courthouse the day of my divorce that I would own my own business within the year, I would have thought they were nuts. But it's true, and I'm really proud of myself."

MLM can be rewarding, or it can be a source of regret. So be sure that getting involved with multilevel marketing is consistent with what you want at this point in your life.

5

Do Business Opportunities
Sound Attractive?

Technically, any venture you buy, or even one you create yourself, is a business opportunity. Franchises and multilevel marketing distributorships are businesses, and they're also opportunities. Business opportunities, as they are called, in common parlance, however, have several unique characteristics that distinguish them from franchises, MLMs, or a business you create on your own. Recognizing these differences is important in determining whether buying a business opportunity would be a better choice for you than starting your own business or buying a franchise or MLM distributorship. The following sections will provide you with information to help you decide whether buying a business opportunity would be right for you.

WHAT ARE BUSINESS OPPORTUNITIES?

If it's not a franchise or a multilevel marketing distributorship, then it must be a business opportunity! This definition may sound a little too general, but it's actually a good place to start. For a business to be considered a franchise, it must meet some very clear rules and conditions, as we spelled out in Chapter 2, such as the rights to use a trademark, the continuing involvement of the parent company, etc. A multilevel marketing distributorship also has some specific defining conditions, such as the downline and upline structure. Business opportunities have no specific conditions in terms of how they're packaged, what they offer, or the way they operate. The very fact that they offer such variety and flexibility is often what people find so attractive about business opportunities, or biz ops, as they're often called. To be more precise, however, a business opportunity is an idea, product, system, or service that someone else has developed and now offers for sale to help someone start a business of some kind. The business may be anything from providing medical billing services to making signs or repairing upholstery. And the relationship you will have with the company you buy a business opportunity from can vary widely as well. You may simply order it over the phone, by mail, or at a business expo and never see or hear from the company again. Or you may find that the business opportunity company offers valuable training, products, and resources. Some biz ops actually even carry out substantial portions of your business's ongoing operations for you and become an ongoing source of support. The cost of a biz op can range from nothing to thousands of dollars.

A Long History

The concept of selling business opportunities has been around throughout history. People have been offering business ideas and formulas for literally thousands of years. The rights to formulas for health elixirs, beauty products such as perfumes, even talismanic good luck charms and potions, for example, were bought and sold in ancient Greece, during the Roman Empire, throughout the Middle Ages in Europe, and in Colonial America. Entrepreneurs across the ages have used biz ops as a way of disseminating their products while increasing their profits. The entrepreneurs who bought these opportunities often became respected members of their business and social communities. Of course there were always the snake oil salesmen. So both legitimate business opportunities and scams have been with us for a very long time.

What's Offered through Business Opportunities?

Of the three types of packaged home businesses you can buy that are profiled in this book, biz ops offer the largest variety of goods and services. While home-based franchises usually offer services as opposed to merchandise and MLMs, offering services, are usually based on a product, biz ops offer any and all of the above—and then some! Billing services, vending machines, mail order, newsletter publishing, financial services, jewelry, advertising, marketing, computer products, insurance, and just about any other product or service you can think of are all sold or rendered through business opportunities.

The Various Types of Business Opportunities

Business opportunities generally fall into several standard business categories based on the nature of what your relationship will be to the company and who your clients and customers will be. So, of course, before you buy, you need to know what kind of business you are buying. The following is a list of standard definitions for commonly agreed-upon terms in standard use throughout the world to help you understand what kind of business someone is offering or operating. These designations define such things as where or from whom you will buy your inventory services or supplies, as well as what your role will be in bringing these products or services to the market.

If it is not clear what category a particular opportunity you're considering falls into, always ask the seller how he or she would categorize the business they're selling. In most cases, that category will be one *or more* of the following:

A Broker

When you buy a business opportunity to operate as a broker, you will buy or sell services or products for the parent company, or parent companies. Brokers are not generally confined to selling for only one company. Brokers for insurance and financial products generally represent several companies. The money you generate will be paid to you in the form of a commission from the company, not the end user. Although you act, for all intents and purposes, as an agent for the parent company or companies, brokers in biz ops are extremely independent. In most cases, your business structure will not differ appreciably from that of any other independently owned business.

For example, for the biz op Intermedia Resources, a telecommunications company listed in Chapter 10, you will be operating as a broker. As a broker, you will find the long-distance carrier best matched to your clients from a number of long-distance companies you will represent.

A Dealership

When you buy a business opportunity to operate as a dealer, you will represent a line of products, and occasionally services, that the parent company provides. You can think of it much like an automobile dealership. As a dealer you will be an independent entity responsible for every aspect of running the company, except for your basic inventory, which you will purchase from the parent company. And as in an auto dealership, you generally will only offer a line of products or services that you purchase from one or a limited number of companies and sell to end users at a profit. So your income will come from the consumer.

For example, Absolute Chemical Corporation, listed in Chapter 10, sells a dealership package that provides you private label ceiling and wall cleaning products.

Direct Sales

Direct-sales business opportunities involve your selling a product or service directly to the end user or consumer. Income is generated by buying products or services from distributors, vendors, brokers, or manufacturers and selling them at a profit. Your own arrangement with the biz op seller will determine if you will sell his or her products exclusively, or if you may sell the products and services of others as well. Your income is derived directly from what you sell to the end user or consumer.

An example of direct-sales biz ops is Conklin Fashions, a jewelry sales business where you can sell over two thousand styles of Conklin's earrings directly to the consumer. You'll find Conklin listed in Chapter 10.

A Distributor

As a distributor you buy products or services from a wholesaler (the company who originally purchased the product or service from a manufacturer) and then sell them to direct-sales organizations, brokers, and sometimes dealers and other business entities. Occasionally distributors buy directly from manufacturers. In other words, as a distributor you are in the middle of the traditional manufacturer-to-wholesaler-to-distributor-to-retailer chain. Your sales will almost never be made to the end user or consumer directly. Your income is derived from the sales you make to retailers, direct sellers, mail-order operations, etc., who will resell whatever they've purchased from you to the end user.

The Ident-a-Kid Program, found in Chapter 10, is a distributorship where you approach public and private schools with the idea providing them with identification cards to sell to students. While the eventual customers are the students' parents, your sales are made to the schools who will sell the card to the parents. This is a classic distributorship.

A Licensee

As a licensee, you buy the right to make, sell, or otherwise use an established brand name, specific technology, or system. This is much like buying a franchise, only you operate without the kinds of rules and regulations required of you by the franchisor. In buying a biz op, to become a licensee, you will have greater independence in regard to how you run your business. Sales can be made to any entity willing to buy, unless otherwise stipulated by the biz op seller.

Chipsaway International, listed in Chapter 10, sells a mobile auto paint restoration business opportunity where you may use the Chipsaway name to form your own auto paint restoration business.

A Mail-Order Business

A mail-order business opportunity consists of your taking orders for particular products (mail order almost never provides services) by mail, or more frequently these days by phone or computer, then sending the products out to the consumer via mail. Mail-order businesses often work with specific distributors, wholesalers, vendors, and manufacturers from which they buy product. In most cases you will be selling directly to the end user. The nice thing about most mail-order businesses is that you can sell products without having to stock inventory. When you receive your order and check, you can place the order with your source and they ship the item to you, or sometimes directly to the end user.

Home-based mail-order businesses found in Chapter 10 include Badge-A-Minute where you will not only be the manufacturer (see next listing) of wearable buttons but can also sell them nationally through the mail using ads you will place in various magazines, publications, or on line.

A Manufacturer

As a manufacturer, you will actually make the product you sell. You sell to wholesalers, vendors, distributors, even end users, depending on how the business is structured. There are not many home-based biz ops to become a manufacturer, for obvious reasons, although you will find a few arts-and-crafts–oriented manufacturing businesses listed in Chapter 6, such as Badge-A-Minute, mentioned above.

A Vendor

When you buy a biz op to operate as a vendor, you will be providing goods or services to other businesses, who then sell them directly to the consumer or use them to create something that will be sold directly to the consumer. Vendors sell to mail-order businesses, retail establishments, manufacturers, and other kinds of businesses. A vendor does not sell directly to the consumer. For example, if you sell computer equipment or advertising consultant services to a business, that business will consider you a vendor. Vendors sell to mail-order businesses, retail establishments, manufacturers, and other kinds of businesses. Vendors do not sell directly to the consumer.

Quantum Technology, Inc., listed in Chapter 10, is an example of a vendor of services. It sells packaged computer businesses in the form of business kits that enable its buyers to "vend" services, such as remote backup, to customers. Beauty by Spector, Inc., enables you to be a vendor of wigs and hair goods for men and women which you can sell to salons and hair-care professionals. If goods are involved, the terms *vendor* and *distributor* may be used interchangeably.

A Wholesaler

A biz op that enables you to operate as a wholesaler enables you to buy directly from manufacturers and sell to vendors, mail-order businesses, distributors, and sometimes manufacturers (if the manufacturer requires the item in the creation of the product). As a wholesaler you make money by buying in bulk from producers of goods and selling to distributors of goods at a profit. Wholesalers never sell directly to the end user or consumer.

A & A Company, Parkway Machine Corporation, listed in Chapter 10, allows you to be a wholesaler, buying vending machine supplies in bulk for resale to vending machine operators.

When a Biz Op Sounds like a Franchise or MLM or Vice Versa

After reading through the descriptions of these categories, you may think, "That franchise I've been looking at is like a licensor business opportunity. What's the difference between this biz op and a franchise?" Again, if the entity who is selling the opportunity does not represent it as a franchise, and there is no specific franchise agreement and you are free to run the business without a lot of company control, then the business you are looking at is a biz op. The same holds true for a multilevel marketing distributorship. Many (if not all) MLMs match the definition of a distributor. If you are considering an opportunity that fits the definition of a distributorship, but there are also downline and upline components, then the opportunity is actually an MLM. Without a downline or upline? You guessed it, it's a biz op.

Another way to tell a biz op from other businesses you can buy comes from Maria Lahm, managing editor of *The Business Opportunity Handbook* and *The Franchising Handbook*. Published since 1988, these quarterly compendiums are available on most newsstands and are a useful source of general information, as well as detailed listings of literally thousands of businesses you can buy. Lahm says, "When someone asks me to define what a biz op is, I tell them it's any means or method that will get you into an established pattern where your chance of success is probably greater than starting on your own."

Biz Ops and Working from Home

Because biz ops are so flexible, you have a lot of leeway in how you run your business. Basically, it's anywhere and any way you wish. So the decision to run a business opportunity you buy from home will most likely be completely up to you. Biz op sellers rarely stipulate that you must rent an office or other facility, whereas franchisors are almost always very specific about where you can and cannot locate your business. For example, most of the larger tax-preparation franchises such as H&R Block and Triple Check Income Tax Service either don't recommend or don't allow their franchisees to run their businesses from home. On the other hand, SAS of Laguna Beach, California, a tax-preparation biz op, *encourages* people to work from home. If you make a quick comparison of the number of biz ops listed in the back of this book with the number of home-based franchises or MLMs listed, you will see that a much greater range of products and services is available to you as business opportunities and MLMs. And according to Maria Lahm, "I definitely see a growing trend for more people to run biz ops from their homes than ever before."

Biz ops are so wide-ranging in terms of the kinds of products and services offered and the amount of time required to start and run the business that you will find most biz ops to be quite compatible with working from home. If you so desire and are committed to it, just about any business opportunity you would select can be operated as a home-based business.

REGULATION OF BUSINESS OPPORTUNITIES

Business opportunities, like almost anything you buy in America, are now subject to a number of laws and regulations. While they are less regulated than franchising, to be sure, biz ops are subject to three areas of regulation: federal, state, and local. Federal laws on biz ops fall within the jurisdiction of the FTC. State laws usually are overseen by each state's attorney general's office. Local laws affecting biz ops vary by locale and are overseen by any number of local agencies. Laws also vary greatly from state to state. In twenty-seven states there are no specific laws governing biz ops on the books, for example. To find out about your state's biz op laws, or if your state even has specific biz op laws, check the chart on page 201, Appendix 5 in the back of this book, as well as the section on trade shows in Chapter 6 on page 194. We also highly recommend that you call your state attorney general's office or, if your state has one, its consumer affairs agency for the details of how the law regulates biz ops in your state and which agencies enforce these laws.

In general, biz op laws take effect when the cost of the business itself is over a prescribed amount, usually somewhere between $200 to $500. In other words, if your state sets the amount at $500, any business opportunity that costs $500 or more to purchase will be subject to state biz op regulations. If your state does not have a specified minimum selling amount, the FTC has set the national amount at $500. This is why you will come across so many biz ops selling at $495. At that price, they're less likely to be subject to federal and state regulation. With circumvention of regulation in mind, some business opportunities are priced lower in states with biz op laws than in states lacking them.

What Do These Laws Cover?

In some states biz op laws are called Seller Assisted Marketing Plan, or SAMP, laws. These laws cover a variety of things and differ from state to state in terms of scope and specifics. In states that regulate business opportunities, however, these laws generally cover three aspects of the biz op sale:

1. A minimum and sometimes a maximum selling price, usually, as we said, over $500, but occasionally as low as $100.
2. What form of disclosure must be presented before the sale. The details of exactly what information is to be included in a disclosure statement vary from state to state. Typically they must include the company's address, phone numbers, principal officers, financial statements, record of complaints and lawsuits, and if the company or any of its officers have ever been convicted of a crime.
3. The specified amount of time that must elapse (usually from forty-eight to seventy-two hours) before the seller can collect the sum total of the sale price. We call this the "consideration period." This mandated "consideration period" allows you time to more fully and completely consider the offer. Commonly, laws specify that the seller can collect some percentage of the selling price after a specified elapsed time, which begins from the time the disclosure documents have been presented to the buyer. The remainder of the selling price can only be collected upon full delivery of all that was promised in the contract, such as training and any products or services required by the buyer to begin operating the business.

For example, let's say that Rachel is interested in a medical billing biz op. She is first given the required disclosure statement form by the seller. After a consideration period of forty-eight hours, required by the state of California, where she lives, she decides to buy the business and gives the seller a 20 percent deposit. Before paying the remainder of the selling price, she first must receive the operations manual, the billing software, a list of potential customers, and three days of training, all of which were stipulated in her contract to be part of the packaged business opportunity. In this case, she would pay the balance when she comes to the training.

How Much to Start?

What you will need to pay to buy a biz op can run the gamut. Biz ops can range from a $30 button-making system to a $10,000 medical billing system. According to what we have found, the average start-up cost of a business opportunity is approximately $2,000 to $10,000. This is considerably more than MLM distributorships, but less than the average franchise. Please remember, however, that we're speaking here only about the cost required to purchase the business itself. Expenses such as office equipment, marketing materials, supplies, inventory, professional services like accounting, and all the other expenses associated with starting and running a business will be additional and ongoing expenses.

IS BUYING A BIZ OP RIGHT FOR YOU?

As you've probably noticed, a biz op offers a lot more freedom in terms of how you will run the business you buy. While rules and procedures are the rule in franchising, they're often optional in a biz op, and sometimes entirely nonexistent. You don't have a sponsor or an MLM upline to teach you the ropes and to turn to for advice. You're usually pretty much on your own when it comes to marketing, strategic planning, customer service, and all the other crucial aspects of your business. However, there are exceptions to this. The more you pay for a biz op, the more support you may get.

You're not starting totally from scratch. Even if there is no support, you have a road map, a business plan, and guidelines. The parent company supplies you with the product, service, or idea. A good biz op will also supply you with a marketing plan, or at least a marketing approach, training materials, and some or even considerable ongoing support. In most cases, though, the guidelines you'll receive are more like suggestions than hard-and-fast rules. If you require a good measure of freedom in making your own decisions, excel at completing tasks, but like the idea that someone else has provided an overall vision of what to do and a procedure for doing it, then a biz op may be well suited to you.

What It Takes to Succeed in a Biz Op

Biz ops, like franchises and multilevel marketing distributorships, lend themselves to certain types of people. In other words, having the right attitudes and personality traits will help increase your chances for success in a biz op. In our research and discussions with successful biz op owners and parent companies, a biz op personality profile began to emerge.

"Eighty-five percent of the people I've seen succeed, succeed because of attitude," says Richard B. Rennick, company founder and president of American Leak Detection. Although American Leak Detection is currently a franchisor, the company began as a biz op. In his experience in working with the people who bought his businesses, Rennick began to recognize a common thread among the traits of successful biz op owners. He eventually began to seek out candidates with just those qualities. "I look for people who have a positive, confident attitude. Not overconfident or unrealistic, but folks who have a basic belief in themselves and a commitment to follow through with their goals," explains Rennick. "I also look for good communicators. You can't go out there and do business if you can't communicate what our service is and its benefits to the customer."

Merry Schiff, president of Medical Management Software, Inc., a medical billing and practice management business opportunity, says that "I look for people who are willing to work. This business is not easy. I'm very upfront about that. Many biz op sellers don't realistically explain to people that they're going to have to work very hard to make the business successful."

Merry also looks for team players, something unusual in the biz op world. "Many biz op sellers sell the business package, and that's it. Buyers never hear from the company again," explains Merry. Buyers of Medical Management Software businesses, however, maintain an ongoing relationship with Merry in terms of continual support and training. She also encourages business owners to network with one another. Another thing Merry looks for in buyers is the openness and willingness to learn new things and the ability to meet challenges. Here's a stirring example of the kind of person she's looking for, Nancie Lee. Nancie has what it takes.

Building Success out of Adversity

Case Study #1:
Nancie Lee Cummins, San Mateo, California
Medical Management Billing, 415-343-9078

Not everyone dreams of going into business for themselves. Three years ago Nancie Lee Cummins was married to a successful contractor and living a comfortable life selling group health and life insurance to corporations. Between her and her husband, they owned several homes and seemed to have had it made. Then things began to unravel. Her husband's business filed for bankruptcy, and her marriage began to fall apart. "At this point I knew I needed to figure something out quickly," she said. "Although I had never considered it before, I began to look at buying a business that I could run myself, and I started doing some serious research. I knew that my home situation was near the breaking point. I went from having everything in terms of material wealth to almost nothing."

Not allowing herself to fall prey to the adversity of her situation, Nancie began to take stock of what she *did* have. She had the drive to succeed, she had a depth of experience in the group insurance business, she had researched home business opportunities, and she had her engagement ring. Nancie picked up her biz op research where she left off and came across Medical Management Software, Inc., coincidentally also located in San Mateo. From her phone conversations with Merry Schiff and other information she gathered, Nancie felt she had found the right opportunity. To finance the purchase of the business, Nancie sold her engagement ring.

The biz op provided three days of training in the use of the medical billing software, a one-year support contract, software for lead management, related books and other resource materials, a business plan, and 1,000 leads within Nancie's territory. She promptly sent out marketing letters to twenty-five of the leads she received from the biz op. Later that week she got her first call from a doctor. "Believe it or not, I haven't sent out a marketing letter since," proclaims Nancie.

For the first three months, Nancie ran her business from her room at a safe haven for women. "It was essentially a living room with a temporary wall dividing it from the rest of the house," she remembers. Her first sale referred her to another medical group, who then referred her to another. She was able to move out into her own apartment and set up her office.

Nancie still works out of her apartment, though things have gotten a bit cramped. "My living room has been completely taken over by the business, so have my dining room and most of the closets!" says Nancie. In business for barely a year, Nancie's company, Medical Management Billing, serves seven practices for a total of over sixty doctors. She built her business through hard work, determination, and, most important, providing excellent, dependable service to every client. And it paid off. She has built her business completely on referrals.

Nancie looks forward to another year of consistent growth, hiring people to help out, and moving to a larger work environment. These days, her credit is restored and, most important, so is her self-confidence.

THE BIZ OP PERSONALITY PROFILE

Since there do seem to be certain personality traits that make someone better suited to succeed, and enjoy succeeding, in a biz op, here's a summary of these traits. In the next chapter you can assess your own personality in relation to this biz op profile.

1. Independence

Biz ops require a higher degree of independence than MLMs or franchises. If you thrive by acting independently, yet like being anchored by an overarching concept, a biz op could be a solution for you. In our research, we've found those who succeed in biz ops rate themselves at being about 75 to 90 percent independent. How much independence do you need?

If currently you're working at a job, you may be thinking, "I'm tired of following orders. I know I would be better off being my own boss." This may be true, but let's consider for a moment. In a biz op, you're buying a service, product, method, or idea. What you do with it and where you take it are entirely up to you. Are you independent enough to follow through on an idea, and make it a reality? Can you set your own rules? As we've said, biz ops, by definition, do not generally include a strict set of procedures for you to follow. Yes, a biz op is essentially based on someone else's idea or formula, so you're not completely on your own. But you have to generate your own plans and action steps for implementing the marketing ideas, strategic plans, and financial guidelines that come with the biz op. Sometimes these blueprints are sketchy or even nonexistent. But if the opportunity is a good one, the parent company will provide advice and suggestions that you can and will do well to follow.

2. Attitude

What is attitude, exactly? As biz op leaders define it, attitude is a realistic awareness of your own abilities and an unshakable confidence in them. If you have the right attitude, you will be able to keep going through the rough times that are inevitable in business. A strong belief in yourself and your goals will also give you the necessary motivation to make your business work, especially during your first year, which is usually the most difficult. Are you motivated to deal with rejection? How about what seems like an endless stream of rejection? To succeed you must believe in yourself even when others don't. When you're on your own, often you're the only one who does, until you prove otherwise.

3. Consistency

Consistency is key to success in any kind of business. In biz ops, with the hands-off approach of most parent companies, being consistent is perhaps the hardest trait to achieve and is one of the most important. So how good are you at follow-through? Not in your golf swing, but in setting goals and seeing them through to their completion. In a biz op, since you're much more on your own than in a franchise or MLM, there's usually no one to remind you what to do and when to do it. Sometimes, it's hard to know just where you stand in terms of achieving your goals and plans. It's easy to get caught up in the day-to-day details and lose sight of the larger picture. In a biz op, the parent company rarely sets quotas for you of sales or other benchmark achievements. You must have the consistency to make and follow through on your plans. Can you accurately and realistically track your progress?

4. Influence

Influence, as described in the franchising personality profile on page 20, is having an outgoing and enthusiastic nature. High-influence people enjoy meeting people, have a positive outlook, and like to communicate. Unlike in franchising, however, high-influence people tend to do well in biz ops. On the one hand, it is essential for a successful business owner to be outgoing, personable, and communicate well. On the other hand, keep in mind that although sales and customer service are important areas that high-influence people excel in, it is also important to be able to keep your nose to the grindstone, as it were, and not avoid the less glamorous sides of running your business. At least at the beginning, you will probably be solely responsible for all aspects of your business. If you would rather sell than keep accurate books, or talk to clients rather than do strategic planning, you may need to consider getting some outside help in these areas.

5. Dominance

How dominant are you? People who consider themselves barely or moderately dominant generally do not have the drive to see a business opportunity through the rough times, or steer it through conflicts. Those who show a high dominance rate, between 75 and 100 percent, have the will and drive to establish a business and enjoy the freedom from the rules, operating procedures, and expectations imposed by franchising or MLM.

Picking the Wrong Company

Case Study #2:
Anne Lohrfink, Wappingers Falls, New York
Association of Certified Liquidators (ACL), 614-291-2103

We met Anne Lohrfink in an on-line discussion group. She's a classic example of someone who chose the wrong business opportunity, and we appreciate her sharing her mistake so others can avoid similar mishaps. The crux of the business she bought involves finding companies and businesses who have merchandise they wish to liquidate, then buying the merchandise at rock-bottom prices and selling it at a higher price. Sounds easy enough. But not according to Anne. Here's what happened and why, for her, it became a bad experience all the way around.

Anne was running her own business, processing medical claims for senior citizens. Nine months ago her father, a retired minister, was having a bout of insomnia one night and saw an infomercial on TV. He thought it looked like a neat business that he and Anne could run together, even though he lives in Virginia and she's in New York.

He convinced her to join him in buying this business opportunity and after an initial payment, Anne received a "how-to" manual, recommending that she become a certified liquidator and offering to sell her the test for becoming certified. Then they recommended that she become a member of the Liquidation Association and offered to sell her the program for that, too. And then she was encouraged to buy a one-year telephone consultation service, which they'd also sell her, for a price. And subscribing to a newsletter would be still another additional cost. Although she was not required to buy any of these add-on services, she felt her chances of their succeeding at the business would be slim if they didn't.

They decided to buy the year of telephone consultation and the manuals. The information they received, however, was outdated. After making a couple of hundred phone calls from the lists provided, she had yet to hook up with anybody she could buy merchandise from. "I've sent out hundreds of letters and made what feels like a gazillion phone calls. Often the response I get is 'Phone disconnected' or 'No forwarding address.'"

In frustration she's tried calling the telephone consultation service for help but can't get through to anyone. She's left messages for people to call her back. But nobody has returned her calls. She's written and gotten no response except a mailing announcing that her year's subscription is up, which it isn't. "It seems like I'm supposed to do all the legwork and they'll take half my profit if I do find some merchandise. If they had told me this up-front, it would be a different story, but that's not how their publicity presents the business. Once you've paid the money and gotten the list of names though, you feel like, well, I invested this much, so I'd better do a little more on it. We're very disappointed."

FINDING A BIZ OP THAT'S RIGHT FOR YOU

As we've mentioned, biz ops require a great deal of independent initiative on your part, with little input from the parent company. But Anne's situation reflects more than not being able to handle the independence. This company did not deliver on specific promises they made that were essential to making the business work. And when Anne tried to resolve the problem, the company basically didn't respond to her at all. It's a good bet that the company wasn't registered with the required regulatory agencies and that Anne didn't check that out before she bought.

In the following chapter, in the sections that tell you how to test a biz op for fitness, honesty, and marketability, we'll give you a set of criteria and research guidelines that will help you avoid problems like the ones Anne encountered.

Because most biz ops do require so much independent initiative, it is essential that you find a business whose Core Function is well suited to you. The Core Function, as we discussed in earlier chapters, is the basic activity that will be at the heart of what you will be doing day in and day out once you're in business. The first of the Fitness Checks will help you determine the Core Function of a biz op you may be considering so you'll know if it's something you can do well on your own and would enjoy doing.

FIRSTHAND EXPERIENCE: CONVERSATIONS WITH OWNERS OF HOME-BASED BUSINESS OPPORTUNITIES

Fortunately, not everyone buying a biz op has an experience like Anne's. Here are a number of stories from people who have succeeded in home-based business opportunities. Our interviews with them cover their experiences in running the business as well as the factors they feel have contributed to their success. A very interesting exercise for you, the reader, is to see how each biz op owner rates in terms of the five traits of the Business Opportunity Personality Profile. Then in the next chapter, you can compare your own personality profile with that of those we've interviewed.

Carving Out a Niche

Case Study #3:
Rick and Joann Landon, Ocean City, Maryland
Hefty Publishing (personalized children's books)

Rick and Joann Landon bought their business opportunity over five years ago. Anticipating starting a family, they looked for a business that would be flexible enough for Joann to work at home and set her own schedule while still providing another income for the household. They had been intrigued with the idea of personalized children's books ever since Joann received one as a gift. After some research into the industry, they decided on Hefty Publishing as they felt the company offered the highest-quality books in terms of artwork and story lines that they had seen.

Their purchase price included a comprehensive manual and set of computer disks that contained the books themselves. Rick was especially impressed with the manual. "The manual is incredible," claims Rick. "It's about five inches thick. It included everything we needed to know: marketing ideas, business formats, everything." After reading the manual and researching their market, they were raring to go. As soon as they actually began marketing their books, the picture changed somewhat. "It turned out to be very hard work," says Rick. "We have to exhibit constantly at places like fairs, craft shows, and trade shows and we have to make the books on-site." Another thing they did not realize is just how seasonal a business it is. Most of their sales have been at Christmastime.

Despite the hard work and challenges, Rick and Joann are satisfied with their business. "We were looking for a part-time income, and we certainly have that," says Rick, "and we sure do love the products we sell. We really believe these books are top of the line, and the people who buy them, they really love them, too." Yet, the Core Function of their business has turned out to be primarily one of sales and marketing. "You have to constantly go out and sell over and over and over again," explains Rick. "We don't make very much per book, about $10. That's a lot of sales to make for it to add up to anything significant." The Landons have found a way to get ongoing repeat business, however. "We have arrangements with a few real estate agents and salespeople. They buy from us every month. When one of them makes a sale, they send a personalized book to their client's kids, if they have them, as a kind of thank you gift." The Landons also send brochures to maternity wards in local hospitals and to local organizations such as the women's auxiliary and have done joint fund-raising ventures with local preschools and charities. "We've even had kids going door-to-door selling our books like Girl Scout cookies," says Rick.

Another important aspect of surviving in business, the Landons have found out, is providing excellent customer service. "If we make a book and misspell something, it sticks out like a sore thumb. If we don't go back and fix it right away, people aren't satisfied with the book and they won't want to pay for it. And they won't recommend us, either. If you don't have a lot of patience, it's not a very good business to be in."

Joann is the one who spends most of the time on the business. In addition to raising two children, she still finds time to devote about five to fifteen hours a week to the business. Rick works full-time in construction and helps out on the weekends. Over the five years they've been in operation, the parent company has provided responsive, ongoing support. In retrospect, the

Landons only point to two disappointments in terms of their expectations. They believe that the company was a little too optimistic when representing potential sales figures, especially for a part-time business, and that their territory is a little crowded. On the whole, though, the Landons are satisfied with their business and the changes it has brought to their lives. Says Rick, "One of most unexpected benefits running this business has given us is that it has made us both feel much more positively about ourselves and our abilities."

Getting Exactly What You Want from a Biz Op

Case Study #4:
Bill Shumaker, Fitchburg, Massachusetts
Auditel (Utility bill auditing)

Bill Shumaker doesn't mince words. When asked why he bought his utility bill auditing business, he simply said, "I got tired of working for somebody else." There were other reasons, too. "I wanted to go out and do something suited to me. This business was something that I could run from home and didn't require a full-time staff, at least to begin with. It also presented some degree of difficulty and it seemed like it was fun to do." Bill chose Auditel, the parent company, after careful research. He liked the way the company presented itself and was impressed with the forthrightness of the representative he spoke with. Whenever he had a question, Auditel answered quickly and comprehensively. What cinched it for Bill was the uniqueness of the bill auditing service: "No one was doing it at the time." (Author's note: Utility bill auditing is no longer unique.)

The company provided training and six months of follow-up support. In addition to learning the mechanics of the business, Bill also received extensive marketing training and support. At first, Bill's intention was to run the business on a part-time basis, but it quickly grew into a full-time situation. Today, six years later, Bill even has a small staff working for him. The Core Function of his business matches Bill's unique personality rather well. He likes the fact that he can work at his own pace and that the work itself is not location dependent. "I can throw a great many bills in my briefcase and take them away for the weekend to work on." explains Bill. He also has a rather exacting set of expectations of himself and his clients. "I guess I have a skill set that doesn't let people off the hook that easily," he points out. Not a "people person," Bill deals with sales and marketing functions by hiring salespeople. "I give them a list of what kinds of customers I'm interested in, and they go knocking on doors."

Growing a Business with Experience, Skill, and Determination

Case Study #5:

Lisa Harmon, Sarasota, Florida

Bizkits by Quantum Technology, Inc. (Formerly Precision Data Corporation)

Remote data backup

Lisa Harmon was an operations manager for Smith Kline in Atlanta when she got married and moved to Florida. This was definitely a time of transition, and Lisa was determined to make as many positive changes as possible. Of course, this extended to her career as well. Although she had never owned or run a business before, the idea had always appealed to her. She began to research general business information through sources such as the Small Business Administration (SBA), local libraries, bookstores, etc. Then she was confronted with the decision as to exactly which kind of business she wanted to get into. She started by taking stock of her own experience. "I did some computer work on the side while I was working for Smith Kline, and I'd always enjoyed that," explains Lisa. "Even after moving to Florida, I was supporting some clients that I'd been helping on the computer via communications software like *PC Anywhere* and *Carbon Copy*. I was doing a backup manually. I was getting on line with them, zipping up their files, and downloading them to my computer, and I knew there had to be an easier way, so I started investigating backup businesses." She claims to have actually gotten the idea from our book *Making Money with Your Computer at Home,* where she saw a reference to Rob Cosgrove's *Bizkits by Precision Data Corp.* She called the phone number listed and "that's how it all started. I just called and asked for information and took it from there."

One and a half years later Lisa is earning a comfortable full-time income from her business. Her initial investment was smaller than most, as she already had much of the computer equipment required. She did buy the special software package from Precision Data, which included extensive technical and marketing support. "I couldn't have done it without them, that's for sure," says Lisa of the company's support. "First, the technical support was extremely crucial, because I'm not technical. I really relied on them for technical support and they always helped me; they were always there." The company also helped her get started as a businessperson. "I'd never run a business or owned a business. I just followed all the instructions Precision Data gave me and used the company's marketing materials. The materials included a sample press release and a sample brochure and that kind of stuff, and I used it all and it all was successful for me."

Lisa has been pleasantly surprised that her business has grown so quickly: "The business has totally exceeded my expectations. I thought because of my inexperience that it was going to take me a little bit longer to get clients and get up and running, but it didn't. I really read a lot and followed the instructions, and things just worked the way they were supposed to. I don't know if that's unusual or normal, but it worked for me. I'm happy."

Lisa attributes her success to a number of factors. The first is the uniqueness of her business. "I don't have any competition. In fact, so many people were interested in the remote backup service in general, I had to ask Precision Data if I could sell their software package for them, and so now I'm a distributor as well as an outside contractor." She also attributes her success to how well her personality and skills match the Core Functions of the business. "The business has everything I like. I like computers, I like helping people, and it's very rewarding, especially if someone has a computer crash and you give them their data back. That feels especially good." Lisa explains further: "I guess I picked up a lot of skills over the years that I didn't know I had, and now they just appear every once in a while. Dealing with the public, being patient. My computer skills. I was a data entry clerk at one time; I was a secretary at another. I think I've been everything at one time, and you've got to be all, you've got to do it all because you've got to wear all the hats when you start your own company."

In terms of specific skills, Lisa credits being well organized as the most important to her success "You have got to stay so organized because the business itself is based on schedules and times and precision. That's really just the basics of the business in general. You have your accounting and your day-to-day routine. Most people start home businesses by themselves, and in a home-based business, there's just so much going on around you, you have to stay organized."

Lisa's research into the world of business also paid off for her. Primarily, it showed the power that knowledge brings. If she encountered something she didn't know, she was never too shy to ask questions: "Like the accounting and the legal stuff. I formed an S corporation, and I did that on my own at first, but then I knew it was getting more serious as I was getting more clients, so I went to an attorney. I didn't know anything about taxes, so I went to an IRS seminar and learned a little bit about that. One field I still don't know anything about is personnel and hiring and that kind of stuff, so that's my next venture."

She also knew very little about marketing and sales Fortunately, the company provided her with extensive training and resources in these areas, and she added her own unique touch. "I use all the Precision Data stuff. They gave us sample brochures, and then I took it a step further. I'm very creative, so I developed my own stuff. I did everything in-house and just had a lot of confidence. I try to stay close to the consumer and customer and try to use my feelings. They say you shouldn't use your feelings in business, but it's worked for me. I create things using my own language and using things I think people can understand." Consequently, Linda finds it easy to get business: "I do find that it's very easy for me to get business. I'm getting lots of business, and I know I'm going to have to hire an administrative assistant or an office manager. So hiring personnel and being able to let go of the things I've been doing is going to be my next step, and I'm going to have to learn how to do that and budget for it." We wish all of you reading this book such problems!

MAKING IT MEANS DOING YOUR HOMEWORK

In reviewing the experiences of people who have been successful in buying a home-based business opportunity, it's clear that the more carefully you look into what you're getting yourself into before you buy, the more satisfied you'll be with whatever decisions you make. That means doing your homework: researching the company, talking to others who have been involved both happily and not so happily, and checking to see if you are positioned to contact people who are interested in and willing to pay for what you'll be offering. Most important, it means assessing yourself, your own motivations, skills, interests, and abilities. In the following chapter, we're going to outline how you can do the needed homework to know if you can succeed in a business opportunity by specifically assessing four key areas:

- *The Company.* Is it a solid opportunity or too good to be true?
- *What You'll Actually Be Doing.* How exactly will you spend most of your time in running the biz op. Is this activity something that's right for you?
- *Your Personal Experience, Skills, and Readiness.* Are you ready to run your own business from home? Do you have the experience, skills, and personality profile to succeed in a biz op you're considering or in running a biz op in general?
- *The Market.* Do people want or need the service or product within the region you propose to operate in?

Starting your own business is one of the most exciting and important decisions you will make in your life. Don't rush into anything. Give yourself at least three to six months to properly complete the necessary homework before making a decision. Research shows that those who do so are more likely to succeed. If someone is pressuring you to make a decision quickly, take this to be a clear warning sign. More frustration results from a hastily made decision to buy a biz op than patiently doing homework that leads to a decision.

If the biz op seller is a solid company offering a solid opportunity, they will appreciate your careful consideration before acting because they will know that's what will make you someone who's serious about your commitment to success should you decide to proceed.

Advantages of Biz Ops

Now that you have something of an understanding of what business opportunities are and how others have made them work, let's list some of the clear-cut advantages of owning one.

- A good business opportunity gives you the freedom to make your own decisions, while still providing you with some training and support from the parent company.
- You can find a wide range of opportunities that have the potential for earning a realistic full-time income.
- There are also many opportunities to select from which will provide you a part-time or supplementary income.
- Part-time biz ops can be run concurrently with a full-time job, another business, or while child rearing.
- Generally, business opportunities have a lower purchase price than franchises.
- Buying a biz op allows you to open a business with much of the legwork already done for you. A good biz op will provide you with a business plan, marketing strategy, operating procedures, training, support, and a great many other resources you won't have to find on your own.
- By working from home you have lower overhead.
- Working from home also allows you to have a more flexible schedule.
- Buying a biz op is buying your own business so, if you build equity in it, you can sell it later at a profit.
- Biz ops allow you to be creative in the way you run and market your business. Unlike franchising, you will not have to follow a strict set of procedures imposed by the parent company.
- Biz ops allow you to be flexible in structuring your business to meet the specific needs of clients, customers, and the market in general.
- Biz ops are available for a wide range of products and services, so you have many more choices for finding something you can feel passionate about.
- With a biz op, your success is often not as intimately tied into the parent company as in franchising and MLM. If the parent isn't doing well, or even goes under, in most cases you can continue operating.

Disadvantages of Biz Ops

There are two sides to everything. Consider the following disadvantages before seriously considering the purchase of a biz op:

- Unlike with franchising, there are no specific laws governing biz ops as an industry group. Seller Assisted Marketing Plan (SAMP) laws and other laws regulating sales in general do exist, but they are not nearly as specific to biz ops as an industry as the Franchising Rule is to franchising.
- Laws that do apply to biz ops vary greatly from state to state and fall under different agencies' jurisdictions. If you run into a problem, it can be confusing to track these laws down and find the appropriate agency to help you resolve it.
- There are no trade or professional organizations specific to the business opportunity industry.
- Because there is little regulation, there is an unending supply of scams and dishonest companies in the biz op world—so beware! There's even a book, *Biz Op: How to Get Rich with Business Opportunity Frauds and Scams,* written specifically by Bruce Easly to tell people how to create their own biz op scams.
- Because the guidelines supplied by many parent companies are not nearly as comprehensive as in franchising and MLM, inexperienced businesspeople may have greater difficulties at first.
- Biz ops nearly never include exclusive territories.
- Often you must find your own sources for vendors, distributors, and essential services. This can take up your time and resources.
- Usually you must create, and pay for, all advertising and marketing materials yourself, although your biz op should provide marketing plans and ideas or samples.
- Most biz ops don't have regional or national recognition for their products or services.
- As in all business, there is a chance you will fail. It's a risk. Are you prepared to lose the money and time you invest in the business?
- You may not make as much money as you expect. Are you ready to make do with less for an indefinite period of time?
- You may have to invest long hours for little return, especially in the beginning. Are you ready to work harder than you now do?
- Having your own business is physically and emotionally taxing. Are you up to the challenge?
- Working from your home requires self-discipline and self-motivation. Can you set goals and follow through?
- Unlike having a job, there are absolutely no guarantees in running your own business. Are you ready for the uncertainty?

- Having your own business means not having any basic-level employer-provided benefits such as health insurance, unemployment insurance, worker's compensation insurance, or the employer's share of Social Security payments. You will be responsible for providing these yourself from your earnings.
- Many biz ops are sold using high-pressure sales techniques. Don't get swept up in the momentary excitement of a dramatic sales pitch.
- Many biz ops are sold by biz op brokers who don't actually work in the company they are selling. They may view their job as that of selling to anyone who will buy, whether the business would be well suited to the buyer or not.

6

Evaluating a Biz
Op for Fitness,
Honesty, and Marketability

"IT'S A REALLY OLD CLICHÉ, but in my fifteen years of experience I've seen it proven over and over again. Those who succeed in business opportunities are those that work at it consistently and diligently—success is 90 percent perspiration and only 10 percent inspiration." That says Terry Smith, Director of Sales and Marketing, of Novus, Inc., an on-site windshield repair service that distributed itself as a business opportunity for over ten years before becoming a franchise. We agree.

Persistence and diligence are the building blocks of success in any business. In order for you to experience enough success to motivate you to persist in the business opportunity of your choice, you need to set yourself up with as many advantages as possible right from in the beginning. And the best way to do that is to test out beforehand if a particular biz op you're considering will be a good "fit" for you, whether the company is an honest and reputable one, and if there is actually a need *you* can meet with what you'll be offering. That's what the tools in this chapter are designed to help you do by providing you with three Before-You-Buy Tests: the Fitness Check, the Honesty Check, and the Market Check.

While many biz ops may "sound" good to you, before you buy any business you're truly interested in, you can use the three tools in this chapter to identify what you'll *actually* be spending your time *doing* if you buy this particular business. You'll know how to assess what you can expect from the company selling you the business and just how much need there is for what you would be offering. So, making sure a biz op passes these three key tests begins with understanding the true nature of any business you're thinking about buying into.

TEST I: THE BIZ OP FITNESS CHECK

Business opportunities, like most MLMs, franchises, and other kinds of businesses, generally have one activity that is at the heart of the business— their raison d'être. Often this activity isn't readily apparent when you first hear about a biz op; biz op ads or seminars may play up other more appealing or interesting aspects of a business. So many people do not realize how they will actually be spending the majority of their time when they get down to operating a particular business. The "main activity" that you will spend most of your time doing is what we call the Core Function of a business and since that's what you'll be spending most of your time doing, you need to make sure that you know what this activity is and that it is something you will truly enjoy and have an affinity for.

What Will You Be Doing?

Because business opportunities have less structure, fewer guidelines, and include a greater range of business choices than home-based franchises or MLMs, it is *especially* important to choose a biz op with a Core Function that is well suited to you. If you truly enjoy the Core Function of a business, you are more likely to have the persistence and motivation to steer it to success. Remember the old saying of Confucius, "Find the perfect occupation and you will never work again"?

We have identified the key elements for success in home-based business opportunities and shared experiences with you through case histories of business owners and parent companies and by monitoring on-line discussion groups. We have found one thing that successful biz op owners have in common: a passion for the day-to-day running of their businesses. To put it succinctly, successful biz op owners *really* like what they do.

In fact, one of the most common problems we see people having with turning their biz op into a success is discovering that what they had imagined themselves doing isn't what they actually ended up doing. This seems to be the main reason that, believe it or not, many biz ops end up collecting dust on the bookshelf instead of becoming flourishing businesses. It also seems to be a primary contributor to why such a high number of people return, or try to return, the business opportunities they buy.

Here's an example of what can happen if you don't check out the Core Function of a biz op carefully before buying. Someone we know bought a sample kit for a business selling beautiful crystal window ornaments thinking it would make an excellent part-time business for her. She had always loved jewelry and decorative household items and was especially fascinated with crystal. So she imagined how wonderful it would be to spend part of every day working with these crystal window hangings.

The Core Function of the business, however, was selling these items to stores and boutiques. As with so many biz ops, selling, not creating, lies at the core of the business. At first, she dutifully lugged her demonstration kit around on Venice's famous boardwalk, as well as to the shops in neighboring Santa Monica. Although she was able to write a fair amount of orders, she quickly became frustrated and bored going from one store to the next, opening her case of wares and saying the same things over and over again. Instead of being surrounded by crystal, she was usually surrounded by traffic. After just a few months she stopped the business. The experience was so upsetting to her that, to this day, she can't look at a crystal window hanging without subconsciously reciting the first few lines of her pitch.

So while our friend thought the Core Function would be handling the crystal she loved, in actuality, the core of her business was a selling/distribution function. Had she taken the time to check this out before she bought the business opportunity, she might still have her windows filled with the lovely crystal art she loved but can no longer stand to look at.

Here's another example of why you need to have a clear idea of what you'll be spending the majority of your time doing before you buy a biz op. A man who came to one of our seminars had purchased a home-based college scholarship matching service. He had been excited at first because, on the surface, it seemed that he would be spending most of his time researching sources of available scholarship funds based on his clients' needs and situations. As a thorough and dedicated researcher, the notion of earning a living in this way appealed to him greatly.

But, after purchasing the business package, he found himself spending 80 percent of his time *locating* people who needed the scholarship service, then submitting their profiles to the biz op vendor who actually did the research. Not being a "people person" himself, he found the whole experience disheartening. By not asking the right questions or researching the business opportunity in enough depth to know what his role would actually be, he found himself in a business that was almost the exact opposite of what he initially though it to be.

In contrast to these stories, however, remember Nancie Lee Cummins? Nancie bought a home-based biz op in medical billing. Although initially she did have to spend time selling her services, once she had a number of clients, she now spends most of her time doing what she had imagined herself doing—helping doctors process their medical claims. That is the core function of that business. It involves problem solving, organizing, and negotiating—all functions she enjoys doing and can do well.

So, you can see why knowing the Core Function of any packaged business you buy, before you buy it, is so important. No matter how interesting or appealing a biz op may sound at face value in an ad or at an expo, you must look more deeply to discover what *you* will be *doing*. Part 1 of the Biz Op Fitness Test is designed to help you answer the question "Is This Biz Op a Good Fit for You?" Then part 2 will help you assess "Are You a Good Fit for This Biz Op?"

PART 1: IS THIS BIZ OP A GOOD FIT FOR YOU? DISCOVERING YOUR CORE FUNCTION

Answering the following questions will enable you to identify what a business opportunity's Core Function is, what your role will be in providing it, and if it's a good "fit" for you. These questions should also help you determine if actually running the business and doing the primary day-to-day tasks involved will actually keep you sufficiently motivated to work long enough and hard enough to succeed

1. What do you think the Core Function of the business is?

See if you can write a brief description of what you think the Core Function of the business you're considering is. What is at the heart of this business? What is its primary focus, its raison d'être? If you can't describe this simply and clearly to yourself, you need to investigate the business further. Here are several examples:

- Selling advertising on golf carts
- Sharpening shears for hair salons
- Teaching children to appreciate music
- Retouching paint jobs on cars
- Conducting sales and management training programs
- Waterproofing decks, balconies, and pools

2. What is your role in providing this Core Function?

All businesses, regardless of their goal, require performing some aspects of the six basic functions listed below:

Creating: Someone must create a product or service of some kind.
Problem Solving: Someone must analyze and research the best solutions.
Building: Someone must build, manage, collect, store, and maintain the materials involved.
Organizing: Someone must gather, organize, record, file, process, and update the details of administering the business.
Leading: Someone must market, promote, and sell the product or service.
Improving: Someone must listen to and take care of client or customer needs.

Once you buy a business opportunity, you will be responsible for running your own business, so you will most likely be involved in performing some of all six of these functions. But, your role in carrying out the Core Function of a particular biz op will focus primarily on one (or perhaps two) of these areas. This will be *your* Core Function. It or may not be the same function as the business itself. For example,

- We just learned that the Core Function of the business our friend bought was to create crystal decorative items (Creating); but her Core Function turned out to be presenting and selling those crystal items (Leading).
- The Core Function of the business the man who came to our workshop purchased was researching scholarships (Problem Solving); but his Core Function was to locate people (Leading) needing scholarships and process their applications for the searches the company would do (Organizing).

So, look over the following six functions and circle which one (or two) will be your primary focus, the one you will be spending most of your time carrying out, *your* role in the business opportunity you're considering. Then check off (√) the specific activities under that function you'll be called upon to spend most of your time performing.

LEADING
___ administering
___ assigning
___ coordinating
___ delegating
___ initiating
___ inspiring
___ managing
___ motivating
___ organizing
___ persuading
___ selling
___ supervising

IMPROVING
___ assisting
___ caring
___ collaborating
___ consulting
___ contributing
___ counseling
___ encouraging
___ explaining
___ helping
___ listening
___ serving
___ supporting

ORGANIZING
___ arranging
___ cataloging
___ compiling
___ evaluating
___ expediting
___ gathering
___ grouping
___ ordering
___ programming
___ recording
___ tabulating
___ updating

CREATING
___ communicating
___ composing
___ designing
___ drawing
___ feeling
___ imaging
___ innovating
___ perceiving
___ performing
___ sensing
___ shaping
___ writing

BUILDING
___ adjusting
___ assembling
___ computing
___ constructing
___ handling
___ maintaining
___ making
___ operating
___ renovating
___ repairing
___ tinkering
___ troubleshooting

PROBLEM SOLVING
___ analyzing
___ classifying
___ defining
___ diagnosing
___ editing
___ investigating
___ reading
___ reasoning
___ researching
___ solving
___ studying
___ thinking

To find out which activities compose a biz op's Core Function you can:

a. Ask the company selling the biz op what people who buy this business actually spend most of their time doing.
b. Ask others who have purchased this same packaged business what they spend most of their time doing.

3. How much time will you spend performing your Core Function?

As we said, in running your own business opportunity you will probably be spending time carrying out some of all six of the above functions, but what proportion of your time will you be devoting to each? Put an asterisk (*) beside all the other activities on the above list you will be performing in running the business you're considering. Then estimate how many hours in an average day, week, and month these functions will involve. For example:

Leading: How much of your time will be spent promoting the business and finding clients and customers? Will you need to develop and place ads and other sales materials? Will you be contacting prospects in person? Doing telemarketing? Giving presentations, demonstrations, or exhibits?

Improving: How much time will be spent working personally helping clients, listening to their concerns, and responding to their needs.

Organizing: How much of your time will be spent doing paperwork, filling out and processing forms, and other administrative tasks?

Building: How much time will you spend purchasing, stocking, fixing, assembling, transporting, carrying, or handling essential materials, goods, or inventory?

Problem Solving: How much time will you spend planning, researching, and analyzing information and solving problems for clients and customers?

Creating: How much time will you spend designing or creating a product, report, service, or printed marketing materials like brochures, flyers, etc.?

3. What functions will the company selling the biz op be providing and what functions, if any, will they carry out for your business?

As we mentioned, often the Core Function of the company selling a biz op and *your* Core Function will be different. Some companies strictly sell and produce the training materials for their biz ops. Others are primarily sales and promotion organizations, locating the merchandise, materials, or supplies those who buy the biz op will sell. Some are primarily administrative arms, pro-

Doing a Time Analysis

Estimate how much time you will be spending each day, week, and month performing each of these functions:

Daily

_____ Leading: i.e., directing/marketing/selling/promoting
_____ Improving: i.e., helping and assisting clients/other customer service
_____ Organizing: i.e., bookkeeping/paperwork/processing information
_____ Building: i.e., assembling/computing/constructing/maintaining
_____ Problem Solving: i.e., planning/research/analyzing
_____ Creating: i.e., innovating/designing/composing

Weekly

_____ Leading: i.e., directing/marketing/selling/promoting
_____ Improving: i.e., helping and assisting clients/other customer service
_____ Organizing: i.e., bookkeeping/paperwork/processing information
_____ Building: i.e., assembling/transporting/packing/constructing/maintaining
_____ Problem Solving: i.e., planning/research/analyzing
_____ Creating: i.e., innovating/designing/composing

Monthly

_____ Leading: i.e., directing/marketing/selling/promoting
_____ Improving: i.e., helping and assisting clients/other customer service
_____ Organizing: i.e., bookkeeping/paperwork/processing information
_____ Building: i.e., assembling/computing/constructing/maintaining
_____ Problem Solving: i.e., planning/research/analyzing
_____ Creating: i.e., innovating/designing/composing

cessing or shipping orders. Still others actually create the product or service that will be sold or administered by those who buy their business opportunities.

What functions will they be providing for you?

a. Is the company's Core Function primarily to provide you with a business support package and ongoing support in running your business through training, written materials, and consultations? Or do they have other primary functions?

b. Is the company's Core Function to perform any of the actual tasks involved in your running of the business you're buying from them? If so, which ones? Will they be doing sales and marketing, creating and shipping products, processing orders, etc.?

c. Will the company be involved in any other way in the running of your business?

Put an (X) beside any of the activities on page 163 that the vendor will be responsible for. The function with the most checks should be a good indication of what the vendor's Core Function is. Confirm your conclusions with the vendor and be sure such functional responsibilities are spelled out clearly in your sales agreement.

4. How will your time be divided among the various key functions you will be spending your time performing?

Now create a pie chart that reflects how much time you will be spending on the various aspects of running the home-based business you're considering purchasing. The area that will be consuming the most time *is* the Core Function of your business, even if it wouldn't seem to be the primary nature of the business.

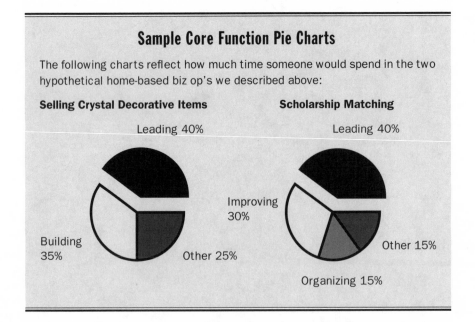

Sample Core Function Pie Charts

The following charts reflect how much time someone would spend in the two hypothetical home-based biz op's we described above:

Selling Crystal Decorative Items

Leading 40%

Improving 30%

Building 35%

Other 25%

Scholarship Matching

Leading 40%

Other 15%

Organizing 15%

PART 2: ARE YOU A GOOD FIT FOR THIS BIZ OP? ASSESSING YOUR NEEDS, MOTIVATION, SKILLS, INTERESTS, KNOWLEDGE, AND PERSONALITY

Do you have what it takes to turn this opportunity into a successful business? This is a key question because, actually, you are not buying a business, you are buying a business *opportunity*. The greatest business opportunity in the world continues to be only an opportunity until you turn it into a business reality. So it is as important to assess your own assets as it is to research the soundness of the opportunity you are considering. You may be perfectly capable of operating a home business, but will you be able to get this one up and running?

If you remember from the last chapter, Anne Lohrfink of Wappingers Falls, New York, bought into a business that required much more initiative, lead time, and legwork than she was willing or suited to do. Rick and Joann Landon of Ocean City, Maryland, had bought several other business opportunities before discovering Hefty Publishing, selling Create-a-Books for children. This business turned out to be the one they were best suited and motivated to do.

So, this part of the **Fitness Check** will help you analyze your own motivations, assess your experience and skills, and examine your expectations. Be as objective as you can. These questions aren't designed to prove you right or wrong but to give you the information you need to help you make an informed decision about whether you're the right person for a particular biz op you're considering.

Your Needs and Motivation

1. Why do you want to buy a business opportunity instead of starting a business yourself?
2. What do you want from this business?
___ a. Satisfaction
___ b. More money
___ c. Independence
___ d. Flexible schedule
___ e. To work less
3. Rate yourself from 1 to 10 on the following questions, 1 being "absolutely not" and 10 being "unequivocally yes." Then add up the points you've given yourself.
___ a. Am I willing to work hard?
___ b. Can I work independently?
___ c. Can I set my own goals and follow through on them?

___ d. Can I overcome frustration and setbacks?

___ e. How well do I get along with other people?

___ f. Do I have good communication skills?

___ g. Do I know how to organize?

___ h. Do I take pride in whatever I do?

___ i. Am I a self-starter?

___ j. Do I welcome responsibility?

___ k. Am I willing to make decisions?

___ l. Am I willing to struggle and make sacrifices?

___ m. Can I control my emotions?

___ n. Am I self-disciplined?

___ o. Do I have enough experience to support my desires?

___ p. Am I more of a doer than a dreamer?

___ Total

A score of 140 to 160 indicates that you have the personal qualities required to succeed at launching a business opportunity if you find one that's suited to you. A score of 120 to 140 indicates that you have many qualities that will help you succeed, but you may need to acquire others to succeed. A score of lower then 120 indicates that you may not be ready, at this time, to take on running a business opportunity full-time.

A score lower than 5 on any of the above could be a possible impediment to your success in a business opportunity. So, if you seriously want to buy a business opportunity, spend some time thinking about why you scored low on any particular questions and what you could do to develop these traits in yourself.

Your Interests, Skills, and Experience

This section is designed to help you discover what particular skills and talents you bring to a particular biz op. Begin by making a list of your talents, skills, and experience related to the business you are considering. Then, read through the lists of skills and place a checkmark next to the ones you feel you can do adequately. Place a second checkmark next to the skills you feel you can handle well. Then circle the skills you most enjoy using. Last, look back at the activities the biz op calls for on pages 160–61 and see if there's a good match. Ideally a business that's well suited to you will make heavy use of your strongest, most-enjoyed skill and draw little if at all on those you don't like or do less well.

LEADING
___ administering
___ assigning
___ coordinating
___ delegating
___ initiating
___ inspiring
___ managing
___ motivating
___ organizing
___ persuading
___ selling
___ supervising

IMPROVING
___ assisting
___ caring
___ collaborating
___ consulting
___ contributing
___ counseling
___ encouraging
___ explaining
___ helping
___ listening
___ serving
___ supporting

ORGANIZING
___ arranging
___ cataloging
___ compiling
___ evaluating
___ expediting
___ gathering
___ grouping
___ ordering
___ programming
___ recording
___ tabulating
___ updating

CREATING
___ communicating
___ composing
___ designing
___ drawing
___ feeling
___ imaging
___ innovating
___ perceiving
___ performing
___ sensing
___ shaping
___ writing

BUILDING
___ adjusting
___ assembling
___ computing
___ constructing
___ handling
___ maintaining
___ making
___ operating
___ renovating
___ repairing
___ tinkering
___ troubleshooting

PROBLEM SOLVING
___ analyzing
___ classifying
___ defining
___ diagnosing
___ editing
___ investigating
___ reading
___ reasoning
___ researching
___ solving
___ studying
___ thinking

Your Knowledge about Business and Biz Ops

It's easy to get focused on the "opportunity" part of a biz op, but it's equally important to remember that to succeed in a biz op, you need to know as much as possible about what's involved in operating it as a business.

Answer the following questions to find out how much business knowledge you currently have. Each one of these questions represents an important aspect of running a business independently. If you are unfamiliar with any terms, concepts, or procedures, you must make it a point to become versed in these areas. It is beyond the scope of this book to give you an overview of these business principles, but the Resources in the Appendices can direct you to the information you need.

1. Does your state regulate biz ops?
2. If so, how long is your state's consideration period?
3. What is an S corporation?
4. Which branch of your state government controls tax collection?
5. What constitutes a business plan?
6. How do you set your prices and make projections as to your expected income?
7. What is the most common reason biz ops fail?
8. What are the most effective ways to market the business you're thinking of buying?
9. What licenses, permits, etc., will you need? Where can you get them?
10. What is cash flow and how do you manage it?
11. What is the difference between gross and net income?
12. Are there any zoning restrictions pertinent to running a home business where you live?
13. What business insurance do you need for this business?
14. If you sell the business, what is your capital gains situation in terms of taxes?
15. What are the demographic and psychographic profiles of your potential customers?

Your Personality Profile

The following questions will help you gain an understanding of your own personality and the traits that might help, or hinder, you in starting and running a business opportunity. If there are areas you find yourself weak in, that doesn't mean you won't ever be able to succeed in a biz op or that there is no hope in trying. Weak areas only indicate areas you have to work on to increase your chances of success.

A. Independence

Thinking about your work, rate yourself from 1 to 100 percent in the following areas, with 1 being "not at all" and 100 being "absolutely":

_____ 1. Do you like the idea of being your own boss?

_____ 2. Do you dislike having to follow someone else's suggestions precisely?

_____ 3. Are you generally interested in following a set of guidelines and seeing them through?

_____ 4. Are you good at managing your time?

_____ 5. Are you good at setting goals?

_____ 6. Are you good at meeting goals?

_____ 7. Do you like working?

_____ 8. Do you feel working with others gets in your way?

_____ 9. Do you work most productively alone?

_____10. Do you hate being told what to do?

_____11. Are you strong willed?

_____12. How much do enjoy starting major projects from scratch?

_____13. Do you enjoy actually following through and completing a project once it is started?

_____14. Do you prefer working without close supervision?

_____15. Is it hard to distract you?

_____16. Does it take a lot to get you frustrated?

_____17. Do you rise to the challenge of adversity?

_____18. Can you keep yourself consistently motivated?

Total ÷ 18 = _____.

Add up the percentage points you've given yourself for each of the above questions, then divide the total by 18. According to most business opportunity companies we spoke with, those scoring between 75 and 100 percent for independence make the best candidates for successful biz op owners. A very high independence score indicates that you have the confidence and the vision to build a business with fewer guidelines and assistance than you would have in franchising or MLM. If you scored 50 to 75 percent, you have the right mix for success in franchising or MLM, where compliance with procedures and rules is a greater requirement. If you scored low, you may not have the self-discipline and self-motivation at this point to run a home-based business.

| 1 | 25 | 50 | 75 | 100 |

B. Attitude

Rate yourself in regard to your work from 1 to 100 percent in the following areas, with 1 being "not at all" and 100 being "absolutely":

_____ 1. How confident are you?

_____ 2. Do you handle rejection well?

_____ 3. Do you act on your decisions?

_____ 4. Do you consider yourself a winner?

_____ 5. When you become discouraged, do you keep trying?

_____ 6. Rate your agreement with the following statement: "I don't care what anyone says, I know when I'm right."

_____ 7. Are you a risk taker?

_____ 8. Are you an optimist?

_____ 9. Do you like yourself?

_____10. Rate your agreement with the following statement: "I believe the only limits we have are set by ourselves."

_____11. How deep are your convictions about having your own business?

_____12. Do you chafe at following rules?

_____13. In stressful situations, do people generally turn to you for advice or guidance?

_____14. Does "Don't play the game; be the game" describe your personal philosophy?

_____15. Do you really believe you have what it takes to succeed?

_____16. Do you prefer setting up your own system as opposed to working within a system?

_____17. Does it take a great deal to get you to give up?

_____18. Do you approach new situations as a fun challenge?

Total ÷ 18 = _____.

Add up the percentage points you've given yourself for each of the above questions, then divide the total by 18. If you achieved a score of between 75 and 100 percent in attitude, you do indeed have the attitude, the personal conviction, and confidence that most business opportunity providers find crucial to success. Biz ops require a lot of you. Your belief in yourself will become the foundation for any business you run on your own.

| 1 | 25 | 50 | 75 | 100 |

C. Consistency

Rate yourself in regard to your work from 1 to 100 percent in the following areas, with 1 being "not at all" and 100 being "absolutely":

_____ 1. Do you finish the projects you start?

_____ 2. Are you good at setting goals?

_____ 3. Are you generally calm?

_____ 4. Do you approach challenges calmly?

_____ 5. Have you met the goals you've set for yourself so far?

_____ 6. Do you consider yourself dependable?

_____ 7. Do you generally react the same way to similar situations?

_____ 8. Does the statement "I'm not easily bored" accurately describe you?

_____ 9. Is the statement "I don't get frustrated often" true for you?

_____10. Do you like to work on big, long-term projects?

_____11. Do you have a set of personal ethics that help guide you through troubling situations?

_____12. Are you a sincere person?

_____13. Are you tolerant of others?

_____14. Do you have long-term relationships in your life?

_____15. Outside of sickness or other factors beyond of your control, have things gotten generally better for you over time?

_____16. Are you emotionally strong?

_____17. Are you easy to talk to?

_____18. Do you usually find yourself outside of trends and fads?

Total ÷ 18 = _____.

Add up the percentage points you've given yourself for each of the above questions, then divide the total by 18. If your score is between 75 and 100 percent in consistency, it bodes well for your success in a biz op. Again, since there are few rules and guidelines, you will need a strong internal compass to help see you through the rough times, meet the challenges, and even deal with the success of running your own business. Consistency is one of the truly beneficial personal assets you can bring to any biz op.

| 1 | 25 | 50 | 75 | 100 |

D. Influence

Rate yourself from 1 to 100 percent in regard to your work in the following areas, with 1 being "not at all" and 100 being "absolutely":

_____ 1. Are you an outgoing person?

_____ 2. How enthusiastic are you, in general?

_____ 3. Do you enjoy meeting new people?

_____ 4. Do you enjoy being in the spotlight?

_____ 5. Is it important for you to be popular?

_____ 6. Do you have a great many friends?

_____ 7. Do you sometimes feel directionless?

_____ 8. Would you rather talk to customers or associates than do the actual work of your business?

_____ 9. Do people generally trust you?

_____10. Rate your sales skills (1 = very poor; 100 = outstanding)

_____11. Do you generally win arguments?

_____12. Do you find that more people agree with you than disagree with you?

_____13. Do you get a strong sense of personal worth from how well you do in the world?

_____14. How much do you care about what people think of you?

_____15. Do you communicate well?

_____16. Do you frequently feel misunderstood?

_____17. Do you actually enjoy sales and customer service?

_____18. Are you a "warm" person?

Total ÷ 18 = _____

Add up the percentage points you've given yourself for each of the above questions, then divide the total by 18. If your score is between 75 and 100 percent, you are a good candidate for a biz op. Sales, promotion, public relations, and customer service are essential skills in business, and high-influence people are quite good in these areas. The disadvantages of being a high-influence personality include having a short attention span and becoming easily bored. That's why a high consistency score is also important.

If your score was low, you may not have the people skills it will take to market a business and deal with the politics of keeping customers satisfied.

| 1 | 25 | 50 | 75 | 100 |

E. Dominance

Rate yourself in regard to your work from 1 to 100 percent in the following areas, with 1 being "not at all" and 100 being "absolutely":

_____ 1. Do you have very high standards?

_____ 2. Are you often critical of those who do not meet your standards?

_____ 3. Do you like to make your own rules?

_____ 4. How true is the following statement for you: "I really don't care what others think when I know I'm right about something."

_____ 5. Would you rather do things yourself because you know they will be done correctly?

_____ 6. Do you think of compromise as something negative, as in "I won't compromise myself."

_____ 7. Is one of the reasons you are considering buying a business so that you won't have do what someone else says?

_____ 8. Do you have frequent conflicts with co-workers or superiors?

_____ 9. Once your mind is made up, do you have difficulty changing it?

_____10. How important is it for you to be right?

_____11. Do you sometimes feel threatened in work-related matters?

_____12. How true is the following statement for you: "I won't play politics just to get ahead."

_____13. Is assistance from others unimportant or not needed?

_____14. Do you like the idea of independence of decision making that self-employment brings?

_____15. Do you feel that in business "too many cooks spoil the broth"?

_____16. Do you feel that, until now, others have hampered your progress?

_____17. Are you easily bored with routines?

_____18. Are you always looking for new challenges?

Total ÷ 18 = _____

Add up the percentage points you've given yourself for each of the above questions, then divide the total by 18. If your score is between 75 and 100 percent in the dominance domain, you will have the best chance of success in a business opportunity according to those who offer them. A low score in dominance usually indicates that you will not have the self-confidence or vision to compete. A score of 50 to 75 percent makes you a good candidate for franchising, as you will have to follow a great many rules imposed by the franchisor. A high dominance rating indicates that you may need to set your own rules in order to be happy—a perfect match for a biz op.

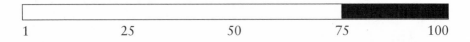

| 1 | 25 | 50 | 75 | 100 |

TEST II: THE BIZ OP HONESTY CHECK

Frustration, disappointment, and sometimes a serious financial setback are just some of the negative results of investing your money and your enthusiasm in a business opportunity that turns out to be less than what was represented to you, or an outright scam. Although a particular biz op may or may not be suited to you, the majority of business opportunities are honest, forthright businesses. Yet, because of the lack of industry standards or federally mandated controls like those that exist for franchising, biz ops do have more than their fair share of shady operators and downright dishonest offers. As a matter of fact, a well-organized underside to the biz op industry has developed that has an entire language of its own for perpetrating frauds and scams. For example, the unfortunate targets of these con artists are called "mooches." "Singers" give fake testimonials when a "mooch" tries to check up on business references provided by the vendor.

The following Biz Op Honesty Check is designed to give you the knowledge you need to make sure you never become a "mooch." It will help you cut right through any hype and skullduggery and get to the bottom line of any biz op company you're considering buying a packaged business from. It gives you the right questions to ask so you can find out if the company is representing itself honestly and openly. This check will also tell you what areas of the company to research, how to do the research, and how to ensure that what they've told you checks out.

PART 1: CHECKING THE INTEGRITY OF THE BIZ OP COMPANY

To maximize your chances of weeding out unscrupulous operators from serious vendors operating in good faith, use the following must-do-procedures to check out each and every biz op you're thinking about buying:

Must-Do Procedures for Weeding Out Scams from Legitimate Business Opportunities

- *Request Disclosure Documents.* Always ask for and review the disclosure documents that are required by the FTC for all business opportunities offered everywhere that cost $500 or more (as little as $100 in one state). These documents provide you with important information about the company and the business opportunity it offers. There are no exceptions to these rules; however, the particular laws governing business opportunities vary from state to state and region to region, so check with your state attorney general's and regional FTC offices to find out what specific disclosure documents a biz op seller is required to provide. (Also review our summary of disclosure laws by state at the end of Chapter 7.)
- *Assure Legal Compliance.* Make sure the biz op seller has complied with all state laws governing biz ops that are covered under the law. Ask for outright proof of compliance.
- *Get Everything in Writing.* If the seller promises something that's not in the written contract, make sure these points are added to the contract and that both you and they initial these additions. You will have a difficult time proving anything in court, should it come down to that, if you don't have every term of the contract in writing.
- *Get Legal Assistance.* If the transaction is greater than $500, or if the sum represents a substantial investment in your estimation, get the advice of an attorney or other trusted business advisor before you buy.

Biz Op Red Flags

An informed business buyer is a smart business buyer. If in your initial negotiations, discussions, or other contacts with the seller of a biz op you see or hear any of the following, consider them red flags for trouble and look elsewhere. These are almost 100 percent sure signs that the opportunity is a rip-off:

- The biz op seller pressures you to decide immediately.
- The biz op seller says that, for whatever reason, federal, state, or local laws do not apply to him or her. A typical example is: "I've never gotten in trouble, so I'm not required to provide a disclosure."
- The biz op seller demands payment immediately.
- The biz op seller lists a local or regional post office box or suite number but won't allow you to visit his or her "office." There probably is no office and while biz op vendors may operate from home, you probably

will be best served by a vendor that is of a size to need an in-house staff.

- The biz op seller discourages you from showing any paperwork to an attorney.
- The seller represents many different kinds of biz ops, not someone who actually does or has done this business him/herself. If you buy from such a person, you will not be dealing with someone directly involved with the business you are buying. Biz op "representatives" or "brokers" have very little stake in whether you succeed in the business you intend to buy and, chances are, will not be there if you need them after the sale.
- Unrealistic claims are made in terms of income and/or amount of hours required, such as: "No selling!" "Easy work!" "This product sells itself!" "If you're not earning $1,000.00 per hour, you're selling yourself short!" "Unlimited retail locations!" In fact, earnings claims cannot be legally made for biz ops.
- Very few states require biz op sellers to give you a list of previous buyers of the business opportunity you are considering. If you are entitled to such a list, it will be of people in your local area. If you don't receive one, beware. If you do receive such a list, be certain to contact the people on it. Find out the experiences of both people who are happy and those who are disappointed. Don't expect everyone on the list to be satisfied or successful—they've bought an opportunity, not a guarantee.
- The biz op seller is new to the business she or he is selling, but not new to selling biz ops.
- The biz op seller has no history of a permanent address (more than six months), changes his or her phone number while you are in negotiations, or otherwise changes location frequently.
- The seller won't take you to see distribution locations or plant operations or otherwise limits or restricts your ability to see his or her operation actually operating.
- Avoid ads in newspapers and magazines that contain only an "enticing" come-on and toll-free (800 or 888) number without reference to who they are or what they're selling.
- The company phone number is answered with a recorded message only and there's no way to speak with a live operator.
- A telemarketer will only take your order if you buy now over the phone. Never make a deal with a telemarketer. If your first contact is a telemarketer, use him or her to start an ongoing dialog with the company. Also, ask to meet with company executives and obtain disclosure statements and other supporting documentation.
- From your first meeting you feel the seller seems somehow secretive or untrustworthy. (Trust your own feelings, they are often dead-on in these kinds of situations).

PART 2: THE BIZ OP SELLERS: WHO ARE THEY?

Going through the Must-Do Procedures is only a first step. Any viable and honest biz op seller will be interested in checking you out. It's only good business. You must do the same. Hopefully, the biz op seller is offering some sort of training or ongoing assistance, so you will be dealing with them in the foreseeable future. Sometimes they'll even be carrying out important functions for your business, such as supplying materials or doing research. So make sure that company officials or the seller are people you can work with, and, most important, make sure they are who they say they are. Finding answers to the following will give you a pretty good idea about where the biz op seller stands in terms of stability, honesty, and fair dealing:

1. How many years has the parent company been in business? If they haven't been around for at least a year, the company is a much higher risk. At best, it is an unproved entity. Most companies fail in their first year of business. If the biz op seller's ongoing support is crucial to the business, you may want to think twice about getting involved with a company that might not be around for long.
2. How many businesses have they sold already? How many in your immediate area? If they have sold many other businesses in your immediate area, you may be in a saturated market, so you will most certainly need to complete the Market Check in the following section.
3. Ask for a detailed breakdown of the parent's management team that lists their experience, background, education, and track record. Poor or inexperienced management is one of the main reasons businesses fail!
4. Ask to see the company's own financial statement; it should be in the disclosure materials.
5. How many businesses have failed? Ask why they failed.
6. Does the seller give you an indication of what you can expect to earn? The FTC does not allow companies to make unreasonable, unjustifiable, or unsupportive claims of potential income. So find out the justification for any income figures and specifically what these figures are based on.
7. Does the seller have benchmark earning figures for an average business in a territory similar to what yours will be? Again, the FTC requires that such benchmarks be reasonable, justifiable, and supported by specific experience.
8. Is the seller's company a large or small one in terms of annual sales, number of employees, and locations.

9. How thoroughly, if at all, has the company checked you out? The more thoroughly a company researches you, the more they care about the success of your enterprise.
10. Is the company well respected in its field? Ask competitors, associates, trade organizations, and publications.
11. How long has the company been selling opportunities? How did the company distribute its products or services before deciding to sell biz ops? Optimally, you want to find a seller that has a history of operating the very type of business they are now selling to you. For example, if you are considering purchasing a business billing system, has the seller actually operated a billing system as their viable business?
12. Is the parent company a leader in their industry? What is their percentage of market share?
13. What is the company's net worth? Do they have the cash reserves to make it through a crisis?

PART 3: DOES THE NAME ON THE DOOR MATCH WHAT HAPPENS ON THE FLOOR?

If no red flags go up in your first phone conversations or meetings, and the biz op seems to be a straightforward business with a solid reputation and track record, it's time to do some research into the inner workings of the company. Finding answers to the following questions will go a long way in helping you determine the forthrightness of the company you are considering:

1. What is the company's record of complaints?
2. What is the company's record of consent orders?
3. Are there any lawsuits or official complaints pending with any regulatory organizations?
   a. attorney general's office
   b. Federal Trade Commission
   c. state, county, and city consumer protection offices
   d. U.S. Postal Inspection Service
4. Are there any complaints lodged or pending with any professional organizations related to the company's industry?
5. Has the company provided you with a list of others who have purchased their biz op?
6. Contact past and existing biz op buyers and distributors. Are they satisfied?

7. Is the list of biz op buyers "highlighted," or do all the parent company's buyers appear on the list? If they don't, why have some been omitted?
8. Are the other biz op buyers of the parent company satisfied?
9. Are the current *customers* of the other biz op buyers satisfied?
10. Some questions to ask past or existing biz op buyers:
    a. What did/do you dislike about the parent company?
    b. In what ways, if any, were you disappointed by the company?
    c. Did the parent company support and assist you as they said they would?
    d. Did you receive the training you were promised?
    e. Did the parent company give you any assistance in marketing?
    f. Did the business perform as you were told it would?
    g. Do you regret buying this business?
11. Will the parent company supply you with references?
12. Can you freely check the company's references?
13. Will the parent company provide you with a business plan?
14. Check your own feelings and impressions:
    a. Do you feel that you're being dealt with honestly?
    b. Are statements made by the company consistent?
    c. How do you feel about the business in general?
    d. Do you like the parent company?
    e. Are you scared?
    f. Are you excited?
    g. Are you raring to go?
    h. Do you have a sense of trepidation?
    i. Do you feel confident?
    j. What are your reservations?

Be as honest as possible with yourself when answering the above questions. Often we ignore our feelings, or dismiss them as irrelevant. This is generally a big mistake. Our feelings almost always give us clues to the fundamental nature of the things that concern us.

PART 4: WHY YOU FEEL THE WAY YOU DO

As you assess your feelings about the company you are considering, it's important to determine why you are feeling the way you do. Don't just take your feelings at their surface value. What desires of your own could be coloring the way you feel? What nonverbal signals could you be picking up from the vendor that are causing you to feel the way you do. For example,

- If you are not feeling confident, figure out why.
  Are you unsure of your own abilities?
  Are you threatened by the unknown?
  Is the business opportunity itself or its Core Function somehow dampening your confidence?
- Examine your positive feelings, too:
  If you're raring to go, look into why you're so raring to go.
  Do the biz op company, its products, and Core Function excite you?
  Are you more motivated by leaving your current situation behind than by what lies ahead?
  Does it all sound too good to be true? If so, it probably is.

Again, we can't express the importance of your feelings enough. Long and careful thought and consideration will lead to some very fruitful insights.

TEST III: THE BIZ OP MARKET CHECK
DISCOVERING IF THE BUSINESS WILL BE
VIABLE FOR YOU

If the biz op you're considering checks out in terms of fitness and honesty that's great, but there still is one more important area you must research before making a decision to buy: the market. The market is the people who want and need your proposed business's product or service. Even if the company you wish to buy is reputable and ideally matched to your strengths, skills, and interest and it has been offering the most comprehensive training and support for over 100 years—if there aren't people whom *you can reach* who need or want the product or service, your chances for turning this opportunity into a successful home business aren't good.

So, who is your market for the business you're considering? That is, who knows they need what you'll be offering and who will be willing and able to pay for it? How much do they need it? How eager will they be to buy it? The better you can answer such questions, the greater your success in this business will be. Doing the following market check before you invest in a biz op will help you answer four key questions: Is there a market? Is it saturated yet? Can you reach and tap into the market? How do you know if you have a viable market?

PART 1: IS THERE A MARKET FOR YOUR INTENDED BUSINESS?

1. Do you use or buy the product or service you will be selling?
2. Do you know other people who do? How many?
3. Do people you know express a desire for the product or service?
4. How do you see people using the product or service?
5. What kind of people do you see using it?
6. Is there a market in your community or proposed territory?
7. Is there a market in outlying or other areas?

To help you find some answers, you will need to do some investigation. There are two ways to gather the information you need: (1) You can communicate directly with potential customers and those already in the business you are considering; or (2) you can check the market by reading statistics and other published figures, looking at census results, and going to the library to look up any published market research for your area of business. We suggest doing both.

Discovering whether there is a market for your business also depends on you. How well positioned or experienced are you to reach your potential market? Will your aptitudes, talents, skills, personality, and current contacts (friends, clubs and organizations, current business contacts) help you find customers? How familiar are you with the market you propose to enter? Here are a few questions to help you find out how easy or difficult finding a market for a particular business will be for *you*:

1. Do you know people right now who need or want the products or services your business will offer?
2. Do you know anyone who is currently offering the same or similar products or services? How busy are they? Might they need someone to take their overload?
3. Do you yourself need or want the product?
4. Is the product or service something you can believe in or get excited about?

PART 2: IS THE MARKET SATURATED?

Market saturation is a term that's used to describe how much competition there is for any product or service you will be offering. If there are already a lot of people providing the same or similar products or services to your market, unless there is an even larger need for these things, your market may be saturated. While many franchise agreements give you a territory protected from competition with other franchisees, that is usually not the case with business opportunities.

Oversaturation can be a real issue in biz ops because when a biz op becomes popular, lots of people rush out and buy it. If there are too many companies selling a particular kind of business, not everyone who buys one will be able to earn a good income from it. In fact, what too often happens in such situations is that everyone starts cutting prices to "heat up" the competition and ultimately no one can earn a good living.

In fact, some business opportunity vendors will sell scores of the same business opportunity in a seminar setting all on the same day. While in some cases there may be plenty of opportunity for multiple new businesses in an area, in many cases there simply is not enough need for everyone who's bought an opportunity to actually be able to make money at it. In such cases, doing business becomes more like playing a game of musical chairs or engaging in a battle for the survival of the fittest. If you're up for that kind of competition, more power to you, but at least you should know beforehand what you are up against. You should know whether you'll have to be battling it out or simply stepping in to develop or fill an existing need. Of course, many businesses in a box sold at seminars are more box than business, and that discourages many people from ever pursuing the opportunity they have purchased.

To find out if your proposed market is already saturated, or is becoming saturated, answer the following:

1. How many people do you know personally who are already offering the same services as you will be?
2. Call ten friends or associates and ask them if they know anybody who is providing the products or services you intend to sell.
3. Look through your local newspaper thoroughly for ads either selling products or services similar to the ones you will be offering, or ads offering "jobs" at companies selling similar services. Also, look for ads placed by people trying to dispose of or unload a biz op they've bought
4. Look through your local Yellow Pages to see how many businesses similar to yours are already in operation.
5. Check with your local Chamber of Commerce and ask for a complete member listing. Look for businesses similar to yours.

PART 3: CAN YOU TAP THIS MARKET?

If it seems that, indeed, there is a need for what you'll be offering, it's time to investigate further. It's time to ascertain how well you're positioned to tap into whatever need there is for what you'll be offering and how you can best go about reaching those who need you. Here are the questions you need to answer:

- Do you feel comfortable asking friends, family, and associates to buy from you or work for you?
- Do you belong to any business, civic, or other organizations whose members might want your products or services?
- Do you have any direct experience with the products or services provided by the biz op you are considering?
- Do you have any direct experience with the industry from which the products or services originate in the biz op you are considering?
- Do you have any hobbies or interests that can lead to desirable contacts for your proposed biz op in terms of sales?
- Do you have any current business contacts that might lead to business or expand your industry knowledge?
- Are there any professional organizations in your area that cater to the market your business will serve?
- Are there local or regional trade publications that cover your proposed business area or appeal to your prospective customer base?
- If your business will be based on providing services to other businesses, how many of those businesses are listed in your local phone book or are members of a national trade association?
- Does your prospective business cater to men more than women, or vice versa?
- Does your prospective business cater to particular age groups that you can relate to?
- Who is your target customer?

Again, the more specifically you can answer that last question, the more information you will be able to gather regarding how many prospective customers you have (the size of your market), what their likes and dislikes are (the psychographic profile), and their age, sex, income level, etc. (demographics). If there are enough people in your market who fit the psychographic and demographic profiles of your target customers, you have a viable market.

PART 4: HOW DO YOU KNOW IF YOU HAVE A VIABLE MARKET?

What happens when you do all the research outlined in the Market Check and you have doubts about whether you have a viable market for the biz op you're considering? A viable market is one that has enough potential customers or clients whom you can reach without undo cost to sustain your business at a level that will enable you to achieve your income and lifestyle goals. But what, exactly, is "not enough" potential? That's a slippery question. To find a solid answer, you have to do a little digging.

1. First, you need to determine the pricing for the product or service you propose to offer. In biz ops, the seller may suggest the pricing of the product or service. Some biz op sellers do not provide you with much guidance, and some cannot due to the variances in regional markets and local economies. If it's up to you to do it, finding the right price is key to getting what you want from your biz op. If what you charge doesn't allow you to earn the income you need or want, it won't matter how good your market is, how good your product or service is, or how well you market your business. On the other hand, your prices by themselves will not enable you to succeed.

   If the biz op involves selling products, your price will need to cover the cost of:

   - The product itself, including all materials used
   - The labor needed to make the product whether it's yours or someone you pay
   - Your overhead, which includes your cost of being in business as well as the cost of doing business

   To these basic costs you then add a profit or a "markup." Thus if you calculate that a product costs you $10 and you add $5 to the cost for a price of $15, you have marked it up 50 percent; if you add $10, you have marked your costs up 100 percent for a price of $20. How much your markup can be varies with the kind of product you offer and your market; that is, "how much the market will bear."

   For biz ops that involve selling services, your price needs to cover:

   - Your labor or time
   - Overhead
   - Direct costs you incur related to delivering the service

   As with products, you then add on your profit, which is money you can use to repay your investment, grow your business, and reward yourself for taking the initiative and risk of being in business.

2. After you've determined your pricing, do some math. How much is enough to both cover your costs and meet your income goals for either supplementing your income or serving as your full-time livelihood? For example, let's say you want to make $3,500. How many sales or customers do you need in a month to earn $3,500? How many hours do you need to bill? Are there enough potential customers in your proposed market and hours in the day to generate that many sales each month?

If you determine there is no real market for the biz op in your area, you need to look for another kind of business or develop something outside your immediate territory, if that's feasible. Don't let the biz op seller pressure you into buying a business package based on an appeal to your emotions. Numbers don't lie.

We again recommend you consult the detailed resources we've listed that deal with these issues in depth. This overview is given only as a way to get you to start thinking about what you will need to do to complete your market test and know what it will take to actually succeed in a particular biz op.

ONE FINAL CHECK

Even if a business opportunity package passes all your tests for fitness, honesty, and marketability, before you decide to buy, ask yourself if, indeed, this is a business you would choose to start, or would you really rather be doing something else but find the pressures in your life right now make buying a biz op seem like some kind of magic bullet to get you out of a tough situation? Rarely will a biz op be a knight in shining armor that will rescue us from life's travails. Usually, like most any business, it will present a whole new batch of travails, but if it's something we really want to do for its own sake, the travails will be interesting challenges we'll want to meet.

Architect Don Carter had been doing well in his business until he ran headlong into the fallout of the early 1990 recession. He found getting the traditional business of an architectural firm was growing more and more difficult by the day. Then, also partly as a result of the recession, his wife, Sue Carol, lost her bid for tenure in her university position and found herself without a job. Feeling the pressure of a dramatic drop in income, Don and Sue Carol went to a business opportunity expo. Don was attracted by a business opportunity for a sign-making business.

Sign making sounded like a excellent business idea for Don. "I can do that!" Don thought. So he requested more information and was seriously considering dropping his practice of architecture to buy the biz op. But he just wasn't sure, so he arranged a consultation with us. We helped him sort out his motivation for wanting to forsake his profession for a new and seemingly exciting business. After considerable evaluation, he realized that marketing a sign-making business would also be a considerable challenge, especially since there already was a lot of competition in the area. He decided that if he was going to have to work his tail to the bone starting a new business in a new field, he might as well work his tail to the bone redefining and marketing himself in his lifelong career, which he truly loved and where he already had a track record and a good reputation to build upon.

He shifted his architectural services designing new commercial and residential construction to helping people transform their existing homes into their dream homes. He found this to be a more creative, marketable, and enjoyable approach for his career. He was able to turn his business around and was thankful that he'd decided against buying into a sign-making business as an escape from the pressures he'd felt at a difficult time in his life.

Lucy Scribner of Salt Lake City, Utah, had an entirely different experience. Having been a teacher, Lucy was looking for a way to make money at home where she could spend more time with her family. While attending a home-business sales seminar she learned about a math tutoring program with which she could help students with math problems improve their skills. This seemed like a perfect match for Lucy. It drew upon her teaching skills, allowed her to work from home, and had good income potential. So she decided to buy the biz op and began handing out flyers in her community about her tutoring program. Within eight weeks she had forty-two students and soon she was generating $2,600 per month while working fewer than twenty hours a week.

Lucy feels quite lucky to have happened upon this biz op. She has gone on to write a book about math tutoring to help others become tutors and turn her newfound passion for helping people with math phobias and anxieties into a full-time income.

7

Important Considerations Before You Buy Any Home-Based Business

As YOU'VE NOW SEEN, franchising, multilevel marketing, and business opportunities are three different kinds of home businesses you can buy. They each have different ways of operating, different rules regulating them, and different kinds of personalities, talents, and skills required to run them successfully. Since we've focused a great deal on their differences, in this chapter, we're going to start off by focusing on what these three types of home businesses have in common.

The commonalties among them are not written into any law or set down in any particular business plan. Instead, the commonalties lie in people's experiences working with these businesses. Almost every person we talked to in researching this book—franchisors, franchisees, MLM uplines or downlines, biz op sellers and buyers—has shared many of the same kind of experiences and given much the same advice to people who are considering the purchase of a home business. Three general areas of commonality began to emerge: What You Can and Can't Expect, Getting the Right Help, and Preparing to Work from Home.

The following considerations are the result of hard-won experiences individuals have had in making their businesses a success, as well as advice from franchisors, MLM distributors, and biz op sellers who provide high-quality, honest business opportunities. No matter which kind of home business you might be attracted to buy, or the nature of the product or service you may wish to provide, the following are important considerations that should be thought through carefully before you make your decision to buy a business. They include guidelines for shopping at a business opportunity expo and one final test we recommend you take before you buy.

WHAT TO EXPECT

Going into business with false or unrealistic expectations is a sure route to frustration and/or failure. Many franchisors and biz op sellers will conduct extensive interviews, of even potential buyers, to ensure that those who buy from them are well-informed and have realistic expectations. The following is a summation of the most important facts they tell us you should be aware of before buying a home business of any kind:

- *There is no such thing as a business that runs itself.* Starting and successfully operating a business, any business, takes a great deal of time, energy, and hard work. If you are considering a business that claims the contrary, the seller is probably manipulating you. This is the first point that nearly everybody we spoke to brought up. It also comes up again and again in the case studies from the previous chapters. When you buy a business, be prepared to work hard for little return in the beginning. Things will probably get easier as time goes on, but the first year is usually the most challenging. Over 90 percent of businesses that fail do so in the first year.
- *If you are looking to buy a job, not a business, you will most likely be disappointed.* If you are buying a business with the expectation that you will be engaged in one kind of activity, such as repairing computers or performing environmental testing, you are setting yourself up for a bad experience. You don't need to pay money to get that. Owning a business means running a business. It means wearing a great many hats: sales, marketing, customer service, accounting, financial planning, legal, and if you're successful, hiring and personnel management. You are also responsible for building the business and increasing its value. If you don't want to be bothered with all this stuff, you will be much happier finding a job, not buying a business.
- *Building a profitable business takes time.* Patience is one of the keys to success in starting any business you buy. If a business claims that you will be making a lot of money in a short amount of time, the

claim is most probably false. When you buy a business, your first goal should be to simply break even; that is, have enough income to cover your expenses. Generating enough business to break even usually takes six months to a year. Businesses that make it through their first year usually see a small profit in their second, with returns gradually increasing on a yearly basis. Don't expect too much at first. It will be far more rewarding if you set small, attainable financial goals and make sure to congratulate yourself when you do attain them. Your franchisor, upline, or biz op seller should be helpful in telling you what you can realistically expect to make at each point in your business's development.

If anyone tries to sell you a chance to make money fast in your own business, consider these facts and figures:

- The New England Business Service found it took a considerable amount of time before small business owners could rely on their company as their primary source of income:
    54 percent—within three years
    77 percent—within three to ten years
    90 percent—more than ten years.
- An *Income Opportunity* magazine survey found:
    1. 21% were profitable almost immediately after launch.
    2. 22% started drawing a salary immediately.
    3. 34% were not yet showing a profit after being in business for two years or more.
    4. 40% had yet to draw a salary after two years.
    5. 58% of self-employed individuals were still uncomfortable taking a vacation even though they had been in business for two or more years.
    6. 77% do not have any other employees after two years.

- *Building a profitable business takes consistency.* Consistency, more than talent, aptitude, or intelligence, is what will lead you to success. Offering consistently good-quality work or high-quality products, providing consistently reliable service and doing what you say you will, every time, and marketing consistently are what will motivate customers to return to you and refer your business to their friends, families, and associates. Given a choice between reliability or cutting-edge product or talent, customers choose reliability nine times out of ten. Consistency also means keeping your doors open (so to speak) during whatever adversity you or your business may be going through. You can't collect the trophy if you quit before the game is over.

GETTING THE RIGHT HELP

In business, you can't go it alone. The following strategies are used by home-business owners, as well as recommended by those selling home-business opportunities.

- Make sure you have enough capital resources not only to buy the business but also to purchase all the equipment you need and to retain, as needed, professional help.
- If you are purchasing a full-time business, *make sure you also have enough to cover your living expenses for at least six months.*
- Unless you are trained in up-to-date accounting procedures, find a good accountant experienced in taxes for small businesses. You will most likely not hire this person but just retain his or her services as needed. Having an accountant available to advise you on tax matters, income management, and general business accounting principles will make managing financial decisions easier. Have your accountant help you develop an accounting system you can manage yourself, preferably a computer-based system. An accountant will help save you money and hassles at tax time, and he or she can even help you through an audit should you face one.
- If you find that the training, business planning, methodology, or support that's available through the company you purchased the business from isn't meeting your needs, don't hesitate to contact an experienced business consultant, especially at the beginning. A business consultant can help you develop a business and marketing plan more tailored to your situation and ease you through rough spots that a selling company doesn't have the time, expertise, or willingness to deal with.
- Obtain the proper legal help. As we mentioned earlier, it's a good idea to have an experienced attorney familiar with the law governing the type of business you are buying (franchise, MLM, or biz op) look over any contracts and agreements you are asked to sign. If you have a good rapport with the attorney, maintain an ongoing relationship with him or her so you will have a legal resource who's familiar with you and your business whenever you ever need it.
- Make allies of your competition. Your competition is a great resource for knowledge about what's happening in your industry and

the trends and movements in your market. With the right approach, you and your competitors can become mutual consultants saving each other countless hours of research and outside consultation. Surprisingly, your competition might also become one your best sources of business, especially when you're starting out. So call them, introduce yourself and, if you perceive the opportunity, ask them if they have any overload you can help out with. Offer to do the same for them when you get busy.

- Get involved. Identify and join one to three organizations. Possibilities include your local chamber of commerce, home business association, a trade or industry association relevant to your business, and formal networking groups. Consider volunteering to serve your community by becoming active in local civic or charitable associations and organizations. Businesspeople, civic leaders, and the community in general will get to know you as a person and business owner, and of course, you will get to know them. This is also a wonderful way to give something back to the society you live in.

- Develop a network of vendors, consultants, and service providers. No matter what kind of business you may purchase, you will need supplies and services to keep it going. Take the time to talk to vendors and service providers. Get to know them. These people can become an invaluable resource for industry and business knowledge, advice, and even business for you.

- Familiarize yourself with your local library and bookstore. There are countless excellent books, videotapes, audio programs, pamphlets, brochures, etc., available on subjects related to business and, quite likely, your business. Go to your local computer and software stores. You can find computer programs that will help you do your accounting; design and produce brochures, flyers, and other marketing materials; manage inventory; track sales leads; manage mailing lists; even write business and marketing plans. Information is power, and it's yours for the asking.

- Get on line. The Internet and on-line services are the single fastest-growing communications medium of the last fifty years. To stay competitive, it is becoming essential that a business utilize it. The great thing about the Internet for a home business is that it levels the playing field. On the Net, small home businesses have access to the same resources and exposure as the big ones. Much of the content on line is business related, and most of this information is free.

PREPARE FOR WORKING FROM HOME

In order to succeed in running a business from your home you have to be prepared, both mentally and physically. Giving attention and care to preparing yourself and your home to accommodate your new business will pay off manyfold. Here are some basic tips to get you started:

- First, select a dedicated space in your home where the business will be located. A separate room such as a spare bedroom, recreation room, or den is best. Many people have also made wonderful office spaces for themselves by modifying basements, attics, and garages. If you cannot devote a separate room to your new enterprise, make sure that the space you do choose is separate in some way from the rest of your home. Use partitions, bookcases, filing cabinets, or other barriers to create this separation. Your office is a place of business. By physically separating it from the normal activities of home life you will have a greater chance of staying focused and reducing distractions. And you'll be more likely to qualify for claiming your home-office tax deduction.
- Buy the proper equipment and furniture. In addition to industry-specific equipment, such as specialized machines and products (often supplied by the parent company), you will need general office equipment, furniture, and supplies. Requirements differ from business to business and office to office, but the minimum home-office requirements include a business-quality computer, a laser or ink-jet printer, a comfortable ergonomic chair, a dedicated business phone, fax machine, filing cabinet(s), and shelving. We recommend having a separate phone line installed for your business telephone and a separate line for your fax machine. See our book *Working from Home* for in-depth information and advice on how to cost-effectively set up and equip your home office.
- Reduce distractions. Though the distractions at home are almost always fewer than at an office, you are still subject to interruptions. After a few weeks of working from your domicile, you might seek out distractions. The best way to keep out the nonbusiness world is to have a door you can close between your home and office. If a separate room isn't feasible, use partitions, etc., as we mentioned above. Use thick-pile carpet and heavy window treatments to reduce noise.
- Discuss your plans for running a business from home with your spouse, children, or roommates. If your mate has an outside job, there won't be much of an issue except perhaps your long hours and your messing up the house more than normally. If your spouse stays

home some or all of the time, however, make sure that he or she understands that even though you're working at home, you're still working. Ask her or him not to disturb you unless it's absolutely necessary. The same goes for roommates and children.

Often it's difficult for children to understand the idea of a new home office. It's very tempting to interrupt Mom or Dad at work when they're right down the hall. So be clear with your children that when you start working from home there will be times when you are not to be disturbed. Set up rules such as always knocking on the door before coming in, not answering your office phone, and not playing in the office—whether you're there or not. And the more you discuss these issues with everyone involved *before* you start working from home, the easier the transition will be for everyone when work begins. Of course, for young children under school age, you will probably need to arrange for some child care either with other family members, friends, or outside help.

USE THIS BOOK AS A TOOL AT HOME-BIZ EXPOS

A quick way to dive right into the world of home-based franchising, MLM, and biz ops is by attending one of the many expos, or trade shows, held with frequency all over the country. You've most likely seen or responded to advertisements on television or in your newspaper for some self-employment expos or trade shows featuring businesses you can buy. Attending such trade shows can be educational, interesting, fun, and a little overwhelming.

Such shows have their own unique atmosphere and feel, even their own language. An average show will take place on a weekend, feature approximately 75 to 100 exhibitors, and reach attendance levels of anywhere from 3,000 to 10,000 people for both days. You can find out a lot at these shows. You might even find the right opportunity to buy, but we advise you to exercise caution before making any kind of decision at a show. In fact, never make a final decision at a show. As you will see, in most states it is actually illegal for a seller to receive any payment at a show or sign you to a binding contract. Use these shows instead as an opportunity to research, gather information, open doors, network, and maybe set the ball rolling for considering the purchase of a business you can run from your home.

When a franchisor, MLM company, or biz op seller registers to exhibit at a trade show, the promoter of the show will ask them to sign a contract or agreement that stipulates that they, the exhibitor, are registered in that state and have met all the requirements that qualify them for the registration. Even though the contract legally binds the exhibitor to be honest, sometimes they are not. Show promoters usually do not double-check to see if the exhibitor is actually in compliance. According to Paul Erhlich of Blenheim Expos, one of the nation's largest organizers and promoters of business expos, "We try hard to impress on our exhibitors the legality of what they're committing to, and almost all of them are honest in doing so. We do, however, see some exceptions, and people need to be aware of that. We run sixty to eighty shows a year across the country. We just don't have the time to check up on every exhibitor to make sure they're telling the truth on their registration forms."

In addition to the occasional outright scammers who exhibit at these shows, some opportunity sellers will use the hubbub of the convention floor to disorient you a bit and pressure you into signing an agreement or collecting some sort of deposit. To protect yourself from being taken advantage of, we recommend that you follow the points on the checklist below. Take this book and the following Business Expo and Trade Show Protection Checklist along with you when you go!

BUSINESS EXPO AND TRADE SHOW PROTECTION CHECKLIST

_____ 1. Is the franchise vendor registered with the state attorney general's office? If the seller of a franchise must register with the attorney general of the state in which he or she is selling the business, ask them if they're properly registered and ask to see proof.

_____ 2. Is the seller offering a "special show price"? *Be skeptical of "show specials." Never give anyone a deposit or payment in full at a trade show. "Show specials" that offer a reduced price if you buy right then and there are usually tricks to get you to commit without properly considering and researching the business.*

_____ 3. Have you been given a disclosure document and is the company giving you a consideration period to think over your decision to buy before taking your money? If you're meeting the seller for the first time at a trade show, they should provide you with disclosure documents and grant you a period of time to think over your decision.

If you live in one of the states listed at the end of this chapter, there are special laws that clearly spell out how long you have to consider your decision to buy before a biz op seller covered by the law is entitled to receive any sort of payment from you. This consideration period begins upon your receipt of the required disclosure documents. These laws apply to any business offered for sale in the state you live in, *even if the seller is headquartered in another state.*

We have provided an overview of the key elements in each state's biz op, or SAMP, laws at the end of this chapter. These laws are for your protection. Make sure any opportunities you consider are in compliance with them.

If your state does not regulate the sale of business opportunities, you can, and should, ask for these same conditions yourself. While sellers won't *have* to provide them in your state, we don't recommend buying from a company that won't.

_____ 4. Has the franchisor provided you with a UFOC (Uniform Franchise Offering Circular)? It's required by the FTC.

_____ 5. Is the company offering proof for any claims they're making? The FTC requires that any income claim be substantiated. Ask for proof!

_____ 6. Do you know your state's laws governing biz ops? Make sure businesses you consider are in compliance. For the appropriate state agency to check with in your state, see Appendix 5 of this book.

_____ 7. Do you know your state's laws governing franchises? Make sure a business you're considering is in compliance. For specific state agencies that regulate franchising, see Appendix 2 of this book.

_____ 8. Is the biz op seller actually involved in the business or is he or she just selling? Sometimes biz op sellers will hire people just to sell for them at trade shows. These salespeople are generally not expert, or even trained in the business they represent, and can not give you the firsthand information you need to make a good decision.

_____ 9. Have you allotted enough time to attend the show? Dedicate at least four hours, if not the entire day, to attending the show. If you feel rushed, you won't have the mental breathing room to ask the right questions and carefully consider the information you're given.

_____ 10. Do you feel rushed or pressured? Don't let anyone pressure or rush you. Shows can be rather hectic, and sellers want to speak with as many people as they can. If at any time you feel you're being rushed or pressured, ask if you can make an appointment to either meet at a later date, or set up a time when you can speak over the phone.

_____ 11. Does the business pass the tests for Fitness, Honesty, and Marketability? Take this book with you to the show and use the Fitness and Honesty checks as a basis for asking questions and requesting information from the seller. If you present yourself as knowledgeable, well researched, and prepared, your negotiations with any seller of an opportunity will start off on a much stronger footing.

THE "WHAT'S WRONG WITH THIS PICTURE?" TEST: ONE FINAL CHECK

Now let's suppose you're at the point where everything looks good for proceeding to buy a particular home business. You've researched the company and it checks out in terms of Fitness, Honesty, and the Market. You've educated yourself about the business and you've prepared your home with a functional office. There is still one more test we suggest taking. We call it the "What's Wrong with This Picture?" check. Or it could also be called the "What's Right with This Picture?" test.

At this point you will have gathered a great body of information regarding the business itself, the kinds of activities you will be performing in running it, and what to realistically expect in terms of income. Now it's time to put everything together into a detailed mental picture. We encourage you to visualize yourself at home, running this business, in as much detail as possible. The more thoroughly creative you can be in constructing this vivid mental picture, the more helpful it will be.

In your visualization, picture yourself performing the activities required to run the business. Picture yourself on the phone talking to a prospective customer, attempting to close a sale. Picture yourself doing the actual work of the business—dying a carpet, selling ads for a newsletter, inspecting a home for environmental hazards, demonstrating products at a party, doing the monthly billing for a busy medical practice. Do you like what you see? Do you like the way you feel? Can you really imagine yourself doing those things?

Imagine yourself working from your home—those same four walls staring at you every day. You're all by yourself. The television and refrigerator are tempting you to distraction. Imagine the long hours and hard work required for success. It's 8:00 P.M., and you're still at work. Your family is down the hall having fun without you. How do you feel about that?

Picture yourself dealing with the franchisor, upline, or biz op seller. You have a problem, and you're asking for their help. Based on their reactions so far to concerns and doubts you've expressed, how do you imagine them responding? Can you see yourself working intimately for a long period of time with the individual(s) involved? Or do you imagine them driving you nuts?

As we said, the more detail you can call up in your visualizations, the more useful information you will receive. If, in your honest estimation, you can't picture yourself performing the activities involved in running the business, and enjoying it, you should keep looking for an opportunity that's a better fit for you.

Visualizations such as this are surprisingly accurate in terms of predicting your actual responses to actual situations. If something doesn't feel right when you actively and realistically imagine it, it probably won't feel right when you actually do it. Scientists such as Sir Isaac Newton and Albert Einstein have long understood the power and efficacy of what science calls "thought experiments," or creative realizations. The theory of relativity itself was proven through a series of such thought experiments.

Take heed of the responses your thought experiments elicit in you. As long as you have gathered accurate information and aren't just relying on wishful thinking, the reactions and emotions you have when visualizing running a prospective business will generally be an accurate reflection of what you will feel and experience when you really do run it. So focus your visualization on what you'll be doing to make money in the business, not on the things you'll do with the money you make. If you're unhappy or dissatisfied in any way with your visualization, you won't be happy with the business. In other words, if you can't picture yourself doing the work, then you probably shouldn't. And best of all, a thought experiment is a lot less expensive in terms of both time and money than buying a business, running it, and then discovering it's not really for you. That's finding out too late.

On a more positive note, your visualizations may show that you will enjoy performing the activities involved in the business and working with the franchisor, upline, or biz op seller. And if your thorough experiments also reveal that you can work from home comfortably and productively, you will have even more proof that the home business you are considering buying is right for you.

In the chapters that follow, you will find a listing of many home-based franchises, multilevel marketing companies, and business opportunities to consider. They are but a few of many possibilities for buying a packaged home-based business. We are not recommending these companies, only providing a directory of opportunities for you to begin exploring.

Even if you don't find a match immediately, each business you explore will bring you closer and closer to knowing what you want and what you will be best suited to pursue. You could find, after exploring many opportunities, that you have an idea of your own you prefer to pursue instead of buying a business. Either way, we wish you the best for thoroughly enjoying the adventure of finding the right business, launching it, and operating it successfully.

Summary of Disclosure of Biz Op Requirements by State

At the time of this book's writing, these are the states that have business opportunity laws on the books, and the following is a summary of what each state's laws cover. State legislatures meet regularly and redefine, refine, and change laws frequently, so call your state's attorney general's office for the most up-to-date information.

Alabama

There is a law on the books called the Unlawful Trade Practices Act that concerns and regulates deceptive practices in connection with the sale of a Seller Assisted Marketing Plan. A Seller Assisted Marketing Plan is any biz op that costs $500 or more.

California

Disclosure documents are required to be given any buyer of a biz op when the initial sum exceeds $500 but is less than $50,000. Disclosure is required to be given forty-eight hours prior to the signing of the agreement or the acceptance of any money, including deposits. Deposits cannot be more than 20 percent unless the money is put in escrow. The terms *buy back* or *secured investment* are not allowed either orally or in writing.

Connecticut

Disclosure is required to be given ten days before the receipt of any money by the seller.

Florida

Disclosure documents are required to be given to the buyer three days before receipt of any money when the initial sum exceeds $500.

Georgia

Disclosure must be given forty-eight hours prior to the receipt of any money by the seller. Deposits are limited to no more than 15 percent of the sale price of the business.

Illinois

Disclosure must be given ten days prior to the signing of an agreement or acceptance of money.

Indiana

Disclosure documents are required to be given to the buyer when the initial sum exceeds $500 but is less than $50,000. Disclosure is required to be given three days prior to receipt of money by the seller. There is a thirty-day cancellation rule. No more than 20 percent of the business's sale price can be taken as a deposit.

Iowa

Disclosure documents are required to be given to the buyer when the initial sum paid for the business exceeds $500. Disclosure is required to be given ten days prior to receipt of money by the seller. There is a three-day cancellation rule.

Kentucky

Disclosure documents are required to be given to the buyer when the initial sum paid for the biz op exceeds $500. There is a thirty-day cancellation rule.

Louisiana

Disclosure documents are required to be given to the buyer when the initial sum paid for the business exceeds $300.

Maine

Disclosure documents are required to be given to the buyer when the initial sum paid for the business exceeds $250. Disclosure is required seventy-two hours prior to receipt of any money by the seller. There is a three-day cancellation rule.

Maryland

Disclosure documents are required to be given to the buyer when the initial sum exceeds $200. Disclosure is required ten days prior to receipt of money by the seller.

Michigan

Disclosure documents are required to be given to the buyer when the initial sum paid for the business exceeds $500.

Minnesota

Disclosures are required ten days prior to receipt of money by the seller for a business opportunity of any amount.

Nebraska

Disclosure documents are required to be given to the buyer when the initial sum exceeds $500. Disclosure is required forty-eight hours prior to the receipt of any money by the seller.

New Hampshire

Disclosure is required seven days prior to the receipt of any money by the seller.

North Carolina

Disclosure is required forty-eight hours prior to receipt of any money by the seller.

Ohio

Disclosure documents are required to be given to the buyer when the initial sum exceeds $100 but is less than $50,000. Disclosure is required ten days prior to receipt of any money by the seller. There is a five-day cancellation rule.

Oklahoma

Disclosure documents are required to be given to the buyer when the initial sum exceeds $250. Disclosure is required ten days prior to receipt of any money by the seller.

Rhode Island

Disclosure documents are required to be given to the buyer when the initial sum exceeds $100. Disclosure is required three days prior to receipt of any money by the seller. This applies only when the operation of the business will be associated with the distributor's trademark, service mark, logo type, etc.; for example, XYZ Medical Billing, a licensee of ACME Electronic Claims Corporation.

South Carolina

Disclosure documents are required to be given to the buyer when the initial sum exceeds $250. Disclosure is required ten days prior to the receipt of any money by the seller.

South Dakota

Disclosure documents are required to be given to the buyer when the initial sum exceeds $250. Disclosure is required ten days prior to receipt of any money by the seller.

Texas

Disclosure documents are required to be given to the buyer when the initial sum exceeds $500. Disclosure is required ten days prior to receipt of any money by the seller.

Utah

Disclosure documents are required to be given to the buyer when the initial sum exceeds $300. Disclosure is required ten days prior to the receipt of any money by the seller.

Virginia

Disclosure documents are required to be given to the buyer when the initial sum exceeds $500. Disclosure is required forty-eight hours prior to the receipt of any money by the seller.

Washington

Disclosure documents are required to be given to the buyer when the initial sum exceeds $300. Disclosure is required forty-eight hours prior to receipt of any money by the seller. There is a seven-day cancellation rule.

Key Provisions for States with Business Opportunity or Seller-Assisted Marketing Plan Laws

	Registration Required	Disclosure to Buyer Required	Limit on Initial Fee or Deposit	Detailed Company Information Needed for Registration and/or Disclosure
Alabama	No	No	No	No
California	Fees over $500	Yes	Yes-20%	Yes
Connecticut	Yes	Yes	No	Yes
Florida	Fees over $500	Yes	No	No
Georgia	No	Yes	Yes-15%	No
Illinois	Fees over $500	Yes	No	Yes
Indiana	Fees over $500	Yes	Yes-20%	Yes
Iowa	Fees over $500	Yes	No	Yes
Kentucky	Fees over $500	Yes	Yes-20%	Yes
Louisiana	No	Yes if over $300	No	No
Maine	Fees over $250	Yes	No	Yes
Maryland	Fees over $200	Yes	No	No
Michigan	Fees over $500	Yes	No	No
Nebraska	Fees over $500	Yes	No	Yes
New Hampshire	Some exemptions	Yes	No	Yes
North Carolina	Yes	Yes	No	No
Ohio	Fees over $100	Yes	Yes-20%	Yes
Oklahoma	Fees over $250	Yes	No	Yes
South Carolina	Fees over $250	Yes	No	Yes
South Dakota	Fees over $250	Yes	No	Yes
Texas	Fees over $500	Yes	No	No
Utah	Fees over $300	Yes	No	Yes
Virginia	Fees over $500	Yes	No	No
Washington	Fees over $300	Yes	No	Yes

8

Home-Based Franchises
You Can Buy

THE FOLLOWING CHAPTER is a list of franchises you can buy and run from your home. We have tried to present you with a wide range of franchises that encompass many different services and business types.

> Please note: We do not endorse these franchises over other franchise opportunities that are not listed here. Their appearance in this book does not mean or imply a recommendation of any sort. We heartily suggest that you apply all the research principles, questions, and techniques we outlined in the Franchising Fitness and Honesty checks in Chapter 2 to any franchisor from this list you contact just as you should with any other franchise.

FRANCHISE CORE FUNCTIONS

Each listing includes basic information about the franchise, as well as a code indicating its Core Function. The Core Function has been determined based on *our* knowledge of the franchise. The franchisors themselves did not specify their Core Function. We have endeavored to compile a listing of home-based franchises that represent a large range of Core Functions for you to choose from. The Core Functions we've chosen are based on the six functions identified earlier as part of the Franchising Fitness Check. The key for the Core Functions code is:

(1) ***Leading*** = marketing/selling/promoting/managing/motivating
(2) ***Improving*** = helping/teaching/counseling/assisting clients and customers
(3) ***Organizing*** = bookkeeping/calculating/paperwork/processing information
(4) ***Creating*** = innovating/designing/composing/imagining
(5) ***Building*** = assembling/handling/constructing/maintaining
(6) ***Problem Solving*** = planning/researching/analyzing

Although a business's Core Function might be listed as something other than Leading (1), please keep in mind that the activities contained under the Core Function (1) figure, such as selling, managing, and motivating, are crucial to the success of any franchise, or any business for that matter.

A DIRECTORY OF HOME-BASED FRANCHISES

PLEASE NOTE: As of the writing of this book, all the following information was current and correct. But things in the business world do change quickly. We apologize in advance if any of these listings are no longer current or contain information that is no longer accurate.

Accounting and Financial

ABS SYSTEMS
1260 Palmetto Ave.
Winter Park, FL 32789; (407)644-5400
Complete accounting and tax service
Number of franchise units: 33 in 11 states
Founded: 1990
Franchise fee: $9,500
Capital requirements: $10,600
Core Function: Organizing

COMPREHENSIVE BUSINESS SERVICES
26722 Plaza Dr.
Mission Viejo, CA 92691; (800)323-9000

Accounting and bookkeeping
Number of franchise units: 280 in 37 states
Founded: 1949
Franchise fee: $12,500
Capital requirements: $30,500
Core Function: Organizing

GENERAL BUSINESS SERVICES
1020 N. University Parks Dr.
P.O. Box 3146
Waco, TX 76707; (800)583-6181; (817)745-2544
Small-business consulting, bookkeeping
Number of franchise units: 309 in 50 states
Founded: 1962
Franchise fee: $30,000
Core Function: Organizing
Capital requirement: $7,500+

PADGETT BUSINESS SERVICES
160 Hawthorne Park
Athens, GA 30606; (800)323-7292
Small-business consulting, bookkeeping
Number of franchise units: 357 in 45 states
Founded: 1966
Franchise fee: $34,500
Capital requirements: $40,000–$60,000
Core Function: Organizing

Advertising and Marketing

BENCH AD
4839 E. Greenway Rd., Ste. 339
Scottsdale, AZ 85254; (602)443-9740
Bench advertising (mini-billboards)
Number of franchise units: 100+ in 20 states in 3 countries
Founded: 1976
Franchise fee: $5,000
Capital requirements: $3,000
Core Function: Leading

BUYING & DINING GUIDE
80 Eighth Ave.
New York, NY 10011; (212)243-6800

Free community guide to dining and shopping
Number of franchise units: 3 in 3 states
Founded: 1980
Franchise fee: $29,000 with guarantee
Capital requirements: franchise fee + $2,000 working capital
Core Function: Leading

CONSUMER NETWORK OF AMERICA
15965 Jeanette Dr.
Southfield, MI 48075; (810)557-2784; (810)557-7931 fax
Short-term advertising program for retailers
Number of franchise units: 13
Founded: 1990
Franchise fee: $15,000
Capital requirements: $20,000+
Core Function: Leading

COUPON TABLOID INTERNATIONAL, INC., THE
5575 S.W. Jean Rd., #101
Lake Oswego, OR 97035; (800)888-8575; (503)697-1968
Direct-mail advertising
Number of franchise units: 27 in 5 states
Founded: 1986
Franchise fee: $3,500
Capital requirements: $5,000
Core Function: Leading

COUPON-CASH SAVER
1020 N. Milwaukee Ave., Ste. 240
Deerfield, IL 60015; (847)537-6420
Direct-mail coupon advertising booklet
Number of franchise units: 4 in 2 states
Founded: 1984
Franchise fee: $9,500
Capital requirements: $17,000
Core Function: Leading

EFFECTIVE MAILERS
1151 Allen Dr.
Troy, MI 48083; (810)588-9880; (810)588-4299 fax
Direct-mail business
Number of franchise units: 4 in 3 states

Founded: 1982
Franchise fee: $500 + $18,000
Capital requirements: $25,000 + start-up
Core Function: Leading

GREETINGS, INC.
P.O. Box 25623
Lexington, KY 40524; (606)272-5624
Target-market advertising in the southeastern United States
Number of franchise units: 5 in 3 states
Founded: 1984
Franchise fee: $15,000
Capital requirements: up to $12,000
Core Function: Leading

MONEY MAILER
14271 Corporate Dr.
Garden Grove, CA 92643; (800)897-3131
Cooperative direct-mail advertising
Number of franchise units: 500+ in 35 states and 2 countries
Founded: 1979
Franchise fee: $22,000
Capital requirements: $5,000
Core Function: Leading

PENNYSAVER
80 Eighth Ave.
New York, NY 10011; (212)243-6800
Free shopping guide
Number of franchise units: 10 in 6 states
Founded: 1979
Franchise fee: $29,900 w/guarantee
Capital requirements: franchise fee + $10,000 working capital
Core Function: Leading

RESORT MAPS
Old High School, Rte. 100, P.O. Box 726
Waitsfield, VT 05673; (800)788-5247; (802)496-6277
Ad-supported business and tourist maps
Number of franchise units: 10 in 7 states
Founded: 1986
Franchise fee: $4,950

Capital requirements: $8,550–$13,650 (includes franchise fee)
Core Function: Leading

RESORT PUBLICATIONS
4839 E. Greenway Rd., Ste. 339
Scottsdale, AZ 85254; (602)443-9740
Hotel guest directory advertising
Number of franchise units: 100+ in 30 states and 5 countries
Founded: 1987
Franchise fee: $1,500-$5,000
Capital requirements: $3,000
Core Function: Leading

TV NEWS MAGAZINE
80 Eighth Ave.
New York, NY 10011; (212)243-6800
Free shopping guide
Number of franchise units: 3 in 1 state
Founded: 1973
Franchise fee: $29,900 w/guarantee
Capital requirements: franchise fee + $5,000 working capital
Core Function: Leading

VAL-PAK DIRECT MARKETING SYSTEMS, INC.
8605 Largo Lakes Dr.
Largo, FL 34643; (800)568-4400
Co-op mail franchisor
Number of franchise units: 253 in 50 states and 2 countries
Founded: 1968
Franchise fee: $500
Capital requirements: varies by territory size
Core Function: Leading

WELCOME HOST OF AMERICA, INC.
13953 Perkins Rd.
Baton Rouge, LA 70810-3438; (504)769-3000
Direct-mail welcoming service
Number of franchise units: 7
Founded: 1987
Franchise fee: $6,000–$8,000
Capital requirements: $6,000–$12,000 (includes franchise fee)
Core Function: Leading

Automotive

NOVUS GLASS REPAIR & REPLACEMENT
10425 Hampshire Ave. S.
Minneapolis, MN 55438; (800)328-1117
Repair and replace damaged windshields
Number of franchise units: 500 in 49 states and 52 countries
Founded: 1972
Franchise fee: $15,000
Capital requirements: $12,000–$17,000
Core Function: Building

PLANET EARTH RECYCLING
7928 State Rd.
P.O. Box 65311
Philadelphia, PA 19155; (800)471-4684; (215)333-6830
Mobile antifreeze recycling
Number of franchise units: 1 in 1 state
Founded: 1990
Franchise fee: $10,000
Capital requirements: $60,000–$85,000
Core Function: Building

Books and Publications

BINGO BUGLE
K&O Publishing Inc.
P.O. Box 51189
Seattle, WA 98115; (800)447-1958
Publish monthly newspaper for bingo players
Number of franchise units: 71 in 32 states and 2 countries
Founded: 1982
Franchise fee: $1,500-$10,000
Capital requirements: $5,000
Core Function: Leading

BRIDE'S DAY MAGAZINE
750 Hamburg Turnpike, #208
Pompton Lakes, NJ 07442; (201)835-6551
Community bridal magazine publishing
Number of franchise units: 10 in 9 states
Founded: 1987
Franchise fee: $14,400

Capital requirements: franchise fee + $5,000
Core Function: Organizing

CATHEDRAL DIRECTORIES FRANCHISES, INC.
Computers Composition Corporations
1401 W. Girard Ave.
Madison Heights, MI 48071; (800)544-6903
Publish church and organization directories
Number of franchise units: 6 in 5 states
Founded: 1952
Franchise fee: $14,500
Capital requirements: $25,000–$30,000 (includes franchise fee)
Core Function: Organizing

FINDERBINDER/SOURCEBOOK DIRECTORIES
California Publishers, Inc.
8546 Chevy Chase Dr.
La Mesa, CA 91941; (800)255-2575
Updated news media and association directories.
Number of franchise units: 24 in 12 states
Founded: 1974
Franchise fee: $1,000
Capital requirements: $8,000–$12,000
Core Function: Leading

HOMESTEADER, THE
P.O. Box 2824
Framingham, MA 01703; (800)941-9907
Newspaper for new homeowners
Number of franchise units: 10 in 3 states
Founded: 1990
Franchise fee: $6,000–$7,500
Capital requirements: $9,000–$25,000 (including franchise fee)
Core Function: Organizing

TV FACTS MAGAZINE
TV Facts of North America, Inc.
Liberty Square
Danvers, MA 01923; (508)777-9225
Free weekly TV magazine and shoppers' guide
Number of franchise units: 170 in 14 states
Founded: 1987

Franchise fee: $24,500
Capital requirements: franchise fee + $4,000–$6,000 working capital
Core Function: Organizing

Business Services and Consulting

BEVINCO
Bevinco Bar Systems, Ltd.
235 Yorkland Blvd. #409
Toronto, ONT M2J 4Y8 CAN; (800)665-1743; (416)490-6266
Liquor inventory control system
Number of franchise units: 40 in 10 states and 4 countries
Founded: 1987
Franchise fee: $15,000
Capital requirements: $20,000–$35,000
Core Function: Organizing

BUSINESS AMERICA
Business America Assoc., Inc.
2120 Greentree Rd.
Pittsburgh, PA 15220; (412)833-1910
Sells over 70 individual home-based franchises
Number of franchise units: 5 in 4 states
Founded: 1984
Franchise fee: $4,995
Capital requirements: $10,000
Core Function: NA

CRESTCOM INTERNATIONAL, LTD.
The Crest Group, Ltd.
6900 E. Belleview Ave.
Englewood, CO 80111; (303)267-8200; (303)267-8207 fax
Video-based management and sales training
Number of franchise units: 74 in 11 states and 36 countries
Founded: 1987
Franchise fee: $32,000–$52,500 in U.S.
Capital requirements: $44,355–$71,960 (including franchise fee)
Core Function: Leading

GENERAL BUSINESS SERVICES
1020 University Parks Dr.
Waco, TX 76707; (800)583-6181; (817)745-2544 fax

Small-business counseling firm
Number of franchise units: 309 in 50 states
Founded: 1962
Franchise fee: $30,000
Core Function: Problem Solving

INTERNATIONAL MERGERS & ACQUISITIONS
4300 N. Miller Rd., Ste. 230
Scottsdale, AZ 85251; (602)990-3899
Serving merger and acquisition–minded companies.
Number of franchise units: 44 in 21 states
Founded: 1969
Franchise fee: $10,000
Capital requirements: $10,000
Core Function: Problem Solving

OMNIWORKS!
FPI
2465 Ridgecrest Ave.
Orange Park, Fl 32065; (904)272-6567; (904)272-6750 fax
Business talent network exchange service
Number of franchise units: 2 in 1 state
Founded: 1991
Franchise fee: $5,000
Capital requirements: $15,000
Core Function: Problem Solving

PARSON-BISHOP SERVICES, INC.
7870 Comargo Rd.
Cincinnati, OH 45243; (800)543-0468; (513)561-5560
Receivable management, A/R financing services
Number of franchise units: 62 in 24 states
Founded: 1973
Franchise fee: $18,500
Capital requirements: 6 months personal living expenses
Core Function: Organizing

PDP, INC. (PROFESSIONAL DYNAMETRIC PROGRAMS)
750 E. Hwy. 24, Building 1, Box 5289
Woodland Park, CO 80866; (719)687-6074; (719)687-8587 fax
Management development tools, sales, training, and consultation
Number of franchise units: 32 in 13 states and 5 countries

Founded: 1978
Franchise fee: $14,900–$29,500
Capital requirements: $5,000–$10,000
Core Function: Leading

PRIORITY MANAGEMENT SYSTEMS
500 108th Ave. N.E., Ste. 1740
Bellevue, WA 98004; (800)221-9031; (206)454-7686
Productivity and effectiveness workshops
Number of franchise units: 302 in 17 countries
Founded: 1981
Franchise fee: $29,500
Capital requirements: franchise fee + $7,500 working capital
Core Function: Leading

WRITER, THE LETTER WRITER
9437 Haggerty Rd.
Plymouth, MI 48170; (313)455-8892
Résumé, secretarial, and letter writing
Founded: 1981
Franchise fee: $15,000
Capital requirements: $10,000
Core Function: Creating

Children's Services

COMPUTERTOTS
13121 Colvin Run Rd.
Great Falls, VA 22066; (703)759-2556
Teach schoolchildren computer skills
Number of franchise units: 46
Founded: 1983
Franchise fee: $19,500
Capital requirements: $10,000
Core Function: Improving

HEAD OVER HEELS
P.O. Box 530744
Birmingham, AL 35200; (205)879-6305
Mobile gymnastics and motor skills
Founded: 1990
Franchise fee: $27,100–$49,000

Capital requirements: $17,000
Core Function: Improving

KINDERDANCE
268 N. Babcock St., Ste. A
Melbourne, FL 32935; (800)666-1595
Mobile group dance instruction
Number of franchise units: 29
Founded: 1979
Franchise fee: $6,000–$9,000, depending on size of territory
Capital requirements: $14,850–$21,000 (including franchise fee)
Core Function: Improving

PEE WEE WORKOUT
34976 Aspen Wood
Willoughby, OH 44094; (800)356-6261
Mobile exercise instruction
Number of franchise units: 25
Founded: 1986
Franchise fee: $1,500
Capital requirements: $2,000
Core Function: Improving

SITTERS UNLIMITED
23015 Del Lago
Laguna Hills, CA 92653; (800)328-1191
In-home child care
Number of franchise units: 8
Founded: 1979
Franchise fee: $8,000
Capital requirements: $10,000
Core Function: Improving

Cleaning

CEILING DOCTOR
17810 Davenport Rd., Suite 108
Dallas, TX 75252; (214)702-8046
Specialty interior cleaning and restoration
Number of franchise units: 150 in 39 states and 30 countries
Founded: 1984
Franchise fee: $12,500

Capital requirements: $25,000
Core Function: Building

Chem Dry Carpet, Drapery & Upholstery Cleaning
Harris Research, Inc.
1530 North 1000 West
Logan, UT 84321; (800)841-6583; (801)755-0099
Carpet, drapery, and upholstery cleaning
Number of franchise units: 3,859 in 50 states and 49 countries
Founded: 1977
Franchise fee: $17,950
Capital requirements: $4,950 down, $13,000 financed 0% interest
Core Function: Building

Cleannet, USA
9861 Broken Land Pkwy., Ste. 208
Columbia, MD 21046; (800)735-8838
Commercial facility cleaning services
Number of franchise units: 1,200+ in 11 states
Founded: 1987
Franchise fee: $3,000–$31,500
Capital requirements: approximately ½ of fee
Core Function: Building

Coustic-Glo International, Inc.
7111 Ohms Ln.
Minneapolis, MN 55439; (800)333-8523; (612)835-1338
Acoustical ceiling, wall, and floor restoration
Number of franchise units: 190 in 50 states and 23 countries
Founded: 1975
Franchise fee: $12,000–$30,000
Core Function: Building

Coverall Cleaning Concepts
3111 Camino Del Rio N., Ste. 950
San Diego, CA 92108; (619)584-1911; (800)537-3371
Commercial cleaning service
Number of franchise units: 3,600+ in 25 states and 7 countries
Founded: 1985
Franchise fee: $3,200–$33,600
Capital requirements: $2,000–$26,200
Core Function: Building

DURACLEAN INTERNATIONAL, INC.
2151 Waukegan Rd.
Deerfield, IL 60015; (800)251-7070
Carpet, upholstery, drapery, janitorial, etc., cleaning services
Number of franchise units: 519 in 50 states and 22 countries
Founded: 1930
Franchise fee: $6,400
Capital requirements: $11,900 (with $5,900 down)
Core Function: Building

KIWI CARPET CLEANING
Tiki, Inc.
4707 140th Avenue N, Ste. 306
Clearwater, FL 34622; (800)577-1551; (800)577-1553
Residential carpet and upholstery cleaning
Number of franchise units: 2 in 2 states
Founded: 1989
Franchise fee: $25,000
Capital requirements: $25,000
Core Function: Building

KWIK DRY CARPET & UPHOLSTERY CLEANING
25665 Canton Farm Rd.
Plainfield, IL 60544; (815)436-0333
Carpet, upholstery cleaning
Number of franchise units: 5 in 3 states
Founded: 1967
Franchise fee: $11,750
Capital requirements: $11,750 (with $5,750 down)
Core Function: Building

LASER CHEM WHITE GLOVE COMMERCIAL CLEANING
Laser Chem Intl. Corp.
7022 South 400 West
Midvale, UT 84047; (800)272-2741
Carpet and upholstery cleaning
Number of franchise units: 6 in 1 state
Founded: 1978
Franchise fee: $7,994+
Capital requirements: $1,500
Core Function: Building

MARBLE RENEWAL
SVI
P.O. Box 56340
Little Rock, AR 72215; (501)663-2080; (501)663-2401 fax
Restoration of marble and hardwood surfaces
Number of franchise units: 20 in 16 states and 3 countries
Founded: 1988
Franchise fee: $17,500+
Capital requirements: $75,000–$100,000
Core Function: Building

O.P.E.N. CLEANING SYSTEMS
O.P.E.N. America, Inc., Ste. 740
2398 E. Camelback Rd.
Phoenix, AZ 85016; (800)777-6736
Office cleaning business
Number of franchise units: 752 in 3 states
Founded: 1983
Franchise fee: $3,800 and up
Capital requirements: $3,000+
Core Function: Building

PROFESSIONAL CARPET SYSTEMS
5182 Old Dixie Hwy.
Forest Park, GA 30050; (404)362-2300; (800)925-5055
Carpet rejuvenation, including cleaning and dyeing
Number of franchise units: 196 in 48 states and 24 countries
Founded: 1978
Franchise fee: $10,000
Capital requirements: $12,000
Core Function: Building

STEAM BROTHERS
933½ Basin Ave.
Bismarck, ND 58504; (701)222-1263
Carpet, upholstery, drapery cleaning
Number of franchise units: 17 in 5 states
Founded: 1977
Franchise fee: $8,990–$16,990
Capital requirements: $4,999–$9,500–$12,995
Core Function: Building

Thee Chimney Sweep, Inc
36 Vernon Rd., NE
Rome, GA 30165; (706)232-5261
Chimney cleaning
Number of franchise units: 1 in 1 state
Founded: 1993
Franchise fee: $8,500
Capital requirements: $12,500
Core Function: Building

Computer

Computer Doctor
105th Ave., S.W.
Aberdeen, SD 57401; (605)225-0054; (605)225-7897 fax
Mobile computer repair and service
Number of franchise units: 9
Founded: 1992
Franchise fee: $15,000
Capital requirements: $27,700–$34,500
Core Function: Building

Construction and Building

Archadeck, Inc.
2112 W. Laburnum Ave., Ste. 100
Richmond, VA 23227; (800)722-4668; (804)353-6999
Design and sell wooden decks to real estate developers and homeowners
Number of franchise units: 60
Founded: 1980
Franchise fee: $32,500
Capital requirements: $47,500–$82,500
Core Function: Leading

B-Dry System, Inc.
1341 Copley Rd.
Akron, OH 44320; (330)216-2576; (800)321-0985
Basement waterproofing
Number of franchise units: 69 in 23 states
Founded: 1958
Franchise fee: $25,000–$60,000

Capital requirements: $50,000
Core Function: Building

HOUSE DOCTORS HANDYMAN SERVICE
4010 Executive Park Dr., Ste. 100
Cincinnati, OH 45241; (800)319-3359; (513)563-0200
Operation of handyman services to homes
Number of franchise units: 32 in 18 states
Founded: 1994
Franchise fee: $11,950–$22,900
Capital requirements: $4,050–$12,750
Core Function: Leading

KOTT KOATINGS, INC.
27161 Burbank St.
Foothill Ranch, CA 92610; (714)770-5055
Resurface kitchen and bathroom fixtures
Number of franchise units: 400 in 44 states and 17 countries
Founded: 1953
Franchise fee: $16,900–$25,995
Capital requirements: $2,200
Core Function: Building

PERMA-GLAZE, INC.
1638 S. Research Loop Rd., Ste. 160
Tucson, AZ 85710; (800)332-7397
Restoration and refinishing of bathroom and kitchen fixtures
Number of franchise units: 175 in 32 states and 10 countries
Founded: 1978
Franchise fee: $27,500
Capital requirements: $2,500
Core Function: Building

PERMA-JACK COMPANY
9066 Watson Rd.
St. Louis, MO 63126; (800)843-1888; (314)843-1957
Foundation stabilization
Number of franchise units: 22
Founded: 1974
Franchise fee: $5,000–$50,000
Capital requirements: $75,000 (maximum)
Core Function: Building

TEMPACO, INC.
P.O. Box 54-7667
Orlando, FL 32854-7667; (407)898-3456; (800)868-7226
Controls and instrumentation distributor
Number of franchise units: 17 in 5 states
Founded: 1946
Franchise fee: $20,000
Capital requirements: $5,000
Core Function: Leading

Entertainment

AMERICAN MOBILE SOUND
AMS Franchise Corp.
5266 Hollister, #105
Santa Barbara, CA 93111; (805)681-8132; (800)788-9007
Professional mobile disc jockey service
Number of franchise units: 5 in 2 states
Founded: 1991
Franchise fee: $6,000–$15,000
Capital requirements: $16,107
Core Function: Leading

AMERICAN POOLPLAYER'S ASSOCIATION
1000 Lake St. Louis Blvd., Ste. 325
Lake St. Louis, MO 63367; (800)3RA-CKEM; (314)625-8611
Organize pool league franchise using handicap system
Number of franchise units: 218 in 43 states
Founded: 1980
Franchise fee: population based
Capital requirements: varies
Core Function: Leading

COMPLETE MUSIC
7877 "L" St.
Omaha, NE 68127; (402)339-0001; (800)843-3866
Disc jockey entertainment service
Number of franchise units: 112 in 29 states and 2 countries
Founded: 1972
Franchise fee: $9,500
Capital requirements: $20,000
Core Function: Leading

PARTY ANIMALS
180 Allen Rd., Ste. 204
Atlanta, GA 30328; (404)303-7789; (404)256-0076 fax
Costumed entertainment for events
Number of franchise units: 17 in 10 states
Founded: 1987
Franchise fee: $12,500
Capital requirements: $20,000
Core Function: Improving

Environmental Cleaning and Inspection

ADVANTAGE RADON CONTROL CENTERS
804 Second Street Pike
Southampton, PA 18966; (800)-535-TEST; (215)953-9200
Testing for Radon and other toxins
Number of franchise units: 7
Founded: 1985
Franchise fee: $17,500
Capital requirements: $25,000
Core Function: Building

ENVIRONMENTAL AIR SERVICES
The Dwyer Group
1010 University Parks Dr.
Waco, TX 76707; (800)583-3828; (817)745-5055 fax
Indoor air quality—residential and commercial
Number of franchise units: 35 in 3 countries
Founded: 1993
Franchise fee: $20,000
Capital requirements: $55,000
Core Function: Problem Solving

FIREMASTER
Master Protection Corporation
520 Broadway, Ste. 650
Santa Monica, CA 90401; (310)451-8888
Fire protection and environmental services
Number of franchise units: 398 in 15 states
Founded: 1935
Franchise fee: $10,000

Capital requirements: $10,000
Core Function: Building

KNOCKOUT PEST CONTROL
1009 Front St.
Uniondale, NY 11553; (800)244-PEST; (516)489-7817
Pest control services
Number of franchise units: 2
Founded: 1975
Franchise fee: $15,000
Capital requirements: $25,000
Core Function: Building

PROFESSIONAL HOUSE DOCTORS, INC.
1406 E. 14th St.
Des Moines, IA 50316; (515)265-6667; (800)288-7437
Environmental/building science services
Number of franchise units: 5 in 3 states
Founded: 1982
Franchise fee: $15,000
Capital requirements: $7,500 + franchise fee
Core Function: Problem Solving

Financial Services

ASSET ONE
Broker One Securities Corp.
1097-C Irongate Ln.
Columbus, OH 43213; (614)864-1440
Financial and investment planning service
Number of franchise units: 5 in 4 states
Founded: 1989
Franchise fee: varies
Capital requirements: varies
Core Function: Problem Solving

CREATIVE ASSET MANAGEMENT
170 Wood Avenue South, Ste. 300
Iselin, NJ 08830; (800)245-0530; (908)549-1011
Long-term savings and investment plans
Number of franchise units: 40

Founded: 1982
Franchise fee: $12,500–$17,500
Capital requirements: $20,000
Core Function: Problem Solving

Home Improvements

BUDGET BLINDS, INC.
1570 Corporate Dr., Ste. B
Costa Mesa, CA 92626; (714)708-3338; (800)420-5374
Mobile window coverings
Number of franchise units: 77 in 12 states
Founded: 1992
Franchise fee: $12,950
Capital requirements: $20,000
Core Functions: Leading/Building

CARPET NETWORK
109 Gaither Dr., #302
Mt. Laurel, NJ 08054; (800)428-1067; (609)273-9393
Mobile retailer of carpet and window treatments
Number of franchise units: 41 in 14 states
Founded: 1992
Franchise fee: $15,500
Capital requirements: $18,900 (including franchise fee)
Core Functions: Leading/Building

CERTA PROPAINTERS
1140 Valley Forge Rd.
Valley Forge, PA 19482; (800)452-3782; (215)983-9884 fax
Residential and commercial painting of single family homes
Number of franchise units: 175
Founded: 1992
Franchise fee: $15,000
Capital requirements: $25,000
Core Functions: Building/Leading

COLOR YOUR CARPET, INC.
2465 Ridgecrest Ave.
Orange Park, FL 32065; (800)321-6567; (904)272-6750 fax
Carpet dyeing and color restoration on site
Number of franchise units: 136 in 15 states and 4 countries

Founded: 1979
Franchise fee: $15,000
Capital requirements: $15,000–$20,000
Core Function: Building

COMPREHENSIVE PAINTING
Comprehensive Franchise Systems, Inc.
4705 Chromium Dr.
Colorado Springs, CO 80918; (800)374-8898; (719)599-7933
Residential painting and staining services
Number of franchise units: 2 in 1 state
Founded: 1986
Franchise fee: $6,500
Capital requirements: $15,000–$20,000
Core Function: Building

DECOR-AT-YOUR-DOOR INTERNATIONAL
Deco Home Stores, Inc.
P.O. Box 1586
Placerville, CA 95667; (800)936-3326; (916)644-6073 fax
Mobile showcase: carpets, blinds, wallpaper, window treatments
Number of franchise units: 15 in 13 states and 2 countries
Founded: 1983
Franchise fee: $4,500
Capital requirements: $1,300 in addition to fee
Core Functions: Leading/Building

DECORATING DEN SYSTEMS
7910 Woodmont Ave., #200
Bethesda, MD 20814; (800)428-1366; (301)652-6393
Shop-at-home interior decorating service
Number of franchise units: 1,000+
Founded: 1969
Franchise fee: $8,900–$23,900
Capital requirements: $8,000–$12,000
Core Function: Leading

DRAPERY WORKS SYSTEM, LTD., THE
4640 Western Ave.
Lilse, IL 60532; (708)963-2820; (800)353-7273
Mobile custom home window treatment sales
Number of franchise units: 1 in 1 state

Founded: 1978
Franchise fee: $7,500
Capital requirements: $27,100–$50,500
Core Functions: Leading/Building

DR. VINYL & ASSOCIATES, LTD.
9501 East 350 Hwy.
Raytown, MO 64133; (800)531-6600
Mobile vinyl and leather repair and dyeing
Number of franchise units: 111
Founded: 1972
Franchise fee: $19,500 and up
Capital requirements: $4,600 to $21,000
Core Function: Building

FLOOR COVERING INTERNATIONAL
5182 Old Dixie Hwy.
Forest Park, GA 30050; (404)361-5047; (800)955-4324
Mobile, in-home floor covering sales
Number of franchise units: 350 in 47 states
Founded: 1988
Franchise fee: as low as $9,000
Capital requirements: as low as $3,500
Core Function: Leading

FURNITURE MEDIC
Furniture Weekend Franchising, Inc.
860 Ridge Lake Blvd.
Memphis, TN 38120 (901)820-8600; (800)877-9933
On-site furniture restoration and repair
Number of franchise units: 439 in 48 states and 4 countries
Founded: 1992
Franchise fee: $9,400
Capital requirements: $5,000
Core Function: Building

GUARDSMAN WOODPRO
Guardsman Products, Inc.
2960 Lucerne S.E.
Grand Rapids, MI 49546; (800)253-3957, ext. 864; (616)285-7870 fax
Mobile, on-site furniture touch-up and repair
Number of franchise units: 15 in 7 states

Founded: 1915
Franchise fee: $18,000
Capital requirements: $18,000–$22,000
Core Function: Building

JET-BLACK SEALCOATING & REPAIR
Jet Black International, Inc.
9033 Lyndale Ave. S.
Bloomington, MN 55420; (612)888-4444
Blacktop driveway maintenance service
Number of franchise units: 5 in 1 state
Founded: 1988
Franchise fee: $6,500
Capital requirements: $20,000–$30,000
Core Function: Building

THE SCREENMOBILE CORP.
457 W. Allen, #107
San Dimas, CA 91773; (818)335-8813
Mobile screening or rescreening
Number of franchise units: 48 in 10 states
Founded: 1982
Franchise fee: $49,300
Capital requirements: $40,000–$50,000
Core Function: Building

SPRING-GREEN CARE CORP.
11927 Spaulding School Dr.
Plainfield, IL 60544; (800)435-4051
Home landscaping service
Number of franchise units: 110
Founded: 1977
Franchise fee: $12,900
Capital requirements: $26,140–$47,000
Core Function: Building

WORLDWIDE WHIRLPOOL SYSTEMS
1020 N. University Parks Dr., P.O. Box 3146
Waco, TX 76707; (817)745-2444; (800)583-9900
Convert existing bathtubs to whirlpools
Number of franchise units: 23 in 10 states
Founded: 1993

Franchise fee: $6,500
Capital requirements: $3,000
Core Functions: Leading/Building

Home and Business Inspection

AMBIC BUILDING INSPECTION CONSULTANTS, INC.
1200 Rte. 130
Robbinsville, NJ 08691; (800)88A-MBIC; (609)448-3900
Residential, commercial, and industrial building inspections
Number of franchise units: 29 in 11 states and 2 countries
Founded: 1987
Franchise fee: $10,000–$16,500
Capital requirements: $8,600–$9,500
Core Function: Problem Solving

AMERICAN LEAK DETECTION
888 Research Dr., Ste. 100
Palm Springs, CA 92262; (800)755-6697; (619)320-9991
Locate leaks in concealed piping systems
Number of franchise units: 229 in 27 states and 9 countries
Founded: 1974
Franchise fee: $45,000
Capital requirements: $29,500
Core Function: Building

AMERISPEC HOME INSPECTION SERVICE
860 Ridge Lake Blvd.
Memphis, TN 38120; (800)426-2270
Residential inspection services
Number of franchise units: 280 in 42 states and 2 countries
Founded: 1987
Franchise fee: $11,900–$22,900
Capital requirements: $5,800–$16,500 + working capital
Core Function: Problem Solving

HOMETEAM INSPECTION SERVICE, INC., THE
6355 E. Kemper Rd., Ste. 250
Cincinnati, OH 45241; (800)598-5297
Home inspection service
Number of franchise units: 230 in 42 states
Founded: 1991

Franchise fee: $11,950–$22,900
Capital requirements: $4,050–$12,750
Core Function: Problem Solving

HOUSEMASTER
421 W. Union Ave.
Bound Brook, NJ 08805; (800)526-3939
Home inspections
Number of franchise units: 172 in 45 states and 2 countries
Founded: 1971
Franchise fee: $5,000–$20,000
Capital requirements: $10,000–$15,000
Core Function: Problem Solving

INSPECTECH
2527 Camino Ramon, Ste. #375
San Ramon, CA 94583; (800)773-2832; (510)358-0250
Computerized home inspection
Number of franchise units: 103 in 6 states
Founded: 1990
Franchise fee: $18,500
Capital requirements: $21,000–$41,550 all-inclusive
Core Function: Problem Solving

WORLD INSPECTION NETWORK
2701 First Ave., Ste. 340
Seattle, WA 98121; (800)967-8127; (206)441-3655 fax
Home inspection service
Number of franchise units: 26 in 10 states
Founded: 1993
Franchise fee: $8,900–$16,900
Capital requirements: $4,595–$8,145
Core Function: Problem Solving

Insurance

PROPERTY DAMAGE APPRAISERS, INC.
P.O. Box 9230
Fort Worth, TX 76147; (817)731-5555; (800)749-7324
Damage appraisers for insurance companies. Must have 2 years auto-appraisal experience
Number of franchise units: 234 in 50 states

Founded: 1963
Franchise fee: none
Capital requirements: $9,250–$23,450
Core Function: Problem Solving

Medical and Fitness

BASIC NEEDS HOME COMPANION SERVICES
P.O. Box 12672
Lexington, KY 40583-2672; (606)269-7611; (800)269-8461
Nonmedical in-home care for the elderly
Number of franchise units: 0
Founded: 1992
Franchise fee: $5,000
Capital requirements: $10,000–$16,000
Core Function: Improving

FITNESS ON WHEELS, INC.
1185 S. Milwaukee
Denver, CO 80210; (303)778-8060
Personal fitness training mobile gym
Number of franchise units: 3 in 1 state
Founded: 1987
Franchise fee: $10,000
Capital requirements: $7,500–$20,000 (royalty—7%, advertising
royalty—1%)
Core Function: Improving

HOME INSTEAD SENIOR CARE
1104 S. 76th Ave.
Omaha, NE 68124; (402)391-2555
Nonmedical care for the elderly
Number of franchise units: 12 in 10 states
Founded: 1994
Franchise fee: $7,500
Capital requirements: $13,000–$18,000
Core Function: Improving

RESPOND SYSTEMS
P.O. Box 39925
Denver, CO 80239; (303)371-6800

Mobile medical supplies
Number of franchise units: 50
Founded: 1979
Franchise fee: no initial fee
Capital requirements: $35,000
Core Function: Leading

Merchandise Sales

K & N MOBILE DISTRIBUTION SYSTEMS
K & N ELECTRIC FRANCHISING, INC.
4909 Rondo Dr.
Fort Worth, TX 76160; (817)626-2885
Sales of electrical parts and hardware
Number of franchise units: 23 in 6 states
Founded: 1972
Franchise fee: $23,500
Capital requirements: $22,400–$82,300
Core Function: Leading

SPORT IT, INC.
4196 Corporate Sq.
Naples, FL 33942; (800)467-8953
Dealers sell brand-name sports equipment from home
Number of franchise units: 7,900 in 50 states
Founded: 1984
Franchise fee: $1,500
Capital requirements: $1,500
Core Function: Leading

Miscellaneous

HIGH TOUCH-HIGH TECH
High Touch Investment Corp.
7908 Wiles Rd.
Coral Springs, FL 33067; (800)444-4968; (305)755-2900
Hands-on science experience that comes to you
Number of franchise units: 14
Founded: 1990
Franchise fee: $50,000
Capital requirements: $8,000–$10,000
Core Function: Improving

MUSIC VENDING, INC.
4000 Hollywood Blvd., Ste. 730-N
Hollywood, FL 33021; (800)JUK-EBOX; (800)-585-3269
Computerized four-function vending/jukebox
Number of franchise units: 2 in 2 states
Founded: 1993
Franchise fee: $26,000
Capital requirements: $377,000
Core Function: Leading

PERSONALIZED DREAM SCENES
NFI Systems, Inc.
3200 S. Andrews Ave., #118
Fort Lauderdale, FL 33316; (800)763-2005; (305)763-3934 fax
Personalized artwork depicting dreams
Number of franchise units: 28 in 14 states
Founded: 1990
Franchise fee: varies
Capital requirements: $11,000–$15,000
Core Function: Creating

YARD CARDS, INC.
49 Willowbrook Dr.
St. Louis, MO 61346; (314)863-6111
8-foot greeting card rentals and gifts
Number of franchise units: 11
Founded: 1983
Franchise fee: varies
Capital requirements: $5,000–$15,000
Core Function: Leading

Pet Care

PET NANNY OF AMERICA, INC.
340 Morgan Lane
Lansing, MI 48912; (517)336-8622
Professional in-home pet-care service
Number of franchise units: 21 in 11 states
Founded: 1983
Franchise fee: $8,700
Capital requirements: $1,400–$4,500
Core Function: Improving

PETS ARE INN
27 N. Fourth Street, Ste. 500
Minneapolis, MN 55401; (800)248-PETS
In-home pet-care placement
Number of franchise units: 30
Founded: 1982
Franchise fee: $2,100–$8,500
Capital requirements: $2,100–$8,500
Core Function: Improving

PET TENDERS
Pet Tenders International, Inc.
P.O. Box 23622
San Diego, CA 92193; (619)298-3033; (800)738-8363
In-home pet and house-sitting service
Number of franchise units: 4 in 2 states
Founded: 1983
Franchise fee: $8,500
Capital requirements: $2,000–$5,400
Core Function: Improving

Photography and Videography

ACTION SPORTS PHOTOS
Chromatech Laboratories, Inc.
4526 N.W. First St.
Oklahoma City, OK 73127; (405)942-7007
Full-service youth sports photography
Number of franchise units: 3
Founded: 1985
Franchise fee: $17,500
Capital requirements: $22,000–$25,000
Core Function: Creating

INTERNATIONAL TELEVISION PRODUCTIONS
448 E. 6400 South, #210
Murray, UT 84107; (800)231-0048
Corporate video productions
Number of franchise units: 11
Founded: 1984
Franchise fee: $28,500
Capital requirements: $10,350–$17,9200
Core Function: Creating

INTERNATIONAL VIDEO YEARBOOKS
25 Century Blvd., #507
Nashville, TN 37214; (800)552-9103
High-school video yearbook
Number of franchise units: 36
Founded: 1989
Franchise fee: $15,000–$35,000
Capital requirements: $3,000–$10,000
Core Function: Organizing

SPECIAL DELIVERY PHOTOS
P.O. Box 34905
Bartlett, TN 38134; (901)829-3555
Provide hospitals with newborns' first picture
Number of franchise units: 6 in 3 states
Founded: 1984
Franchise fee: $10,000
Capital requirements: $16,850–$22,050 incl. franchise fee
Core Functions: Leading/Building

SPORTS SECTION, INC., THE
H&B Products
3871 Lakefield Dr., Ste. 100
Suwanee, GA 30174; (800)321-9127; (770)622-4900
Children/sports photography products
Number of franchise units: 105 in 40 states and 2 countries
Founded: 1983
Franchise fee: $9,900–$29,500
Capital requirements: operating capital to cover one month's living
Core Functions: Leading/Building

VISUAL IMAGE
203 Indiana Ave.
Maryville, TN 37803; (615)370-1505
Mobile photography, preschool, pet markets
Number of franchise units: 5 in 2 states
Founded: 1994
Franchise fee: $13,500
Capital requirements: $11,500
Core Function: Creating

Security

ALLIANCE SECURITY SYSTEMS, INC.
6-140 McGovern Dr.
Cambridge, ONT N3H 4R7 Canada; (519)650-5353
Wireless-burglar and medical 24-hr. monitoring
Number of franchise units: 80
Founded: 1970
Franchise fee: $17,900
Capital requirements: $24,000
Core Function: Building

CITIZENS AGAINST CRIME
1111 Jupiter Rd., Ste. 101C
Plano, TX 75074; (972)578-2287; (800)466-1010
Personal safety seminars and products
Number of franchise units: 40 in 21 states and 2 countries
Founded: 1980
Franchise fee: $12,500 and up
Capital requirements: $10,000–$20,000
Core Function: Leading

Travel

CRUISEONE, INC.
10 Fairway Dr., Ste. 200
Deerfield Beach, FL 33441; (954)428-8433; (800)892-3928
Putting together cruises and association tours travel service
Number of franchise units: 320 in 43 states and 2 countries
Founded: 1989
Franchise fee: $6,800
Capital requirements: $10,000–$20,000
Core Function: Organizing

OUTDOOR CONNECTION
1001 E. Cliff Road
Burnsville, MN 55337; (612)890-0407
Sell fishing and hunting trips
Number of franchise units: 70 in 16 states
Founded: 1988
Franchise fee: varies
Capital requirements: ½ of franchise fee
Core Function: Leading

TRAVEL NETWORK
560 Sylvan Ave.
Englewood Cliffs, NJ 07632; (201)567-8500; (800)TRA-VNET
Travel agencies
Number of franchise units: 374 in 33 states and 7 countries
Founded: 1982
Franchise fee: $10,000–$29,000
Capital requirements: $15,000 home based, $80,000+ full service
Core Function: Leading

9

MLMs You Can Join

THE FOLLOWING LIST of multilevel marketing opportunities represents just a few of the literally thousands of MLMs available. If you are so inclined, this list should provide you with a starting point for finding an MLM that's right for you.

> We do not imply that these opportunities are in any way superior to companies we have not listed, and we do not imply or suggest any sort of recommendation by their inclusion. We advise you to apply all the tests and criteria outlined in the previous chapters to any company you consider.

CORE FUNCTIONS IN MLM

The Core Function of MLMs, in our opinion, is always (1) **Leading**. Period. No matter what kind of product or service you will be distributing, your primary Core Function in an MLM will always consist of the tasks associated with this function, such as administering, assigning, coordinating, initiating, inspiring, motivating, persuading, and, most important, selling. For further analysis of determining an MLM's Core Function, please review the Fitness Check section in Chapter 4. If you are in any way uncomfortable with the activities of Leading as a Core Function including all the skills associated with it, we suggest you consider purchasing a franchise opportunity or perhaps a biz op.

A DIRECTORY OF MULTILEVEL MARKETING COMPANIES

PLEASE NOTE: As of the writing of this book, all the following information was current and correct. The business world often changes quickly, however, so we apologize in advance if any of these listings are no longer current or contain information that is no longer accurate.

ADVANTAGE MARKETING SYSTEMS, INC. (AMS)
2601 Northwest Expressway, Ste. 1210
Oklahoma City, OK 73112; (405)842-0131
Membership buying service; card holder obtains various discounts
Founded: 1988

ALLIANCE
1302 Champion Circle
Carrollton, TX 75006; (972)969-6400
Herbal and nutritional dietary supplements, skin care
Founded: 1993

ALPINE INDUSTRIES
9199 Central Ave., N.E.
Blaine, MN 55434-3422; (800)989-2299
Air and water purification systems
Founded: 1986

AMERICAN COMMUNICATIONS NETWORK
100 West Big Beaver, Ste. 400, P.O. Box 5000
Troy, MI 48007-5000; (810)528-2500; (810)528-6790 fax
Telephone service
Founded: 1992

INC (AIM)
3904 E. Flamingo
Nampa, ID 83687; (800)456-2682; (800)766-5133 fax
Nutritional and skin-care products
Founded: 1982

AMWAY CORPORATION
7575 Fulton Street
Ada, MI 49355-0001; (616)787-6000; (616)787-8140 fax
Manufactures several hundred goods and services from cleaning products to personal shoppers service
Founded: 1959

ARTISTIC IMPRESSIONS
240 Corland Ave.
Lombard, IL 60148; (630)916-0050
Framed paintings
Founded: 1985

BODYWISE
6350 Palomar Oaks Ct.
Carlsbad, CA 92009; (619)438-8977
Salon products, health and nutritional products
Founded: 1993

CELL TECH
1300 Main St.
Klamath Falls, OR 97601; (800)800-1300; (503)884-1869 fax
Freeze-dried Super Blue Green(TM) algae, skin-care, and nutritional products
Founded: 1982

CHANGES INTERNATIONAL
548 Mary Ester Cutoff, Ste. 325
Fort Walton Beach, FL 32548; (904)837-1956; (904)654-2877 fax
Nutritional products
Founded: 1994

CLUB ATLANTA TRAVEL, INC.
2440 Sandy Plains Rd., Bldg #7
Marietta, GA 30066; (770) 579-5551; (770) 579-5885 fax
Travel service
Founded: 1995

CONSUMER POWER UNLIMITED
1414 East Susquehanna St., Ste. 11
Allentown, PA 18103; (610)791-5483
Discounted coffee and cereal, and manufacturers' coupons
Founded: 1995

COUNTRY PEDDLER
5625 W. 115th St.
Alsip, IL 60482; (800)873-3537
Decorative country items for the home
Founded: 1983

DESIGNER NUTRITION AMERICA—DNA
3535 Hwy. 66, Bldg. 2
Neptune, NJ 07753; (908)922-0777; (908)922-5329 fax
Nutritional products
Founded: 1994

DISCOVERY TOYS, INC.
6400 Brisa St.
Livermore, CA 94550; (510)606-2600; (510)447-0626 fax
Manufactures and distributes games and toys designed to enhance learning
through play
Founded: 1978

ELYSEE COSMETICS
6804 Seybold Rd.
Madison, WI 53719; (608)271-3664; (800)235-9733
Alpha-hydroxy creams, lotions, and other skin-care products, fragrances,
and cosmetics
Founded: 1940

ENRICH INTERNATIONAL
748 N. 1340 West
Orem, UT 84057; (801)226-2600; (801)226-8232 fax
Herbs and health-oriented products
Founded: 1977

ENVIRO-TECH INTERNATIONAL, INC.
3930 West Ali Baba
Las Vegas, NV 89118; (702)262-5555
Waterless car wash and home care
Founded: 1991

EXCEL TELECOMMUNICATIONS, INC.
8750 N. Central Expressway
Dallas, TX 75231-6428; (214)863-8000; (214)863-8843 fax
Long-distance reseller
Founded: 1988

THE FULLER BRUSH COMPANY
P.O. Box 729, One Fuller Way
Great Bend, KS 67530; (316)792-1711; (800)523-3794
Home and personal-care products
Founded: 1906

FREEDOMSTARR COMMUNICATIONS, INC.
657 North Broadway, #1
Escondido, CA 92025; (619)492-8080; (619)432-9700 fax
Discount domestic long-distance service, international long distance, global
calling card, Internet on-ramp
Founded: 1995

FREELIFE INTERNATIONAL, INC.
333 Quarry Rd.
Milford, CT 06460; (203)882-7250; (203)882-7255 fax
Nutritional products
Founded: 1995

GLENNET
8501 Commerce St.
Burnaby, BC V5A 4N3 Canada; (604)668-5151; (800)661-6698 fax
Residential and business long-distance service
Founded: 1993

GLOBAL HEALTH & WELLNESS, INC.
624 Military Trail
Deerfield Beach, FL 33442; (954)427-6565 fax
Stop-smoking program, weight-management system
Founded: 1995

THE GROCERY CLUB
8350 East Evans, Bldg. C
Scottsdale, AZ 85260; (602)614-3500; (602)614-2902 fax
Grocery co-op saving consumers 30–40% on supermarket prices + $340 in
free groceries.
Founded: 1995

HEALTH TECHNOLOGIES NETWORK
150 Research Dr.
Hampton, VA 23666; (757)868-4600; (800)851-7486
Health and nutritional products, dental hygiene products
Founded: 1995

HERBALIFE INTERNATIONAL
P.O. Box 80210
Los Angeles, CA 90080-0210; (310)410-9600; (310)216-7454 fax
Herbal and nutritional products
Founded: 1980

INNOVATE COMMUNICATIONS
Houston, TX 77040; (713)460-1976; (713)460-9049 fax
One-Plus Long Distance, prepaid calling card, prepaid cellular time, prepaid Internet access, etc.
Founded: 1992

GAFFER COSMETICS, INC.
2451 Townsgate Rd.
West Lake Village, CA 91361; (800)551-2345
Skin-care, color-care, personal-care and fragrance products
Founded: 1956

JAPAN LIFE AMERICA CORPORATION
4160 Wilshire Blvd.
Los Angeles, CA 90010; (213)954-1781; (213)954-1758 fax
Manufactures and markets futons, futon comforters, pillows, bed frames, and personal comfort items
Founded: 1975

JEWELWAY INTERNATIONAL
5151 E. Broadway, Ste. 500
Tucson, AZ 85711; (520)747-9900; (520)745-0551 fax
Fine jewelry
Founded: 1990

LIFE EXTENSIONS INTERNATIONAL
12005 Ford Road, Ste. 800
Dallas, TX 75234; (214)484-7000; (214)488-9124 fax
Nutrition and weight loss
Founded: 1994

LIFE FORCE INTERNATIONAL
P.O. Box 1980
Spring Valley, CA 91979; (800)531-4877
Advanced nutritional products
Founded: 1981

LIFE PLUS
P.O. Box 3749
Batesville, AR 72503; (800)572-8446; (501)698-2379 fax
Nutritional products /Pycongenol
Founded: 1992

LIFEWORKS! USA
7361 Topanga Canyon Blvd.
Canoga Park, CA 91303; (818)884-5090; (818)884-5225 fax
Internet and telecommunications, travel and leisure, health and beauty,
personal development, financial products
Founded: 1996

LONGEVITY NETWORK, LTD.
15 Cactus Garden Drive
Henderson, NV 89014; (702)454-7000; (702)435-4786 fax
Vitamins and bodycare products
Founded: 1994

MARKET AMERICA
7605A Business Park Drive #5
Greensboro, NC 27409; (910)605-0040; (910)605-0041 fax
Nutritional, personal, and auto care products
Founded: 1992

MARY KAY COSMETICS, INC.
16251 N. Dallas Pkwy.
Dallas, TX 75248-2696; (972)687-6300
Skin-care products and cosmetics
Founded: 1963

MATOL BOTANICAL INTERNATIONAL, LTD.
1111, 46E Ave.
Lachine, Quebec H8T 3C5, Canada; (514)639-0730; (514)637-0576 fax
Nutritional products: bars, shakes, supplements, cereal, etc.
Founded: 1986

MELALEUCA, INC.
3910 South Yellowstone
Idaho Falls, ID 83402; (800)282-3000
Nutritional, medicinal, personal-care, and home-hygiene products
Founded: 1985

MULTI-PURE CORPORATION
21339 Nordhoff St.
Chatsworth, CA 91311; (818)341-7577
Drinking-water treatment systems
Founded: 1982

N/A/T/O-INTERNATIONAL
1380 Burrard St., #250
Vancouver, BC V6Z 2H3, Canada; (604)689-9553; (604)689-5662 fax
Car-care products, fuel-saving products
Founded: 1994

NATURAL PRODUCTS, INC.
2512 W. Main St.
Jeffersonville, PA 19403; (610)630-0100; (610)630-0800 fax
Distributor of odor neutralizer
Founded: 1992

NETEL TELECOMMUNICATIONS & TECHNOLOGY
6300 N.E. First Ave.
Ft. Lauderdale, FL 33334; (888)333-TEL3; (800)355-6080 fax
Long-distance telecommunication
Founded: 1994

NETSAFE, INC.
2077 North Collins Blvd., Ste. 202-R
Richardson, TX 75080; (214)690-7233; (214)644-6388 fax
Full-service Internet provider
Founded: 1995

NEWAYS
150 East 400 North, P.O. Box 651
Salem, UT 84653; (801)423-2800; (801)423-2350
Personal-care, cosmetics, nutritional and weight-loss products
Founded: 1987

NIKKEN USA, INC.
15363 Barranca Pkwy.
Irvine, CA 92618; (714)789-2043; (800)669-8859
KenkOpillow, Kinkicreator, and other personal-comfort items.
Founded: 1975

NOEVIR USA, INC.
1095 S.E. Main Street
Irvine, CA 92714; (714)660-1111; (714)660-9562 fax
Natural and herbal skin-care products, cosmetics, personal-care and
nutritional products
Founded: 1964

NONSCENTS
Krueger's Enterprises
5057 American Legion Rd., S.E.
Iowa City, IA 52440-9071; (319)351-2808
Odor removal/clean-air products
Founded: 1987

NSA, INC.
4260 East Raines Rd.
Memphis, TN 38118; (901)366-9288
Water filtration, air filtration systems and educational products
Founded: 1970

NU SKIN INTERNATIONAL, INC.
75 W. Center
Provo, UT 84601; (800)487-1500; (801)345-8000 fax
Personal-care, skin-care, and nutritional supplements and formulas
Founded: 1984

NUTRICARE
910 West Battlefield
Springfield, MO 65807; (888)NUTRICARE; (417)882-7710
Innovative heart, health, and immune-system nutritionals
Founded: 1996

NUTRITION FOR LIFE INTERNATIONAL
9101 Jameel, Ste. 180
Houston, TX 77040; (713)460-1976; (713)460-9049 fax
Antioxidants and nutritional, personal-care, and weight-management
products
Founded: 1984

OMNITRITION INTERNATIONAL, INC.
2855 Trinity Sq.
Carrollton, TX 75006; (972)702-7600; (972)417-9240 fax

Nutritional products, dietary food and drinks, herbal teas, diet cookies
Founded: 1989

ORIFLAME USA
4434 Cerritos Ave.
Los Alamitos, CA 90720; (714)229-1160; (714)229-1590 fax
Cosmetics, fragrances, hair- and skin-care products combining Scandinavian
and Swiss beauty secrets
Founded: 1967

OXYFRESH WORLDWIDE, INC.
P.O. Box 3723
Spokane, WA 99220; (509)924-4999; (509)924-5285 fax
Dental hygiene, personal care, skin care, household hygiene, and pet care
Founded: 1984

THE PEOPLE'S NETWORK
2045 Chenault Dr.
Carrollton, TX 75006; (972)860-0400; (800)860-0480 fax
Satellite television, home shopping and entertainment, personal achievement
Founded: 1995

PRE-PAID LEGAL SERVICES
321 East Main St.
Ada, OK 74820; (800)654-7757; (405)436-7409 fax
Preferred legal plan
Founded: 1972

PRIMERICA FINANCIAL SERVICES
3120 Breckinridge Blvd.
Duluth, GA 30199; (770)381-1000
Term insurance and financial services
Founded: 1977

PROSTEP
P.O. Box 5678
Destin, FL 32540-5678; (904)654-4444; (904)654-5585 fax
Lead generation, training, and support for network marketers
Founded: 1995

QUORUM INTERNATIONAL
1550 West Deer Valley Rd.

Phoenix, AZ 85027; (602)780-5500; (602)883-8533 fax
Security alarms for home, office, and car
Founded: 1991

RE-VITA
153 Industrial Loop S.
Orange Park, FL 32073; (904)278-0222; (904)269-7661 fax
Liquid vitamins and powdered nutrient mousse
Founded: 1986

RELIV
P.O. Box 405
Chesterfield, MO 63005-0405; (314)537-9715
Nutritional products
Founded: 1988

REXALL SHOWCASE INTERNATIONAL
853 Broken Sound Pkwy., N.W.
Boca Raton, FL 33487; (561)241-9400
Bios Life Diet, nutritional supplements, water filtration systems, homeo-
pathic remedies, and traditional remedies
Founded: 1990

S&K GROUP, INC.
55 W. Port Plaza, Ste. 555
St. Louis, MO 63146; (800)660-0330; (314)453-0330
Capital acquisition and expense reduction
Founded: 1966

SHAKLEE U.S., INC.
444 Market Street
San Francisco, CA 94111; (415)954-3000; (800)Shaklee
Nutritional supplements, household and personal-care products, water
treatment systems, and career tapes/seminars
Founded: 1956

SUNRIDER INTERNATIONAL
1625 Abalone Ave.
Torrance, CA 90501; (310)781-3808
Herbal foods, beverages, personal care, skin care, and cosmetics
Founded: 1982

USANA
3838 W. Parkway Blvd.
West Valley City, UT 84120; (801)954-7100
Nutritional weight loss
Founded: 1992

VH$ NETWORK
P.O. Box 291989
Nashville, TN 37229; (615)883-5500; (615) 883-5504 fax
Products and services featured in a videocassette catalog
Founded: 1995

VITOL INTERNATIONAL
Box 16200-313
Mesa, AZ 85201; (800)488-4865
Herbal formula, food extract wafers, skin-care products, and weight-management system
Founded: 1987

WATKINS
150 Liberty St.
Winona, MN 55987; (800)533-8018
Imitation vanilla extract, spices, flavorings and condiments, foods, nutritional supplements
Founded: 1968

YOUNGER LIVING, INC.
P.O. Box 1561
Watertown, SD 57201; (605)886-7203; (800)657-4346
Car care, water treatment, homeopathic medicines, and vitamin and mineral supplements
Founded: 1961

LEADING DIRECT-SELLING COMPANIES THAT DON'T USE MULTILEVEL MARKETING

AVON PRODUCTS, INC.
9 West 57th Street
New York, NY 10019; (212)546-6015
http://www.getbuzy.com/avon/avon.htm
Cosmetics, jewelry, fashions, toys, fitness videos
Founded: 1886

ELECTROLUX CORPORATION
2300 Windy Ridge Parkway, Ste. 900
Atlanta, GA 30339; (770)993-1000
Vacuum cleaners
Founded: 1919

THE KIRBY COMPANY
1920 West 114th Street
Cleveland, OH 44102; (216)228-2400; (216)221-3162
Vacuum cleaners
Founded: 1919

TUPPERWARE WORLDWIDE
P.O. Box 2353
Orlando, FL 32802; (407)847-3111; (407)826-5050 fax
http://www.tupperware.com
Tupperware, toys
Founded: 1946

10

Home-Based Biz Ops
You Can Buy

The listings in this chapter in no way imply a recommendation or endorsement of any kind. We advise you to apply all the tests and criteria outlined in the previous chapters to any company you consider.

IN THIS CHAPTER we have compiled a directory of business opportunities you can buy and run from your home. Each listing includes basic information about the biz op, as well as a code indicating its Core Function. The Core Functions are derived from the six function headings listed in the Business Opportunities Fitness Check. The key for the Core Function symbols is:

(1) **Leading** = marketing/selling/promoting/managing/motivating
(2) **Improving** = helping/teaching/counseling/assisting clients and customers
(3) **Organizing** = bookkeeping/calculating/paperwork/processing information
(4) **Creating** = innovating/designing/composing/imagining

(5) **Building** = assembling/handling/constructing/maintaining

(6) **Problem Solving** = planning/researching/analyzing

As in franchising, the Core Function **Leading (1)** will be a significant part of running any of the biz ops listed here, or anywhere for that matter. Even if the biz op is listed as having another Core Function, please keep in mind that Leading (1) will always be a close second. If you are not comfortable with the skills of administering, motivating, managing, and, most important, *selling*, you may wish to reconsider the purchase of a biz op and instead focus on starting some type of business of your own for which you are so well positioned that you'll have little competition and will be able to attract business primarily through the value of what you do. To find out how to create such a unique self-employment career, see *Finding Your Perfect Work*, which appears in Appendix 7, "General Resources for Home-Business Success."

We do not endorse the following business opportunities over other biz ops that are not listed here. This compendium is intended to give you a starting point from which to begin looking for a business opportunity that is well suited to you. **We in no way imply or suggest a recommendation of the Business Opportunities listed here.**

A DIRECTORY OF HOME-BASED BUSINESS OPPORTUNITIES

PLEASE NOTE: As of the writing of this book, all the following information was current and correct. Things in the business world sometimes change fast, however, so we apologize in advance if any of these listings are no longer current or contain information that is no longer accurate.

Advertising and Marketing

AMERICAN MEDIA ASSOCIATES
Wes-State Mortgage, Inc.
1450 W. 7th Ave.
Eugene, OR 97402; (541)485-4741
Compile mailing lists
Number of units: over 150
Founded: 1976
Capital requirements: $29
Core Function: Leading

BADGE-A-MINT LTD.
P.O. Box 800

Department BBY597
LaSalle, IL 61301; (800)223-4103
Button-making machines
Number of units: over 1,000
Founded: 1972
Capital requirements: $29.95 and up
Core Functions: Leading/Building

CAPTIVE AUDIENCE INDOOR ADVERTISING
STRATEGIC ADVERTISING, INC.
Ford Centre, 420 N. 5th St., Ste. 345
Minneapolis, MN 55401; (612)333-3411; (800)416-7559
Place ads in restaurant restrooms
Number of units: 27 in 20 states and 3 countries
Founded: 1987
Capital requirements: $5,000–$20,000
Core Function: Leading

INFORMATIONAL DISPLAY SYSTEMS
STRATEGIC ADVERTISING, INC.
Ford Centre, 420 N. 5th St., Ste. 345
Minneapolis, MN 55401; (612)333-3411; (800)416-7559
Placing advertising in elevators
Number of units: 15 in 15 states
Founded: 1987
Capital requirements: $12,000–$17,000
Core Function: Leading

Q-PON BOOK, THE
Mid-Michigan Direct Mail, Inc.
1827 N. Michigan Ave.
Saginaw, MI 48602; (517)754-0000; (517)754-0898
Direct-mail advertising coupon book
Number of units: 44 in 17 states
Founded: 1989
Capital requirements: $495
Core Function: Leading

SO CAL MARKETING
1722 LaHoud Dr., Ste. 101
Cardiff, CA 92007; (619)942-0289; (619)942-6338
Manufacture changeable banner systems

Number of units: 16 in 12 states and 4 countries
Founded: 1989
Capital requirements: $1,000–$2,000
Core Function: Leading

THRIFTY ADVERTISING SYSTEMS
Thrifty Instant Print
13199 Brookhurst St.
Garden Grove, CA 92843; (714)636-6711
System to imprint advertising specialties
Number of units: 4
Founded: 1996
Capital requirements: $3,250
Core Functions: Leading/Building

Automotive

AUTOMOTIVE APPRAISAL SERVICES GROUP
91398 World Way Ctr.
Los Angeles, CA 90009-1398; (800)495-2525, ext. 71; (310)640-2525
Used-vehicle prepurchase inspections
Number of units: 56 in 16 states
Founded: 1987
Capital requirements: $700–$15,000
Core Function: Problem Solving

AUTOPLUS WINDOW STICKERS
Tanner Communications
12570 Yacht Club Circle
Ft. Myers, FL 33919; (941)466-7641; (800)825-4838
http://www.autoplusnet.com
New-car–type window sticker for used-car departments and independent dealers
Number of units: 90 in 18 states and 3 countries
Founded: 1991
Capital requirements: $499–$5,000
Core Function: Leading

CHIPSAWAY INTERNATIONAL
1536 Saw Mill Run Blvd.
Pittsburgh, PA 15210; (412)885-9000; (800)837-2447
Mobile auto paint restoration business

Number of units: 625 in 5 countries
Founded: 1989
Capital requirements: $7,000–$12,000
Core Function: Building

GLAS-WELD SYSTEMS, INC.
20578 Empire Blvd., Dept. N
Bend, OR 97701; (541)388-1156; (800)321-2597
Glass repair—mobile business
Number of units: 2,000
Founded: 1978
Capital requirements: $2,000–$3,000
Core Function: Building

M.A.R.S. 2000 MOBILE AUTOMOBILE RECONDITIONING SYSTEMS
1581 Solomon Run Rd.
Johnstown, PA 15904; (800)676-6277; (814)539-4228
Repair of auto paint chips, vandal key scratches, scuffs, rust, etc.
Number of units: 250 in 30 states and 6 countries
Founded: 1979
Capital requirements: $3,995
Core Function: Building

MOBILE LUBE SYSTEMS, INC.
3140-K S. Peoria, Ste. 228
Aurora, CO 80014; (800)368-9339
Mobile oil change business
Number of units: 137 in 40 states
Founded: 1991
Capital requirements: $29,450
Core Function: Building

Beauty

BEAUTY BY SPECTOR, INCORPORATED
Dept. PB-97, McKeesport, PA 15134-0502; (412)673-3259
Wigs and hair goods
Founded: 1994
Capital requirements: none
Core Function: Leading

CONCEPT NOW COSMETICS
10200 Pioneer Blvd., #100

Santa Fe Springs, CA 90670; (310)903-1450
Cosmetics
Number of units: 20,000 in 50 states and 6 countries
Founded: 1971
Capital requirements: none
Core Function: Leading

GOUBAUD DE PARIS
Fern Laboratories, Inc.
280 Smith St.
Farmingdale, NY 11735; (516)420-8000
Price-value family hair care and products
Number of units: 30 in 2 countries
Founded: 1946
Capital requirements: none
Core Function: Leading

TOTAL SOLUTIONS, INC.
2400 S.W. Jefferson
Peoria, IL 61605; (309)637-0600
Total shaving solution for men and women
Number of units: over 1,000
Founded: 1988
Capital requirements: $45–$490
Core Function: Leading

Books and Publications

AMERICAN INSTITUTE OF SMALL BUSINESS
7515 Wayzata Blvd., Ste. 201
Minneapolis, MN 55426; (612)545-7001
Hold seminars on small-business start-up
Number of units: 8 in 4 states and 2 countries
Founded: 1986
Capital requirements: $5,000
Core Function: Leading

CALAGRAPHICS
247 Old Belgan Rd.
Jersey City, NJ 07305; (201)435-9339; (201)435-9848 fax
Direct-mail marketing success system
Number of units: 1

Founded: 1983
Capital requirements: $19.95 for operations manual
Core Function: Leading

INFOPRENEUR PUBLISHING
Reprintable Reports Division
306 W. Jefferson
Prudy, MO 65734-0096; (417)442-3547; (417)442-3771 fax
Over 1,001 printable reports
Number of units: 1,001
Founded: 1984
Capital requirements: under $20
Core Function: Leading

JEFFREY LANT ASSOCIATES, INC.
50 Follen St., #507
Cambridge, MA 02138; (617)547-6372; (617)547-0061 fax
Business development and "get ahead" titles
Number of units: over 1,000
Founded: 1979
Capital requirements: $75
Core Function: Leading

LOOKING AHEAD
Professional Salutations
1100 Lincoln Ave., #100
Napa, CA 94558; (707)226-2475
Publication aimed at active seniors
Number of units: 2 in 2 states
Founded: 1992
Capital requirements: $5,000
Core Function: Leading

RENAISSANCE VISION
10555 St. Hubert, Ste. 1
Montreal, QUE H2C 2H9 Canada; (514)388-7898
Home-based opportunities
Number of units: 3 worldwide
Founded: 1988
Capital requirements: $300 and up
Core Function: Leading

SUNNYSIDE PUBLISHERS
P.O. Box 29
Lynn, MA 01903; (617)595-4742; (617)593-2718
How-to-win gambling books
Number of units: 1,200 in 42 states and 4 countries
Founded: 1955
Capital requirements: $200 and up
Core Function: Leading

Business Services

AMALISA SERVICES
Dept. AS, Block A-5, P.O. Box 24
Fayetteville, AR 72702; (501)443-9785; (501)443-4024 fax
Office/business equipment and supplies
Number of units: 200 in 50 states and 15 countries
Founded: 1987
Capital requirements: $50–$10,000
Core Function: Leading

BLUEJAY SYSTEMS
3 Meca Way
Norcross, GA 30093; (770)564-5592
Billing service, invoice preparation, and accounts receivable management services
Number of units: 4,100 in 50 states and 13 countries
Founded: 1987
Capital requirements: $289
Core Function: Organizing

BUSINESS ADVERTISING SPECIALTIES CORP. (BASCO)
9401 Desoto Ave.
Chatsworth, CA 91311; (818)718-1506; (800)642-1090
Advertising supplier, distributor, and imprinter
Number of units: 6,000
Founded: 1987
Capital requirements: $24.95 to start
Core function: Leading

BUSINESS ARBITRATION
Banks, Bentley & Cross

1500 Quail St., Ste. 550
Newport Beach, CA 92660; (800)866-8865
Business arbitration and debt negotiation
Number of units: 250+ in 39 states and 2 countries
Founded: 1983
Capital requirements: $195 registration fee and $500 capital
Core Function: Improving

BUTLER LEARNING SYSTEMS
1325 W. Dorothy Ln.
Dayton, OH 45409-1385; (513)298-7462
Sales and management-training programs
Number of units: 68 in 50 states and 4 countries
Founded: 1959
Capital requirements: $475
Core Function: Leading

ELECTRONIC CLAIMS & FUNDING, INC.
2865 Amwiler Rd., Ste. 200
Atlanta, GA 30360-3607; (770)416-0673
Electronic claims-processing services
Number of units: 1,000
Founded: 1990
Capital requirements: $1,995
Core Function: Organizing

EXPRESS BUSINESS CARDS PLUS
652 Bair Island Rd., Ste. 306
Redwood City, CA 94063; (415)369-1430 fax
Make business cards with personal computer
Number of units: 39 in 14 states and 5 countries
Founded: 1993
Capital requirements: $1,000–$2,500
Core Functions: Leading/Building

I.D. USA- I.S.A INC.
2810 Sherer Dr., Ste. 100
St. Petersburg, FL 33716; (800)890-1000
Photo ID badge-making system
Number of units: 5
Founded: 1994

Capital requirements: $2,995
Core Function: Building

MELLINGER CO., THE
25620 Rye Cnyn Rd., Unit B
Valencia, CA 91355; (805)257-2700
Import-export mail-order business plan
Founded: 1947
Capital requirements: $225
Core Function: Leading

PRE-PAID LEGAL SERVICES, INC.
5600 Wisconsin Ave., Ste. 404
Chevy Chase, MD 20815; (301)951-0211
Market memberships in legal service plans
Founded: 1972
Capital requirements: $249
Core Function: Leading

SHRED TECH LIMITED
295 Pinebush Rd.
Cambridge, ONT N1T 1B2 Canada; (800)465-3214
Mobile document-shredding truck
Number of units: 120
Founded: 1976
Capital requirements: $125,000–$150,000
Core Function: Building

UTILITY AND TAX REDUCTION CONSULTANTS
Bill Barrett CPA Consulting Group
1240 Iroquois Dr., Ste. 106
Naperville, IL 60563; (630)369-3072 fax; (800)321-7872
Home-based auditing business
Number of units: 400+ in 45 states and 2 countries
Founded: 1981
Capital requirements: $3,995
Core Function: Problem Solving

WORK MEASUREMENT SYSTEMS, INC.
8511 N. Pennsylvania St.
Indianapolis, IN 46240-2251; (317)253-2043

Labor-productivity improvement services
Number of units: 18 in 8 states
Founded: 1983
Capital requirements: $7,500
Core Function: Problem Solving

Children's Services

CHILD SHIELD, USA
103 W. Spring St.
Titusville, PA 16345; (800)488-2445
Videotape registration service for protection of children
Number of units: 609 in 50 states
Founded: 1990
Capital requirements: $495–$3,000
Core Functions: Leading/Building

COMPUCHILD
406 Rushwood Dr.
Murfreesboro, TN 37130; (615)893-5216; (800) 619-KIDS
Kids' computer training classes
Number of units: 65 in 26 states
Founded: 1994
Capital requirements: $9,900
Core Function: Improving

HEFTY PUBLISHING
1232 Paula Circle
Gulf Breeze, FL 32561; (904)934-1599; (800)732-3009; (904)934-8903 fax
Printing personalized children's books
Number of units: 3,000
Founded: 1980
Capital requirements: $3,000
Core Function: Leading

IDENT-A-KID PROGRAM, THE
2810 Scherer Dr., Ste. 100
St. Petersburg, FL 33716; (813)577-4646
Laminated child ID cards
Number of units: 195 in 38 states
Founded: 1986

Capital requirements: $12,500
Core Functions: Leading/Building

Music Experience for Young Children, The
PJM Associates
910 Bent Ln.
Glenside, PA 19038; (800)350-9504; (215)233-5795
Children's music enrichment program
Number of units: 40 nationally
Founded: 1990
Capital requirements: $6,000–$10,000
Core Function: Improving

Wee Watch Private Home Day Care
105 Main St.
Unionville, ONT L3R 2G1 Canada; (905)479-4274
Supervised private day-care agencies
Number of units: 45
Founded: 1986
Capital requirements: $20,000
Core Function: Improving

Computers & Technology

Alpha Services
400 Parque Dr.
Ormond Beach, FL 32174; (904)677-1601; (800) 627-2574;
(904)677-8901 fax
Recycling, repair-servicing of laser printers
Number of units: 96 in 49 states and 2 countries
Founded: 1986
Capital Requirements: $1,000–$6,000
Core Function: Building

Applied Technologies, Inc.
Computer Products Division, Lyndon Way
Kittery, ME 03904; (207)439-5074
Computer software and hardware
Number of units: 1
Founded: 1979
Capital requirements: computer plus $75 minimum order
Core Function: Leading

COMPUTER MAINTENANCE SERVICE
P.O. Box 8
San Marcos, TX 78667; (210)629-1400; (512)353-5337 fax
Sell and maintain computer peripherals
Number of units: 1
Founded: 1987
Capital requirements: $10,000
Core Functions: Leading/Building

QUANTUM TECHNOLOGY, INC.
1720 Harbor Ave.
Memphis, TN 38113; (901)774-9900; (800)833-4732
Complete business kits for computer-based businesses
Number of units: 3,000 worldwide
Founded: 1984
Capital requirements: $329–$900, not including computer and modem
Core Function: Leading

Dating and Relationships

SINGLE SEARCH NATIONAL
13176 N. Dale Mabry, Ste. 202
Tampa, FL 33618; (813)264-1705; (800)779-8362
Mail-order computer matchmaking service
Number of units: 151 in 42 states; 28 in 10 countries
Founded: 1989
Capital requirements: $1,200–$1,800
Core Function: Leading

Environmental Services

AGRONICS, INC.
6808 Academy Parkway, N.E., Bldg. A, Ste. 3
Albuquerque, NM 87109; (505)761-1454
Landscapers, livestock producers
Number of units: 34 in 23 states and 3 countries
Founded: 1987
Capital requirements: $5,000
Core Function: Building

CLEAN-AIRE INTERNATIONAL
2223 Handley Ederville Rd.
Fort Worth, TX 76118; (817)589-7873; (817)595-0240 fax

Video-assisted duct-cleaning equipment
Number of units: 184 in 34 states
Founded: 1982
Capital requirements: $18,850
Core Function: Building

HOMEPRO SYSTEMS, INC.
2841 Hartland Rd., Ste. 201
Falls Church, VA 22043; (800)966-4555; (703)560-4663
Network of home inspection companies
Number of units: 1
Founded: 1981
Capital requirements: $7,500
Core Function: Improving

Financial Services

AMERICAN SECURITY FINANCIAL
4132 Shoreline Dr., Ste. J
Earth City, MO 63045; (314)344-1111; (314)298-9110
Financing of credit-rejected receivables
Number of units: 263 in 23 states and 3 countries
Founded: 1976
Capital requirements: $500
Core Function: Problem Solving

CARDSERVICE INTERNATIONAL
2516 34th St.
Santa Monica, CA 90405; (310)392-5433; (310)392-6733; (800)898-9048
Set up businesses to accept credit cards
Founded: 1988
Capital requirements: $199 for training manual and registration
Core Function: Leading

COLLEGE FINANCIAL AID SERVICES, INC.
1615 Union St.
Schenectady, NY 12309; (800)869-0220; (518)382-0240
College financial aid consulting
Number of units: 85 in 32 states
Founded: 1991
Capital requirements: $495
Core Function: Leading

WORLDWIDE INFORMATION SERVICES, INC.
P.O. Box 21261
Ft. Lauderdale, FL 33335-1261; (954)764-7942
Home-based computer information consultant
Number of units: 13 in 7 states
Founded: 1990
Capital requirements: $12,500
Core Function: Problem Solving

General Merchandise

BRIDAL ACCENTS™
38 Pond St., Ste. 104
Franklin, MA 02038; (800)865-2228; (508)528-2530
In-home sales of bridal accessories
Founded: 1992
Capital requirements: $9,500–$11,500
Core Function: Leading

CONKLIN FASHIONS, INC.
72 Main St.
Sidney, NY 13838; (800)437-1161
Boutique earrings, 2,000 styles
Founded: 1985
Capital requirements: $500
Core Function: Leading

HANKINS MARKETING CORP.
128 N. Merritt Ave.
Salisbury, NC 28144; (704)637-3589
Tear-gas sales to retail stores and chains
Number of units: 6,900 in 49 states
Founded: 1974
Capital requirements: $25
Core Function: Leading

LAKESIDE PRODUCTS COMPANY
6646 N. Western Ave.
Chicago, IL 60645; (773)761-5495
Selling imported and manufactured gifts

Founded: 1959
Capital requirements: no minimum required
Core Function: Leading

RESPOND FIRST AID SYSTEMS
3650-C Fraser St.
Aurora, CO 80011; (303)371-6800; (800)942-6022
Sales and service of first-aid kits
Number of units: 65 in 36 states
Founded: 1979
Capital requirements: $35,000
Core Function: Leading

SPECTOR'S FLEA MARKET SUPREME
Dept. PB-97
McKeesport, PA 15134-0502; (412)673-3259
Flea-market items, wholesale
Founded: 1994
Capital requirements: none
Core Function: Leading

SPORTSFORCE
3023 Hwy. 80 E.
Jackson, MS 39206; (800)898-2855
Sell brand-name sporting goods at wholesale prices
Number of units: 21 in 9 states
Founded: 1984
Capital requirements: $1,200+
Core Function: Leading

Home Improvement

BRENTWOOD LOG HOMES
427 River Rock Blvd.
Murfreesboro, TN 37128; (615)895-0720; (800)264-5647
Selling manufactured log homes
Number of units: 340 in 35 states and 3 countries
Founded: 1980
Capital requirements: $5,000
Core Function: Leading

CABINET DOCTOR KITCHEN RESTYLERS
85 County Rd. 75
Mechanicville, NY 12118; (518)664-6949; (518)664-7096 fax
Kitchen cabinet refacing
Number of units: 14 in 3 states
Founded: 1958
Capital requirements: $4,895
Core Function: Building

COUNTER TOPPERS, INC.
1248 Englewood St., Ste. 1
Lynchburg, VA 24501; (804)525-8462
Kitchen cabinet and counter refinishing
Number of units: 4
Founded: 1993
Capital requirements: $4,000–$7,000
Core Function: Building

FABRICMATE SYSTEMS
2192 Channel Dr.
Ventura, CA 93001; (805)643-9281
Fabric wall-covering system
Number of units: 2 in 1 state
Founded: 1988
Capital requirements: $3,000–$5,000
Core Function: Building

PERFORMAHOME
317 Hwy. 620 S., Ste. 200
Austin, TX 78734; (512)263-5199, ext. 103
Voice-activated home automation distributorship
Number of units: 1,000+ in 50 states and 20 countries
Founded: 1987
Capital requirements: $6,900 and up
Core Function: Leading

SERR-EDGE MACHINE CO.
4471 W. 160th St.
Cleveland, OH 44135; (216)267-6333
Scissors, shears, and knife sharpeners
Founded: 1940

Capital requirements: $275
Core Function: Building

UNIQUE REFINISHERS, INC.
5171 Nelson Brogdon Blvd.
Sugar Hill, GA 30518; (770)945-0072; (800)332-0048
Bathtub and tile reglazing corp.
Number of units: 325 in 50 states and 3 countries
Founded: 1962
Capital requirements: $3,000
Core Function: Building

Home Furnishings

ALL-AMERICAN BLIND SALES
23052 Alicia Pkwy., #H202
Mission Viejo, CA 92692; (714)-258-7069
Discount shop-at-home miniblind sales
Number of units: 25 in 6 states
Founded: 1985
Capital requirements: $1,700
Core Function: Leading

Cleaning Technologies and Services

ABSOLUTE CHEMICAL CORP.
1555 Sunshine Dr.
Clearwater, FL 34625; (813)449-1776; (800)762-5326
Ceiling and wall cleaning, private label
Number of units: 1,000 in 50 states and 5 countries
Founded: 1988
Capital requirements: $500–$12,900
Core Function: Building

AIR CARE
DPL Enterprises, Inc.
5115 S. Industrial Rd., #506
Las Vegas, NV 89118; (800)322-9919; (702)736-4063
Manufacture clean air-conditioning and heating systems
Number of units: 98 in 36 states and 3 countries
Founded: 1979

Capital requirements: $20,500
Core Function: Building

ALL-AMERICAN MOBILE MINI-BLIND SYSTEMS
23052 Alicia Pkwy., #H202
Mission Viejo, CA 92692; (714)258-7068
Wash miniblind, wood blind, etc., systems
Number of units: 400+ in 35 states and 2 countries
Founded: 1985
Capital requirements: $2,400
Core Function: Building

AMERICAN ROOF-BRITE, INC.
4492 Acworth Ind. Dr., Ste. 102
Acworth, GA 30101; (800)476-9271; (770)966-1080
Removal of stains and fungus from roofs
Number of units: 45 in 15 states
Founded: 1973
Capital requirements: $5,995
Core Function: Building

Medical Billing & Management

MEDICAL MANAGEMENT SOFTWARE, INC.
1730 S. Amphlett Blvd., Ste. 217
San Mateo, CA 94402; (415) 341-6101
Medical billing and practice management software and procedures
Number of units: more than 1,000
Founded: 1992
Capital requirements: $4,000–$7,000
Core Function: Organizing

Miscellaneous

ADVENTURE QUEST, LLC.
P.O. Box 9224
Fargo, ND 58106; (701)277-1332; (800)990-8377
Portable motion simulator
Number of units: 6 in 4 states and 2 countries
Founded: 1993
Capital requirements: $75,000–$85,000
Core Function: Building

BUSINESS OF DOG TRAINING, THE
Matthew Margolis Enterprises, Inc.
11275 National Blvd.
Los Angeles, CA 90064; (310)445-4671
Dog-training program
Founded: 1969
Number of units: over 50
Capital requirements: $1,000
Core Function: Improving

CLASSIC CREATIONS, INC.
2169 West 7420 South
West Jordan, UT 84084; (801)255-3875; http://www.classiccreations.com
Founded: 1996
Capital requirements: $3,500 and up
Core Function: Creating/Leading

COMPREHENSIVE HOME INCARCERATION PROGRAMS (CHIP)
8038 Winton Rd.
Cincinnati, OH 45224; (800)253-2447, ext. 146
Selling electronically monitored house-arrest systems
Founded: 1984
Capital requirements: $20,000
Core Function: Leading

DON LING'S REMOVABLE TATTOOS
P.O. Box 309
Butterfild, MN 56120; (507)956-2024; (800)247-6817
Sell fake tattoos at fairs, festivals, resorts, etc.
Number of units: 1,500 in 50 states and 30 countries
Founded: 1984
Capital requirements: $50–$300
Core Function: Leading

IMAGES IN TIME
Martek, Ltd.
P.O. Box 15160
Charlotte, NC 28211; (704)364-7213; (704)364-7253 fax
Clocks from photos, business cards, and logos
Number of units: 6 in 2 states
Founded: 1980

Capital requirements: $4,000
Core Function: Leading

MEMORABLE AFFAIRS
209 Gibbons St.
Dunmore, PA 18512; (717)344-6799
Reunion planning, memory books
Founded: 1989
Capital requirements: none
Core Function: Organizing

PRESSXPRESS
P.O. Box 4516
Boston, MA 02101; (617)471-7233; (617)471-7611 fax
Publish information on events going on up to a year in advance in an
exclusive territory
Number of units: 12
Founded: 1989
Capital requirements: $5,000–$9,000
Core Function: Organizing

SPACE WALK
The Inflatable Zoo, Inc.
P.O. Box 641479
Kenner, LA 70064; (504)464-6026; (800)622-6026
Rent air-inflated rides for events
Number of units: 43 in 24 states
Founded: 1980
Capital requirements: $500 security deposit
Core Function: Leading

THRIFTY INSTANT SIGNS
13199 Brookhurst St.
Garden Grove, CA 92643; (714)636-6711; (800)659-SIGN
Home-based or storefront production of signs, banners, etc.
Number of units: 37 in 11 states
Founded: 1989
Capital requirements: $10,000–$28,500
Core Function: Creating

Telephone and Communications

INTERMEDIA RESOURCES
6114 LaSalle Ave., #505
Oakland, CA 94611; (415)435-7905
900 numbers
Number of units: 100 in 15 states
Founded: 1991
Capital requirements: $500
Core Function: Leading

ON-HOLD INTERNATIONAL
Executive Business Group, Inc.
5650 Breckenridge Park Dr., #104
Tampa, FL 33610; (800)401-HOLD; (813)622-7770
Digital message "on-hold" system
Number of units: 90 in 30 states and 5 countries
Founded: 1989
Capital requirements: $8,750-$29,750
Core Function: Leading

TELE-SAVE USA
5999 Central Ave., Ste. 302
St. Petersburg, FL 33710; (813)347-2200
Sell rechargeable phone cards
Number of units: 75+ in 26 states
Founded: 1994
Capital requirements: $1,000
Core Function: Leading

Travel

AMERICAN TRAVEL INCENTIVES
301 E. Burnsville Pkwy.
Burnsville, MN 55337; (612)648-1460
Low-price-fare hotel cruises
Number of units: 1,102 in 50 states
Founded: 1993
Capital requirements: $50–$500
Core Function: Leading

TRAVEL SERVICE NETWORK
2560 Foxfield Rd., Ste. 302

St. Charles, IL 60174; (630)443-8834; (800)820-0428
Home- or office-based full-service travel agency
Number of units: 295 in 12 states
Founded: 1990
Capital requirements: $4,995
Core Function: Leading

WILDWOOD TRAVEL, INC.
5218 Yonge St.
North York, ONT M2N 5P6 Canada; (416)223-8111; (800)461-8111
Home-based travel business
Number of units: 21 in 3 countries
Founded: 1990
Capital requirements: $12,500
Core Function: Leading

Vending Machines

A & A COMPANY PARKWAY MACHINE CORP.
2301 York Rd.
Timonium, MD 21093; (410)252-1020; (800)638-6000
Full-line and bulk vending suppliers
Founded: 1941
Capital requirements: none
Core Function: Leading

Video & Photography

HI-SHOTS AERIAL PHOTOGRAPHY LTD.
1040 Airport Rd.
Salem, IL 62881; (618)548-6691; (618)548-6250 fax
Selling patented aerial photography
Number of units: 150+ in 32 states and 16 countries
Founded: 1989
Capital requirements: $8,000–$ 26,000
Core Function: Leading

VIDEO EDITOR
5000 Beltline Rd., Ste. 210
Dallas, TX 75240; (214)788-4988
Video production and postproduction
Number of units: 8 in 6 states

Founded: 1985
Capital requirements: $100,000
Core Function: Creating

VIDEO LEARNING LIBRARY
15838 N. 62nd St., Ste. 101
Scottsdale, AZ 85254-1988; (602)596-9970; (602)596-9973 fax
Home-based video superstore
Number of units: 50 in 29 states
Founded: 1988
Capital requirements: $195
Core Function: Leading

APPENDIX 1

Attorneys General Offices and Federal Trade Commission Regional Offices

THE FOLLOWING ARE detailed lists of U.S. attorneys general offices and FTC regional offices. These two government agencies are both powerful advocates for honesty in business and offer extensive information and resources on how you can protect yourself from fraud and scams. Check out any franchise, MLM, or biz op with both of these organizations before deciding to buy.

ATTORNEYS GENERAL OFFICES

STATE OF ALABAMA
Office of the Attorney General
State House, 11 S. Union
Montgomery, AL 36130
Telephone: (334)242-7300

STATE OF ALASKA
Office of the Attorney General
P.O. Box 110300

Juneau, AK 99811-0300
Telephone: (907)465-3600

STATE OF ARIZONA
Office of the Attorney General
1275 W. Washington,
Phoenix, AZ 85007
Telephone: (602)542-4266

STATE OF ARKANSAS
Office of the Attorney General
200 Tower Building
323 Center Street
Little Rock, AR 72201
Telephone: (501)682-2007

STATE OF CALIFORNIA
Office of the Attorney General
P.O. Box 944255
Sacramento, CA 94244-2550
Telephone: (916)445-9555;
(800)952-5225

STATE OF COLORADO
Office of the Attorney General
1525 Sherman Street
Denver, CO 80203
Telephone: (303)866-4500

STATE OF CONNECTICUT
Office of the Attorney General
55 Elm Street
Hartford, CT 06106
Telephone: (860)566-2026

STATE OF DELAWARE
Office of the Attorney General
820 N. French Street
6th Floor
Wilmington, DE 19801
Telephone: (302)577-8338

STATE OF FLORIDA
Office of the Attorney General
PL01 State Capitol
Tallahassee, FL 32399-1050
Telephone: (904)487-1963

STATE OF GEORGIA
Office of the Attorney General

40 Capitol Square, S.W.
Atlanta, GA 30334
Telephone: (404)656-4585

STATE OF HAWAII
Office of the Attorney General
425 Queen Street
Honolulu, HI 96813
Telephone: (808)586-1282

STATE OF IDAHO
Office of the Attorney General
P.O. Box 83720
Boise, ID 83720-0010
Telephone: (208)334-2400

STATE OF ILLINOIS
Office of the Attorney General
500 S. 2d Street
Springfield, IL 62706
Telephone: (217)782-1090

STATE OF INDIANA
Office of the Attorney General
219 State House
Indianapolis, IN 46204
Telephone: (317)232-6201

STATE OF IOWA
Office of the Attorney General
Hoover State Building, 2d Floor
Des Moines, IA 50319
Telephone: (515)281-5164

STATE OF KANSAS
Office of the Attorney General
Judicial Center, 2d Floor
Topeka, KS 66612
Telephone: (913)296-2215

STATE OF KENTUCKY
Office of the Attorney General
116 State Capitol
Frankfort, KY 40601
Telephone: (502)564-7600

STATE OF LOUISIANA
Office of the Attorney General
Department of Justice,
234 Loyola Dr., 7th Floor
New Orleans, LA 70112
Telephone: (504)568-8778

STATE OF MAINE
Office of the Attorney General
6 State House Station
Augusta, ME 04330
Telephone: (207)626-8800

STATE OF MARYLAND
Office of the Attorney General
200 St. Paul Place
Baltimore, MD 21202
Telephone: (410)576-6300

STATE OF MASSACHUSETTS
Office of the Attorney General
1 Ashburton Place
Boston, MA 02108
Telephone: (617)727-2200

STATE OF MICHIGAN
Office of the Attorney General
525 W. Ottawa, P.O. Box 30212
Lansing, MI 48909
Telephone: (517)373-1110

STATE OF MINNESOTA
Office of the Attorney General
102 State Capitol
St. Paul, MN 55155
Telephone: (612)296-6196

STATE OF MISSISSIPPI
Office of the Attorney General
P.O. Box 220
Jackson, MS 39205
Telephone: (601)359-3680

STATE OF MISSOURI
Office of the Attorney General
Missouri Supreme Court Building
Jefferson City, MO 65102
Telephone: (573)751-3321

STATE OF MONTANA
Office of the Attorney General
P.O. Box 201401, 215 N. Sanders
Helena, MT 59620
Telephone: (406)444-2026

STATE OF NEBRASKA
Office of the Attorney General
State Capitol, P.O. Box 98920
Lincoln, NE 68509
Telephone: (402)471-2682

STATE OF NEVADA
Office of the Attorney General
198 S. Carson Street
Carson City, NV 89710
Telephone: (702)687-4170

STATE OF NEW HAMPSHIRE
Office of the Attorney General
33 Capitol St.
Concord, NH 03301
Telephone: (603)271-3641

STATE OF NEW JERSEY
Office of the Attorney General
Dept. of Law and Public Safety
CN080
Trenton, NJ 08625
Telephone: (609)292-4925

STATE OF NEW MEXICO
Office of the Attorney General
Bataan Building, Galisteo Street
P.O. Drawer 1508
Santa Fe, NM 87504-1508
Telephone: (505)827-6792

STATE OF NEW YORK
Office of the Attorney General
120 Broadway, Floor 3
New York, NY 10271
Telephone: (212)416-8345

STATE OF NORTH CAROLINA
Office of the Attorney General
CB 2953, 693 Palmer Drive
Raleigh, NC 27626
Telephone: (919)733-3983

STATE OF NORTH DAKOTA
Office of the Attorney General
State Capitol, 600 East Boulevard
1st Floor
Bismarck, ND 58505
Telephone: (701)328-2210

STATE OF OHIO
Office of the Attorney General
State Office Tower, Floor 17
30 E. Broad Street
Columbus, OH 43266
Telephone: (614)466-3376

STATE OF OKLAHOMA
Office of the Attorney General
2300 N. Lincoln, Ste. 112
Oklahoma City, OK 73105
Telephone: (405)521-3921

STATE OF OREGON
Office of the Attorney General
116 Court St., N.E.

Salem, OR 97310
Telephone: (503)378-6002

STATE OF PENNSYLVANIA
Office of the Attorney General
Strawberry Square, 16th Floor
Harrisburg, PA 17120
Telephone: (717)787-3391

STATE OF RHODE ISLAND
Office of the Attorney General
150 South Main St.
Providence, RI 02903
Telephone: (401)274-4400

STATE OF SOUTH CAROLINA
Office of the Attorney General
Rembert Dennis Office Building
P.O. Box 11549
Columbia, SC 29211
Telephone: (803)734-3970

STATE OF SOUTH DAKOTA
Office of the Attorney General
State Capitol, 500 E. Capitol
Pierre, SD 57501
Telephone: (605)773-3215

STATE OF TENNESSEE
Office of the Attorney General
450 James Robertson Parkway
Nashville, TN 37243
Telephone: (615)741-3491

STATE OF TEXAS
Office of the Attorney General
Capitol Station, P.O. Box 12548
Austin, TX 78711
Telephone: (512)463-2100

STATE OF UTAH
Office of the Attorney General

236 State Capitol
Salt Lake City, UT 84114
Telephone: (801)538-1015

STATE OF VERMONT
Office of the Attorney General
109 State Street
Montpelier, VT 05609
Telephone: (802)828-3171

STATE OF VIRGINIA
Office of the Attorney General
900 E. Main St.
Richmond, VA 23219
Telephone: (804)786-2071

STATE OF WASHINGTON
Office of the Attorney General
P.O. Box 40100
Olympia, WA 98504-0100
Telephone: (360)753-6200

STATE OF WEST VIRGINIA
Office of the Attorney General
State Capitol, Bldg. 1, Room E-26
Charleston, WV 25305
Telephone: (304)558-2021

STATE OF WISCONSIN
Office of the Attorney General
114 East State Capitol
P.O. Box 7857
Madison, WI 53707
Telephone: (608)266-1221

STATE OF WYOMING
Office of the Attorney General
123 State Capitol
Cheyenne, WY 82002
Telephone: (307)777-7841

FEDERAL TRADE COMMISSION REGIONAL OFFICES

FTC HEADQUARTERS
6th and Pennsylvania Avenue, NW
Washington, D.C. 20580
(202)326-2222

FTC ATLANTA
1718 Peachtree Street, N.W.
Suite 1000
Atlanta, GA 30367
(404) 347-4837

FTC BOSTON
101 Merrimac Street, Suite 810
Boston, MA 02114-4719
(617)424-5960

FTC CHICAGO
55 East Monroe Street
Suite 1860
Chicago, IL 60603
(312)353-4423

FTC CLEVELAND
668 Euclid Avenue, Suite 520-A
Cleveland, OH 44114
(216)522-4207

FTC DALLAS
100 N. Central Expressway
Suite 500
Dallas, TX 75201
(214)979-9350

FTC Denver
1961 Trout Street
Suite 1523
Denver, CO 80294
(303)844-2272

FTC Los Angeles
11000 Wilshire Boulevard
Ste. 13209
Los Angeles, CA 90025
(310)235-4000

FTC New York
150 William Street, Suite 1300

New York, NY 10038
(212)264-1207

FTC San Francisco
901 Market Street, Suite 570
San Francisco, CA 94103
(310)235-4000

FTC Seattle
2809 Federal Building
915 Second Avenue
Seattle, WA 98174
(206)220-6350

Resources for
Home-Based Franchises

BOOKS, PERIODICALS, AND OTHER PUBLICATIONS

The Best Home-Based Franchises. Gregory Matusky and the Philip Lief Group. The Philip Lief Group, Inc., 6 West 20th Street, New York, NY 10011.

Buying Your First Franchise. Rebecca Luhn, Ph.D. Crisp Publications, Inc., 1200 Hamilton Court, Menlo Park, CA 94025.

Checklist for Going into Business. Small Business Administration, Washington, DC 20416.

The Complete Franchise Book. Dennis L. Foster. Prima Publishing, P.O. Box 1260BK, Rocklin, CA 95677.

A Consumer Guide to Buying a Franchise, a free reference from the Federal Trade Commission, Washington, DC 20580.

Directory of Franchising Organizations. Pilot Industries, Inc., 103 Cooper Street, Babylon, NY 11702.

Encyclopedia of Associations. Lists trade and professional organizations throughout the United States. This book will be available in the reference section of your local library.

The Franchise Handbook. Enterprise Magazines, Inc., 1020 North Broadway, Suite 111, Milwaukee, WI 53202.

Franchise Opportunity Handbook. U.S. Department of Commerce.

Franchise Times. Bimonthly magazine, International Franchise Association, 1350 New York Avenue N.W., Suite 900, Washington, DC 20005-4709.

Franchises You Can Run From Home. Lynie Arden. John Wiley & Sons, Inc., 605 Third Avenue, New York, NY 10158.
Franchise Investigation—Contract Negotiation. Harry Gross and Robert S. Levy. Pilot Industries, Inc., 103 Cooper Street, Babylon, NY 11702.

FTC Franchising Rule: The IFA Compliance Kit. International Franchise Association, 1350 New York Avenue N.W., Suite 900, Washington DC 20005.

Guide to Understanding an Offering Circular and Negotiating a Franchise Agreement. Keith J. Kanouse, Esq., Professional Press (407)392-0001.

How to Select a Franchise. Robert McIntosh. International Franchise Association, 1350 New York Avenue N.W., Suite 900, Washington DC 20005.

Successful Franchising. Bimonthly magazine, HIS Publishing, Inc., 1224 Westwind Trail, Berne, IN 46711

Twenty-one Questions. International Franchise Association, 1350 New York Avenue N.W., Suite 900, Washington DC 20005.

STATE AGENCIES THAT REGULATE FRANCHISING

Fifteen states have franchise investment laws that require franchisors to provide presale disclosures, known as "offering circulars," to potential purchasers. According to the FTC, these states "typically prohibit the offer or sale of a franchise within their state until a franchise offering circular has been filed on the public record with, and registered by, a designated state agency." Two of the fifteen states do not require a filing of offering circulars, as noted in the list of state offices below.

California (filing required)
Franchise Division
980 9th St.
Ste. 500
Sacramento, CA 95814
(916) 445-7205

Hawaii (filing required)
Franchise & Securities Division
State Department of Commerce
P.O. Box 40
Honolulu, HI 96810
(808) 586-2722

Illinois (filing required)
Securities Division
Office of Attorney General
500 South Second Street
Springfield, IL 62706
(217) 782-4465

Indiana (filing required)
Office of Secretary of State
Securities Division
302 W. Washington
Rm. E111
Indianapolis, IN 46204
(317) 232-6688

Maryland (filing required)
Franchise Office
Division of Securities
200 St. Paul Place—20th Floor
Baltimore, MD 21202
(410) 576-6360

Michigan (only notice required)
Antitrust and Franchise Unit
Office of Attorney General
670 Law Building
Lansing, MI 48913
(517) 373-7117

Minnesota (filing required)
Franchise Division
Department of Commerce
133 East Seventh St.
St. Paul, MN 55101
(612) 296-6328

New York (filing required)
Franchise & Securities Division
State Department of Law
120 Broadway—23d Floor
New York NY 10271
(212) 416-8211

North Dakota (filing required)
Franchise Division
Office of Securities Commission
600 East Boulevard—5th Floor
Bismarck, ND 58505
(701) 328-2910

Oregon (no filing)
Division of Financial and Corporate
Securities
350 Winter St. N.E.
Rm. 21
Salem, OR 97310
(503) 378-4387

Rhode Island (filing required)
Franchise Office
Division of Securities
233 Richmond St.—Suite 232
Providence, RI 02903
(401) 277-3048

South Dakota (filing required)
Franchise Office
Division of Securities
118 W. Capitol Ave.
Pierre, SD 57501-2017
(605) 773-4013

Virginia (filing required)
Franchise Office
State Corporation Commission
1300 E. Main St.
Richmond, VA 23219
(804) 371-9276

Washington (filing required)
Franchise Office
Business License Services
State Securities Division
P.O. Box 648
Olympia, WA 98504
(360) 753-6928

Wisconsin (filing required)
Franchise Office
Dept. of Financial Institutions
Division of Securities

P.O. Box 1768
Madison, WI 53701
(608) 266-3364

TRADE AND PROFESSIONAL ASSOCIATIONS

American Association of Franchisees and Dealers
1420 Kettner
Suite 415
San Diego, CA 92101
Voice: (800) 733-9858
Fax: (619) 235-2565
Web Site: http://www.gateads.com/aafd/index.htm

American Franchisee Association
53 W. Jackson Blvd
Suite 205, Chicago, Illinois 60604
(800) 334-4232; (312) 431-0545
Web Site: http://infonews.com/franchise/afa

Capital Area Franchise Association
1150 18th Street, N.W., Suite 875
Washington, D.C. 20036
Phone: (202)331-3444

Federal Communications Commission
Office of Communications Business Opportunities
1919 M Street, N.W.
Washington, D.C. 20554
Voice: (202) 418-0990; fax: (202) 418-0235, Rm. 644
E-mail: a kbeverly@fcc.gov.

Federal Trade Commission
Bureau of Consumer Protection
6th Street and Pennsylvania Ave., N.W.
Washington, D.C. 20580
Phone: (202)326-2222

Franchise Information Network
1709 B Hillyer Robinson Parkway South

Oxford, AL 36203
Phone: 1-(800)444-6670; (205)235-2987

International Franchise Association
1350 New York Ave., N.W., Suite 900
Washington, D.C. 20005-4709
Phone: (202)628-8000
Fax: (202)628-0812
Fax on-Demand: (202)628-3432

CSC-the United States Corporation Company
(formerly Prentice-Hall Legal and Financial Service)
375 Hudson St.
11th Floor
New York, NY 10014
Phone: (800)221-0770
Prentice Hall will provide a litigation history on any company for a small fee.
The search must occur in the county where the business is located. The report
will indicate any proceeding against the company, criminal or civil.

Small Business Administration
409 3d Street, S.W., Room 7177
Washington, D.C. 20416
Phone: (800)8-ASK-SBA; (800)827-5722
Fax: (202)205-7067
Web Site: //www.sba.online.sba.gov

TIMS Management Systems
P.O. Box 36360
Tucson, AZ 85740
Phone: (800)528-5153

FRANCHISING ON-LINE RESOURCES

Better Business Bureau Web Server
—*http://www.bbb.org/bbb/index.*
Home page for the Better Business Bureau. File a consumer complaint on
line.

Business and Franchise Opportunity Directory
—*http://www.teleport.com/~ryton/BizOpndx.html*
A commercial site that offers extensive listings of franchises you can buy, as well as MLMs and biz ops.

The Business Researcher's Interests
—*http://www.bint.com*
Compiled by University of Pittsburgh doctoral student Yogesh Malhotra, the meta-site is one of the most useful locations on the World Wide Web. With literally thousands of links to all kinds of business-related information, we advise you to use this site as an intro to any research you do on line.

E X P O
—*http://130.102.169.38/expo*
Another commercial site that offers a wide variety of home-based businesses, including franchises.

Franchise Category FRANCHISE ATTORNEY
—*http://www.franchise1.com/categ/catno25.html*
Maintained by the FRANCHISE HANDBOOK: On Line, this site offers a comprehensive list of franchise attorneys.

FRANCHISE HANDBOOK: On Line
—*http://www.execpc.com/franchise1/*
The FRANCHISE HANDBOOK: On-Line site is a franchise listing and information service provided by the Franchise Handbook publication. Very extensive.

Franchising Research WWW Site — IFRC, University of Westminster, London
—*http://www.wmin.ac.uk/~purdyd/)*
This site is maintained by the International Franchise Research Centre of the University of Westminster, London, U.K. Although somewhat European in perspective, this site offers solid information regarding business and marketing trends and legislative issues concerning franchising.

FRANCHISE SOLUTIONS
—*http://www.bluefin.net/~fransol/*
This commercial site is maintained by Franchise Solutions, a franchise infor-

mation company that offers a variety of services to potential franchise buyers.

Franchise UPDATE Online
—*http://www.franchise-update.com/*
Franchise UPDATE is recognized around the world for their coverage of the franchise trade, management, and investment activity. The site includes excellent information and editorial content and a listing of over 1,000 franchises available for purchase.

FranNet Home Page
—*http://www.frannet.com*
A commercial site that promotes: "Everything you ever wanted to know about this industry is at this site." This site includes information on franchising in general, provides franchising personality profiles, and also lists many franchises available for sale.

International Franchise Internet Service (IFIS)
—*http://www.ifis.com/*
Information about the franchising industry—directories, news, events.

Revised IFA Page
—*http://www.entremkt.com/ifa/*
The official Web site of the International Franchising Association. Good editorial information and helpful links make this a must-see site.

SBA: Small Business Administration Home Page — Text Only
—*http://www.sbaonline.sba.gov/lynx/index-lynx.html*
The United States Small Business Administration maintains one of the largest, most comprehensive, and downright useful sites on the World Wide Web. Specific information regarding franchising, business law, marketing and finance, and much more is available.

Small & Home-Based Business Links
—*http://www.gnn.com/gnn/wic/wics/bus.74.html*
A page of links to Web sites related to small and home-based businesses and franchises, maintained by Renaissance Internet Services.

U. S. & International Law
—*http://members.aol.com/DangeLaw/homepage.html*
Although a commercial home page, this site does offer some useful infor-

mation regarding U.S. and international law as it relates to franchising as a business.

The World Wide Web Virtual Library: Law: Law Firms
—http://www.law.indiana.edu/law/v-lib/lawfirms.html
This page is maintained by the Indiana University School of Law—Bloomington. It contains a comprehensive list of links that is fully searchable as well as alphabetically arranged.

APPENDIX 3

Resources for MLMs

BOOKS, PERIODICALS, AND OTHER PUBLICATIONS

Encyclopedia of Associations. Lists trade and professional organizations throughout the United States. This multivolume encclopedia will be available in the reference section of your local library.

Get Rich Through Multi-Level Selling. Dr. Gini Graham-Scott, Bellingham, WA: Self-Counsel Press

Multi-Level Marketing: The Definitive Guide to America's Top MLM Companies. The Summit Group, 1227 West Magnolia, Suite 500, Fort Worth, TX 76104, 1994

National Trade and Professional Associations of the United States, Columbia Books, Inc., Washington, DC. This annual directory may be available in the reference section of your local library.

The Network Marketer's Guide to Success. Jeffrey A. Babener and David Stewart, Forum Network Marketing, 1990

Upline: The Journal for Network Marketing Sales Leaders. 400 East Jefferson, Charlottesville, VA 22902; (804)979-7856; (804)979-1602 fax.

Wave 3: The New Era in Network Marketing. Richard Poe, Rocklin, CA: Prima, 1994.

The Wave 3 Way to Building Your Downline. Richard Poe, Prima Publishing, Rocklin, CA: Prima, 1996.

The Multi-Level Marketing International Association, 1101 Dove Street, Suite 170, Newport Beach, CA 92660; (714)622-0300, fax (714)251-1319, offers a number of privately published books not available in bookstores. These include:

A History of Multi-Level Markteing, Doris Wood
Multi-Level Marketing Law, D. Jack Smith, Jr.
Putting on the Best Opportunity Meeting, Doris Wood
The Tax Guide for Network Marketing Entrepreneurs, Dale Quale

In addition, the Association publishes for a $25 fee its list of currently operating MLM companies.

TRADE AND PROFESSIONAL ASSOCIATIONS

Direct Selling Association and Foundation (DSA)
1666 K Street, N.W., Suite 1010
Washington, DC 20006-2808
Phone: (202)293-5760; fax: (714)463-4569

Federal Communications Commission
Office of Communications Business Opportunities
1919 M Street, N.W.
Washington, DC 20554
Voice: (202)418-0990; fax: (202)418-0235, Rm. 644
E-mail: a kbeverly@fcc.gov.

Federal Trade Commission
Bureau of Consumer Protection
6th Street and Pennsylvania Ave., N.W.
Washington, DC 20580
Phone: (202)326-2222

MLMIA Multi-Level Marketing International Association (MLMIA)
1101 Dove Street, #170
Newport Beach, CA 92660
Phone: (714)622-0300; fax: (714)251-1319

Prentice Hall Legal and Financial Service
Phone: (800)221-0770
Prentice Hall will provide a litigation history on any company for a small fee. The search must occur in the county where the business is located. The report will indicate any proceedings against the company, criminal or civil.

Small Business Administration
1441 L Street, N.W.
Washington, DC 20416
Phone: (800)8-ASK-SBA; (800)827-5722
Web Site: //www.sba.online.sba.gov

Small Business Foundation of America
20 Park Plaza
Boston, MA 02116

MULTILEVEL MARKETING ON-LINE RESOURCES

BBB Consumer Information Series: Multilevel Marketing
—*http://www.bbb.org/pubs/tippyra.html*
The Better Business Bureau Web Server. Tips on multilevel marketing.

Better Business Bureau Web Server
—*http://www.bbb.org/bbb/index.*
Home page for the Better Business Bureau. File a consumer complaint on line.

The Business Researcher's Interests
—*http://www.bint.com*
Compiled by University of Pittsburgh professor Yogesh Malhotra, this meta-site is one of the most useful locations on the World Wide Web. With literally thousands of links to all kinds of business-related information, we advise you to use this site as an intro to any research you do online.

Home Business Resources
—*http://www2.networkmarketing.com/networkmarketing/*
Another commercial site that lists over 190 MLM opportunities and calls itself the "Entrepreneur's guide to Network Marketing (MLM/Multi-Level Marketing)." Includes extensive catalog of tools and resources.

The MLM Advertiser
—http://www.mlmads.com/
Claims to be the "First Electronic Multi-Level Marketing Magazine."

Multilevel Marketing
—http://www.cris.com/~Sbis/mlm.html
A commercial that offers a series of articles and books on MLM. Some of this information is slanted to getting you to buy into one program or another, but the site does offer many MLM businesses to choose from.

Multilevel Marketing
—http://www.usps.gov/websites/depart/inspect/pyramid.htm
Provided by the United States Postal Service. Concentrates on MLM pyramid schemes and how they violate postal law.

Multilevel Marketing and Pyramid Schemes
—http://www.bosbbb.org/lit/0003.htm
Consumer information sponsored by member businesses, tips on multilevel marketing and how to tell a legitimate opportunity from a pyramid scheme.

Multi-Level Marketing Resources
—http://www.scott.net/~sw-etc/tm/mlm.html
A commercial site that claims it's "Your One-Stop MLM Homepage." This site includes many informational resources, MLM companies, and MLM links.

Multilevel Marketing YellowPages
—http://www.bestmall.com/mall/
A well-maintained, easy-to-use, on-line directory of MLM companies.

Multilevel Marketing Yellow Pages
—http://www.mlm-directory.com/mlyp/mlyp.htm
A commercial site that offers comprehensive research tools for details on many home business opportunities in network marketing (multilevel marketing.)

The Network Marketing Emporium
—http://www.cashflow.com/index.
A commercial site that nevertheless provides a good place to find potential MLM opportunities and gain some background information on the MLM industry.

NIC—alt.business.multi-level
—http://sunsite.unc.edu/usenet-i/groups-html/alt.business.multi-level.html
alt.business.multi-level
The multilevel marketing businesses usegroup.

Online Index
—http://www.primenet.com/~magrath/test.html
Index of articles, publications, and other writings on MLM, its history,
companies, legal issues, and more.

Working from Home Forum on CompuServe Interactive.
Go Work.
Message section and library.

Resources for Home-Based Business Opportunities

BOOKS, PERIODICALS, AND OTHER PUBLICATIONS

Biz Op: How to Get RICH with "Business Opportunity" Frauds and Scams. Bruce Easly. Loopmanics, Port Townsend, WA. (This book is a how-to on putting together biz op scams. Although you don't want to try any of these rip-offs at home, the techniques Easly outlines are textbook examples of how scammers operate.)

Business Opportunities Handbook. Enterprise Magazines, Inc., 1020 North Broadway, Suite 111, Milwaukee, WI 53202

Encyclopedia of Associations. Lists trade and professional organizations throughout the United States. This book will be available in the reference section of your local library.

Finding Your Perfect Work. Paul and Sarah Edwards, New York: Tarcher/Putnam, 1996.

National Trade and Professional Associations of the United States. Columbia Books, Inc., Washington, DC.

Start Your Own Business Magazine. Harris Publications, 1115 Broadway, 8th Floor, New York, NY 10010; (212) 807-7100.

Today's Business Owner Magazine. TD, Inc., 1151 Dove Street, Suite 100, Newport Beach, CA 92660.·

TRADE AND BUSINESS ORGANIZATIONS

Federal Communications Commission
Office of Communications Business Opportunities
1919 M Street, N.W.
Washington, DC 20554
Voice: (202)418-0990; fax: (202)418-0235, Room 644
E-mail: a kbeverly@fcc.gov.

Federal Trade Commission
Bureau of Consumer Protection
6th Street and Pennsylvania Ave., N.W.
Washington, DC 20580
Phone: (202)326-2222

National Business Opportunities Bureau
2064 Peachtree Industrial Court, Ste. 404,
Atlanta, GA 30341
Phone: (800) 829-3547
Business opportunities can register with this organization. Not all do. Those that do submit their materials and agreements for use in reporting by the bureau.

National Federation of Independent Business
600 Maryland Avenue, S.W., Suite 700
Washington, DC 20024
Phone: (202)554-9000

CSC-the United States Corporation Company
(formerly Prentice-Hall Legal and Financial Services)
375 Hudson St.
11th Floor
New York, NY 10014
Phone: (800)221-0770
Prentice Hall will provide a litigation history on any company for a small fee. The search must occur in the county where the business is located. The report will indicate any proceedings against the company, criminal or civil.

Small Business Administration
409 3d Street, S.W., Room 7177
Washington, D.C. 20416
Phone: (800)8-ASK-SBA; (800)827-5722
Fax: (202)205-7067
Web Site: http://www.sbaonline.sba.gov

ON-LINE RESOURCES

Better Business Bureau Web Server
—*http://www.bbb.org/bbb/index.*
Home page for the Better Business Bureau. File a consumer complaint on line.

Business Opportunities
—*http://www.webcom.com/cfnet/keywords/busopp.html*
Another commercial site that has databases listing over 500 business opportunities.

Business Opportunities News Home Page
—*http://www.business-Opps-news.com/*
Business Opportunities News on-line magazine. Comprehensive listings of biz ops and interesting editorials and other resources.

Business Opportunity Page
—*http://www.galaxy-net.com/bus-Opp/*
A commercial site that offers quite a bit of good info on business and marketing in general. It also includes listings for MLM and franchising. Look for free business reports and stock market and stock quotes.

The Entrepreneurs Bookstore
—*http://www.kwicsys.com/kwicsys/books*
This site lists over 600 titles of "information-packed" reports which are of interest to entrepreneurs, starting from $2.

The Internetwork Classified Business & MLM Directory
—*http://www-edin.easynet.co.uk/internetwork/int.*
Another on-line business-opportunity magazine, this one based in the UK. Features relevant articles, news, biz ops, Internet, and computer-related resources.

SBA: Hotlist
—http://www.sbaonline.sba.gov/hotlist
A hotlist of biz ops provided by the U.S. Small Business Administration. Part of a very extensive site maintained by the SBA.

State Biz Op Seller-Assisted Marketing Plan (SAMP) Agencies by State

As we mentioned in Chapter 5, at the time of this book's writing, twenty-six states in the U.S. have SAMP laws on their books. Check with your state's attorney general for specific information regarding the SAMP laws in your state.

PLEASE NOTE: Earning claims (telling you how much you can make), even with a disclaimer that these figures are approximate, are absolutely forbidden in all states. The Federal Trade Commission enforces this rule.

California (filing required)
Consumer Law Section
Attorney General's Office
P.O. Box 94255
Sacramento, CA 94244-2550
(916) 445-9555

Connecticut (filing required)
Department of Banking
Securities Division
260 Constitution Plaza

Hartford, CT 06103
(860)240-8299, ext. 8322

Florida (filing required)
Dept. of Agriculture and Consumer Services
Division of Consumer Services
Attention: Biz Op
Mayo Building
2nd Floor
Tallahassee, FL 32399-0800

(904) 488-2221
(800) 342-2176 (in-state only)

Georgia (no filing required)
Office of Consumer Affairs
2 Martin Luther King, Jr., Dr.
S-356
Atlanta, GA 30334
(404) 656-3790

Indiana (filing required)
Consumer Protection Division
Attorney General's Office
219 State House
Indianapolis, IN 46204
(317) 232-6331

Iowa (filing required)
Securities Bureau
Second Floor
Lucas State office Building
Des Moines, IA 50319
(515) 281-4441

Kentucky (filing required)
Attorney General's Office
Consumer Protection Division
1024 Capitol Center Dr.
Frankfort, KY 40601
(502) 573-2200

Louisiana (bond filing required)
Office of the Attorney General
Consumer Protection Division
301 Main St.
Suite 1250
1 American Place
Baton Rouge, LA 70801
(504) 342-7186

Maine (filing required)
Banking Bureau
Securities Division

State House—Station 121
Augusta, ME 04333
(207) 624-8551

Maryland (filing required)
Attorney General's Office
Securities Division
200 St. Paul Pl.—20th Floor
Baltimore, MD 21202
(410) 576-6360

Michigan (notice required)
Consumer Protection Division
Dept. of the Attorney General
525 West Ottawa
P.O. Box 30213
Lansing, MI 48909
(517) 373-7117

Minnesota (filing required)
Department of Commerce
Registration Division
133 East 7th Street
St. Paul, MN 55101
(612) 296-6328

Nebraska (filing required)
Dept. of Banking & Finance
P.O. Box 95006
Lincoln, NE 68509
(402) 471-2171 or
(402) 471-3445

New Hampshire (filing required)
Attorney General's Office
Consumer Protection Division
33 Capitol St.
Concord, NH 03301
(603) 271-3641

North Carolina (filing required)
Department of Justice

Consumer Protection Division
P.O. Box 629
Raleigh, NC 27602
(919) 733-7741

Ohio (no filing required)
Attorney General's Office
25th Floor, State Office Tower
30 East Broad Street
Columbus, OH 43215-3428
(614) 466-8831
(800) 282-0515 (in-state only)

Oklahoma (filing required)
Dept. of Securities
120 N. Robinson
First National Center
Suite 860
P.O. Box 53595
Oklahoma City, OK 73102
(405) 280-7700 #2

South Carolina (filing required)
Secretary of State's Office
P.O. Box 11350
Columbia, SC 29211
(803) 734-2170

South Dakota (filing required)
Division of Securities
118 W. Capitol

Pierre, SD 57501
(605) 773-4013

Texas (filing required)
Secretary of State's Office
Statutory Documents Section
P.O. Box 12887
Austin, TX 78711
(512) 475-1769

Utah
Consumer Protection Division
160 East 300 South
P.O. Box 146704
Salt Lake City, UT 84114-6704
(801) 530-6601

Virginia (no filing required)
Consumer Affairs Office
900 E. Main St.
Richmond, VA 23219
(804) 786-0594
(800) 451-1525 (in-state only)

Washington (filing required)
Department of Financial Institutions
Securities Division
P.O. Box 9033
Olympia, WA 98507-9033
(360) 902-8760

APPENDIX 6

On-Line Fraud
Protection Resources

Consumer Fraud Alert Network
—*http://www.world-wide.com/HomeBiz/Fraud.htm*
A few tips on how not to be a victim of consumer fraud and how to recognize fraud. It also contains some more specific links on similar subjects.

Home Business Scam Alert Network
—*http://www.world-wide.com/HomeBiz/Scams.htm*
Same author as above, but this has more specific links and information specifically on home business scams (one of the few about home businesss).

Distributorship and Franchise Fraud
—*http://www.usps.gov/websites/depart/inspect/emplmenu.htm*
Some tips to prevent and recognize lots of kinds of fraud. A U.S. government page.

Hang Up on Fraud
—*http://www.emich.edu/public/coe/nice/hangup.html*
Lots of tips, resources, and books on how to prevent franchise fraud. (This one came up a lot.)

National Fraud Information Center
—*http://www.fraud.org*

A list of newsletters, books, and resources on how to prevent fraud. Some tips also.

Consumer Scam Alert
—*http://www.world-wide.com/homeBiz/invest.htm*
Fraud protection for the Internet.

Frauds against Businesses
—*http://www.usps.gov/websites/depart/inspect/infomenu.htm*
Business fraud protection, with section on home-based fraud. (This one came up a lot, too.)

The Fraud Prevention Detection Kit
—*http://www.quiknet.com/fraud/*
A do-it-yourself test to see how well you are defending against fraud, and more.

Investor Bulletin: On-Line Investment Schemes
—*http://www.state.ct.us/dob/pages/cyberblt.htm*
Protection against on-line investment fraud.

A Whistleblowers' Web Site
—*http://www.whistleblowers.com/def.html*
Ways that contracters commit fraud against the government.

UCRPD Crime Alert: Pyramid Schemes
—*http://police2.ucr.edu/pyramid.html*
Advice on how to prevent pyramid schemes.

The Insurance Fraud Research Register
—*http://www.ifb.org/ifrr.htm*
Insurance fraud.

The Fraud Information Center
—*http://www.echotech.com/*
Lots of more specific links of fraud protection and informationlike books.

Financial Scandals
—*http://www.ex.ac.uk/~RDavies/arian/scandals.html*
This page contains more specific links to sources of information on various financial scandals, prievously commited.

FCSC International
—*http://www.vir.com/~catrahal/fraud2.htm*
This page has a bit of information on fraud victims and ways not to become one.

Pyramid Schemes
—*http://www.ag.state.mn.us/consumer/fraud/pyramid.html*
A page that talks about pyramid schemes.

Multilevel Marketing and Pyramid Schemes
—*http://www.bosbbb.org/lit/0003.htm*
Tips on how to tell a multilevel marketing fraud.

APPENDIX 7

General Resources for Home Business Success

BOOKS, PERIODICALS, TAPES, AND OTHER PUBLICATIONS

Choosing, Starting, and Running a Home Business

Checklist for Going into Business. Small Business Administration, Washington, DC 20416.

Finding Your Perfect Work Making a Living, Creating a Life. Paul and Sarah Edwards, Jeremy P. Tarcher/Putnam, 200 Madison Avenue, New York NY 10016, 1996.

Goverment Assistance Almanac: The Guide to All Federal Financial and Other Domestic Programs. J. Robert Dumouchel, Omigraphics, Detroit, annual.

Homemade Money. Barbara Brabec, Betterway Publications, Whitehall, VA, 1994.

Honey, I Want to Start My Own Business. Azriella Jaffe, Harper Business, New York, NY 1996.

Schemes and Scams. Douglas P. Shadel and John T., Newcastle Publishing, North Hollywood, CA, 1994.

Succeeding in Business. Jane Applegate, Plume, New York, NY, 1994.

Working from Home. Paul and Sarah Edwards, Jeremy P. Tarcher/Putnam, 200 Madison Avenue, New York, NY 10016, 1994.

Legal Matters

Forming Corporations and Partnerships. John C. Howell, Liberty Hall Press, Summit, PA, 1991.

Self-help legal books by Nolo Press:

Everybody's Guide to Small Claims Court
How to Form a Nonprofit Corporation
It Yourself, The Partnership Book
Simple Contracts for Personal Use.

Most of these book are written for national readership, others for a particular state such as California, Florida, New York, and Texas. For a free catalog, write to Nolo Press, 950 Parker Street, Berkeley, CA 94710; (510)549-1976, (800)992-6656.

Money Matters

Basic Accounting for the Small Business. Clive G. Cornish, Self Counsel Press, Bellingham, WA 1992.

Desktop Credit Manager. Lord Publishing, Dana Point, CA (software).

Estimating and Invoicing. Lord Publishing, Dana Point, CA (software).

Financial Freedom in 8 Minutes a Day. Ron and Mary Hulnick, Rodale, Emmaus, NY, 1994.

Personal Finance for Dummies. Eric Tyson, IDG Books, San Mateo, CA, 1994.

Save Your Business a Bundle. Daniel Kehrer, Simon & Schuster, New York, NY, 1994.

Small Time Operator. Bernard Kamoroff, Bell Springs, Laytonville, CA, 1993.

Getting and Staying Organized

Home Storage Projects for Every Room. David H. Jacobs, McGraw-Hill, New York, NY, 1996.

Organized to Be the Best. Susan Silver, Adams Hall, Los Angeles, CA, 1995.

Organizing Your Home Office for Success. Lisa Kanarek, Plume, New York, NY, 1993.

Make Your House Do the Housework. Don Aslett and Laura Aslett Simons, Writer's Digest, New York, NY, 1986.

Sunset Complete Home Storage. Sunset Publishing Co., Menlo Park, CA, 1986.

Sunset Home Offices & Workspaces, Sunset Publishing Co., Menlo Park, CA, 1986.

Time Management for Dummies. Jeff Mayer, IDG Book, Foster City, CA, 1995.

Winning the Fight Between You and Your Desk. Jeff Mayer, Harper Business, New York, NY 1993.

Home Office Technology

Computer Power for Your Small Business. Nick Sullivan, Random House, New York, NY, 1993.

The Computer User Survival Guide. Joan Stigliani, O'Reilly, Sebastapol, CA, 1995.

Doing Business on the Internet. Mary J. Cronin, Van Nostrand Reinhold, New York, NY, 1994.

Healthy Computing. Dr. Ronald Harwin and Colin Haynes, American Management Association, AMACOM, P.O. Box 1026, Saranac Lake, NY 12983.

The Office Computing Bible. Nancy E. Dunn, Prentice Hall, Englewood Cliffs, NJ, 1995.

Your First Book of Personal Computing. Joe Kraynak, Alpha Books, Indianapolis, IN, 1995.

Marketing and Promoting Your Home Business

Do It Yourself Marketing Research. George Breen and A.B. Blankenship, Mc-Graw-Hill, New York, NY, 1989.

Don't Slurp Your Soup: A Basic Guide to Business Etiquette. Betty Craig, Brighton Publications, New Brighton, NM, 1991.

Getting Business to Come to You. Paul and Sarah Edwards, Jeremy P. Tarcher/Putnam, 200 Madison Avenue, New York, NY 10016, 1991.

Getting Business to Come to You (CD-ROM). Paul and Sarah Edwards, Info Business, Orem, UT; (800)221-1194.

Getting Business to Come to You (audiotape). Paul and Sarah Edwards, Nightingale Conant, 7300 North Lehigh Avenue, Niles, IL 60714; (800) 525-9000.

The Hiring and Firing Book: The Complete Legal Guide for Employers. Steven Mitchell, Legal Strategies, Inc., Merrick, NY.

Look Before You Leap: Market Research Made Easy. Don Doman, Dell Dennison, Margaret Doman, Self-Counsel Press, Bellingham, WA 1993.

Paul and Sarah Edwards' Business Generator. Includes the Edwards's book *Getting Business to Come to You*, a seventy-five-minute video, *Top of the Mind Marketing*, and *The Marketing Partner*, a sixty-four-page workbook and guide for developing and following through on a marketing plan tailored to your personality and your business. Here's How, P.O. Box 5091, Santa Monica, CA 90409.

The World's Best Known Marketing Secret. Ivan Misner, Bard Productions, Austin, TX, 1994.

Self-Management

Emotional Intelligence. Daniel Goleman, Bantam, New York, NY, 1995.

Getting It Done: The Transforming Power of Self-Discipline. Andrew J. Dubrin, Petterson's/Pacesetter, Princeton, NJ, 1995.

How Good People Make Tough Choices: Resolving the Dilemmas of Ethical Living. Rushworth M. Kidder, Morrow, New York, NY, 1995

How to Stay Up No Matter What Goes Down. Sarah Edwards, P.O. Box 5091, Santa Monica, CA 90409 (audiotape).

Idea Fisher. Idea Fisher Systems, Inc., 2222 Martin St., #110; Irvine, CA 92612; (714)474-8111.

Managing Your Anxiety. Christopher McCullough and Robert Woods Mann, Tarcher/Putnam, New York, NY, 1995.

Secrets of Self-Employment, Surviving and Thriving on the Ups and Downs of Being Your Own Boss. Paul and Sarah Edwards, Tarcher/Putnam, New York, NY, 1996.

Secrets of Successful Self-Employment. Paul and Sarah Edwards, Nightingale Conant, 7300 North Lehigh Avenue, Niles, IL 60714; (800)525-9000 (audiotape).

The Survivor Personality. Al Siebert, Practical Psychology Press, Portland, OR, 1994.

True Success: A New Philosophy of Excellence. Tome Morris, Grosset/Putnam, New York, NY, 1994.

MAIL-ORDER HOME OFFICE AND COMPUTER SUPPLIES

Hello Direct, 5884 Eden Park Place, San Jose, CA 95138; (800)444-3556 (telephone products).

Inmac Inc., 55 United States Ave., Gibbsboro, NJ 08026, (800)547-5444.

MacWarehouse, (800)255-6227 and *MicroWarehouse,* 1720 Oak Street, Lakewood, NJ 08701; (800)367-7080.

PC Connection, Mill Street, Marlow, NH 03456; (800)800-0004; and *Mac Connection,* Mill Street, Marlow, NH 03456; (800)800-0002.

Quill, 100 South Schelter Road, Lincolnshire, IL 60069; (847)634-4800 or (800)789-1331.

Reliable Home Office, P.O. Box 1502, Ottawa, IL 61350; (800)869-6000.

Viking Office Products, 13809 South Figuroa, P.O. Box 61144, Los Angeles, CA 90061; (800)248-6111 and (800)421-1222.

Wholesale Supply Company, P.O. Box 23437, Nashville, TN 37202; (800)962-9162.

TIME MANAGEMENT SYSTEMS

Day Runner, Inc. 2750 West Moor Ave., Fullerton, CA 92633; (800)232-9786.

Day Timer. Day-Timer Concepts, Inc., 794 Roble Rd. LVIP III, Allentown, PA 18103; (800)317-9152.

The Franklin Planner. Franklin Quest, P.O. Box 31406, Salt Lake City, UT 84131; (800)544-1776.

TIME MANAGEMENT SOFTWARE

Anytime. Individual Software, 5870 Stoneridge Drive, #1, Pleasanton, CA 94588; (800)331-3313.

Ascend. Franklin Quest, P.O. Box 31406, Salt Lake City, UT 84131; (800)544-1776.

Lotus Organizer. Lotus Development Company, 55 Cambridge Parkway, Cambridge, MA 02142; (800)635-6887.

Outlook. Microsoft Corporation, 1 Microsoft Way, Redmond, WA 98052; (800)426-9400.

MAGAZINES

Entrepreneur Magazine, 2392 Morse Ave., Irvine, CA 92714.

Home Office Computing Magazine, Scholastic, Inc., 730 Broadway, New York, NY 10003.

Small Business Opportunities Magazine, Harris Publications, 1115 Broadway, New York, NY 10010.

RADIO AND TELEVISION

Working from Home with Paul and Sarah Edwards on the Home and Garden Cable Network.

"*Working from Home*" is heard weekly on Business News Network Sundays at 10:00 P.M. Eastern, 7:00 P.M. Pacific. If you do not have an affiliated station near you, you can listen live on the Internet at http://www.cfra.com or using your satellite dish, tuning to Digital: SATCOM C-5, Transponder 15, Channel 11.0.

NATIONAL SMALL OFFICE–HOME BUSINESS ASSOCIATIONS

American Association of Home-Based Businesses
P.O. Box 10023
Rockville, MD 20849
(202)310-3130; (800)447-9710

Independent Business Alliance
111 John Street, Suite 1210
New York, NY 10038
(212)513-1446

National Home Office Association
1828 L Street, NW, Suite 402
Washington, DC 20036
(800)664-6462
http://www.nhoa1.org

Small Office Home Office Association
1767 Business Center Drive
Reston, VA 22090
(703)438-3060; (888)SOHOA11

PARENTS-WORKING-AT-HOME ASSOCIATIONS

Association of Enterprising Mothers
6965 El Camino Road
Suite 105-612
Carlsbad, CA 92009
(800)223-9260; (619)434-9225

Dads at Home
61 Brightwood Ave.
North Andover, MA 01845
(508)685-7931

Mother's Home Business Network
P.O. Box 423
East Meadow, NY 11590
(516)997-7394

Home-Based Working Moms
P.O. Box 500464
Austin, TX 78750
(512)918-0670

ON-LINE RESOURCES

Better Business Bureau Web Server
—*http://www.bbb.org/bbb/index.*
Home page for the Better Business Bureau.

The Business Researcher's Interests
—*http://www.pitt.edu/~malhotra/interest.html*
Compiled by University of Pittsburgh doctoral student Yogesh Malhotra, the meta-site is one of the most useful locations on the World Wide Web. With literally thousands of links to all kinds of business-related information, we advise you to use this site as intro to any research you do on-line.

Paul and Sarah Edwards's Web site located at *http://www.homeworks.com,* providing links to many small-business resources.

SBA: Small Business Administration Home Page
—*http://www.sbaonline.sba.gov/lynx/index-lynx.html* (text only)
The United States Small Business Administration maintains one of the largest, most comprehensive, and downright useful sites on the World Wide Web. Specific information regarding franchising, business law, marketing and finance, and much more is available.

Small and Home-Based Business Links
—*http://www.gnn.com/gnn/wic/wics/bus.74.html*
A page of links to Web sites related to small and home-based businesses and franchises, maintained by Renaissance Internet Services.

Small Business Development Centers
Funded by the Small Business Administration, Small Business Development Centers (SBDCs) operate in all fifty states and U.S. territories. Centers are listed on the SBA's Web site at *http://www.sbaonline.sba.gov/regions/states.html.*

U.S. and International Law
—http://members.aol.com/DangeLaw/homepage.html
Although a commercial home page, this site does offer some useful information regarding U.S. and international law as it relates to franchising and business.

Working from Home Forum
On CompuServe Interactive. **GO WORK.** Message section and library.
www.workingfromhome.com

The World Wide Web Virtual Library: Law: Law Firms
—http://www.law.indiana.edu/law/v-lib/lawfirms.html
This page is maintained by the Indiana School of Law at Bloomington. It contains a comprehensive list of links that is fully searchable as well as alphabetically arranged.

Index

Other Books by Paul and Sarah Edwards

Use the table below to locate other books that contain the information you need for your business interests.

Subject	Best Home Businesses for the 90s	Getting Business to Come to You	Secrets of Self-Employment	Making Money with Your Computer at Home	Working from Home	Finding Your Perfect Work
Advertising		Yes				
Business opportunities					Yes	
Business planning				Yes		
Children and child care					Yes	
Closing sales		Yes	Yes			
Credit					Yes	
Employees					Yes	
Ergonomics				Yes	Yes	
Failure			Yes			
Family and marriage issues					Yes	
Financing your business		Yes		Yes	Yes	
Franchise named					Yes	
Getting referrals		Yes			Yes	
Handling emotional/psychological issues			Yes			
Housecleaning					Yes	
Insurance					Yes	
Legal issues					Yes	
Loneliness, isolation					Yes	
Managing information				Yes	Yes	
Marketing	Specific techniques by business	Yes Focus of book	Yes Attitude	Yes Technology tools	Yes	
Marketing materials		Yes		Yes		
Money			Yes	Yes	Yes	
Naming your business		Yes				
Networking		Yes			Yes	
Office space, furniture, equipment					Yes	
Outgrowing your home					Yes	
Overcoming setbacks			Yes			
Pricing	Yes Specific			Yes Specific	Yes Principles	
Profiles of specific businesses	Yes			Yes		
Public relations and publicity		Yes			Yes	
Resource Directory			Yes			
Selecting a business/career	Yes			Yes	Yes	Yes Focus of book
Software				Yes	Yes	
Speaking		Yes				
Start-up costs	Yes			Yes		
Success issues			Yes			
Taxes					Yes	
Time management			Yes	Yes	Yes	
Zoning					Yes	

Do You Have Questions or Feedback?

The authors of this book, Paul and Sarah Edwards, want to answer your questions. They can respond to you directly, usually within twenty-four hours, if you leave a message for them on the Working From Home Forum on CompuServe Information Service. If you have a computer and access to CompuServe, simply type "GO WORK" at any "!" prompt; their ID is 76703,242. You can also visit Paul and Sarah's resources offered on the Internet's World Wide Web at *http://www.workingfromhome.com*.

If you do not have a computer, you can write to Paul and Sarah in care of "Q&A," Home Office Computing magazine, 730 Broadway, New York, NY 10003. Your questions may be selected to be answered in their monthly column or they may respond to it on their radio or TV show. However, they cannot respond to every letter.

Complete Your Library of the Working from Home Series by Paul and Sarah Edwards

These books are available at your local bookstore or wherever books are sold. Ordering is also easy and convenient. To order, call 1-800-788-6262, prompt #1, or send your order to:

Jeremy P. Tarcher, Inc.
Mail Order Department
PO Box 12289
Newark, NJ 07101-5289

For Canadian orders:
PO Box 25000
Postal Station 'A'
Toronto, Ontario M5W 2X8

		Price
_____ The Best Home Businesses for the 90s, Revised Edition	0-87477-784-4	$12.95
_____ Finding Your Perfect Work	0-87477-795-X	$16.95
_____ Getting Business to Come to You	0-87477-629-5	$11.95
_____ Making Money with Your Computer at Home	0-87477-736-4	$12.95
_____ Secrets of Self-Employment	0-87477-837-9	$13.95
_____ Teaming Up	0-87477-842-5	$13.95
_____ Working from Home	0-87477-764-X	$15.95

Subtotal _____

Shipping and handling* _____

Sales tax (CA, NJ, NY, PA) _____

Total amount due _____

Payable in U.S. funds (no cash orders accepted). $15.00 minimum for credit card orders. *Shipping and handling: $3.50 for one book, $1.00 for each additional book. Not to exceed $8.50.

Payment method:

☐ Visa   ☐ MasterCard   ☐ American Express

☐ Check or money order

☐ International money order or bank draft check

Card # _____ Expiration date _____

Signature as on charge card _____

Daytime phone number _____

Name _____

Address _____

City _____ State _____ Zip _____

Please allow six weeks for delivery. Prices subject to change without notice. Source key WORK